I0833993

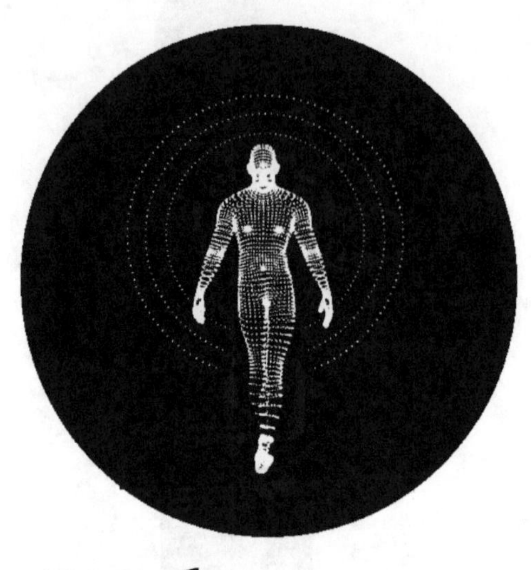

Welcome

More resources from the author

SIGNAL
AND
NOISE
ADVANCED
PSYCHIC TRAINING
for Remote Viewing,
Clairvoyance, and ESP
SEAN MCNAMARA

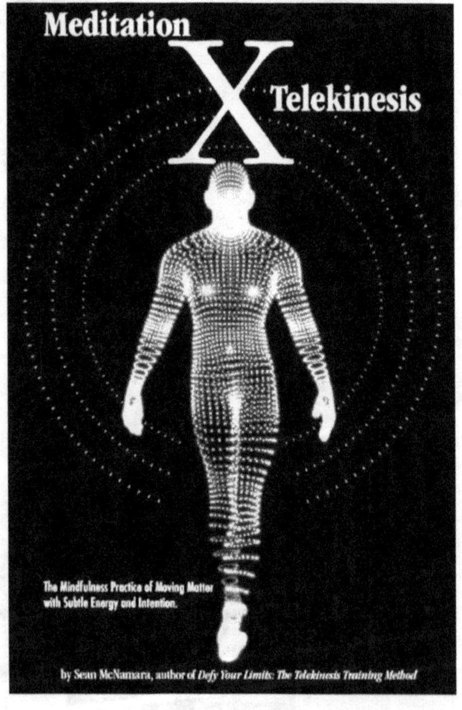
Meditation
X
Telekinesis
The Mindfulness Practice of Moving Matter
with Subtle Energy and Intention.
by Sean McNamara, author of Defy Your Limits: The Telekinesis Training Method

Concise Instructions for

Lucid Dreaming

and the

Out of Body Experience

Dewdrops of Infinity
Psychedelics, Psychic Abilities, UFOs, and
THE PUHARICH PROJECT
Sean McNamara

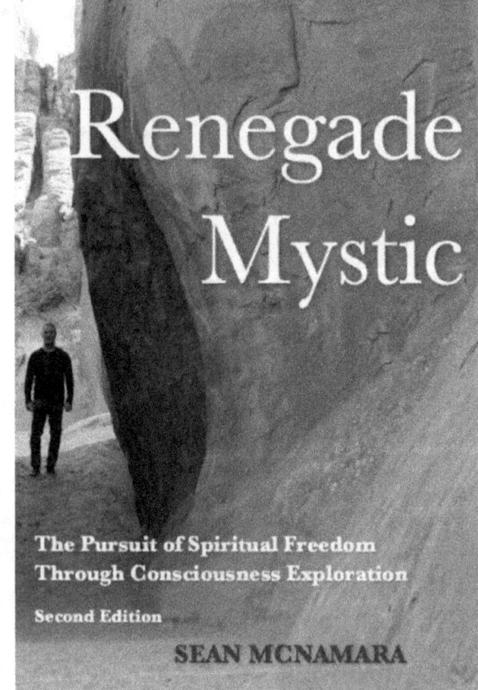
Renegade Mystic
The Pursuit of Spiritual Freedom Through Consciousness Exploration
Second Edition
SEAN MCNAMARA

BLUE THUMB
How to Grow Psilocybin Mushrooms at Home
Sean McNamara
The Experiential Step-by-Step, Picture-by-Picture Guide
Color Edition

Path of the Golden Teacher
Integrating MEDITATION with PSILOCYBIN and other psychedelics
Sean McNamara

Online Training Courses

with Sean McNamara at www.MindPossible.com

- Telekinesis
- Remote Viewing
- Guided Meditation
- Telepathy Training
- Vagus Nerve Stimulation
- Guidance for Telepathy Teachers
- Lucid Dreaming and the Out-of-Body Experience

Mind Sight II

TELEPATHY TRAINING

for Neurotypicals

THE ESTES PARK SESSIONS

SEAN MCNAMARA

The writing, editing, layout, and other aspects of preparing the manuscript for publishing was 100% human (non-AI).

First Edition

Published by Mind Possible

www.MindPossible.com

ISBN: 979-8-9883119-6-6

Non-fiction

Parapsychology | Consciousness Studies | Psychic Development

0216A

TABLE OF CONTENTS

Participant Names and Privacy iii
Acknowledgments v

PART 1
This Life and the Next 1
Typical and Divergent, Together 19
Transmission 32
Establishing Set and Setting 38
A Note to Scientists 47

PART 2
Cheryl's Dream 49
Telepathy Instructions 53
Observed Attributes of Telepathy 77

PART 3
DAY 1 Individual Telepathy with Line Drawings 81
Telepathy Target 1: Two trees and a path 83
Telepathy Target 2: Coliseum with pennants 96
Telepathy Target 3: Sun and ocean waves 107
Telepathy Target 4: Spider 116
Telepathy Target 5: Two hearts 123
Telepathy Target 6: Shower head / lamp 128

DAY 2 Clairvoyance with Colors 135
DAY 2 Clairvoyance with Small Objects 139
DAY 2 Telepathy with Complex Images 142

DAY 2 Remote Viewing as Autotelepathy 146
The Lucky Thread of Autotelepathy 152
Coordinate 271765: Sahrawi Horsemen 153
Coordinate 453191: The Blue Mosque 165
Coordinate 522931: Dragon 2 Hover Test 180
Coordinate 553904: Light Rail 208

DAY 2 Psychokinesis with Random Event Generators: The Owls 216

DAYS 2 and 3 Outbounder Remote Viewing 218

DAY 3 Team Telepathy Events 226

DAY 3 What's in the Box? #1 234

DAY 4 Heart Rate Telepathy (DMILS) 241

DAY 4 What's in the Box? #2 269

DAY 5 Team Telepathy with Blinking Shapes 279
Team Telepathy with Color-Matching Abacus Test 283

DAY 5 Team Telepathy with Line Drawings 286
Telepathy Target: Hand 288
Telepathy Target: Radiation symbol 291
Telepathy Target: Rainbow and two clouds 295
Telepathy Target: Roller coaster 300
Telepathy Target: Rose bud with leaf 304
Telepathy Target: Submarine 309
Telepathy Target: Radio 313
Telepathy Target: Award ribbon 317

PART 4
The Closing Circle 322

Appendix 1: Notes from the call with Dalia and Lidu Burgoin 327
Appendix 2: 2025 Psychic Training Intensive's Complete Schedule 329
Appendix 3: QR codes to see the Remote Viewing targets in color 331
Appendix 4: QR code for various videos & 360-degree RV targets 332
Appendix 5: QR codes for recommended contacts and teachers 333

Please Leave a Book Review 334

About the Author 335

PARTICIPANT NAMES AND PRIVACY

Many of the participants' names have been replaced with code names. This occurs mostly in the transcript headings in Part 3.

The purpose of the code names is to protect their privacy as well as to reduce the tendency of a participant to compare their work to someone else's, which can negatively affect self-esteem.

The participants know their own code names, and it is their choice to publicly disclose their identities.

Some participants asked to remain anonymous and did not submit their transcripts for use in this book.

ACKNOWLEDGMENTS

Left to right: Edie W., Cheryl M., Wendy G., Marta R., Rhonda W., Donna F., Chris K., Blake F., the author, Melissa G., Austin S., Owen M. Desi M., Ivy V., Neal C., Su S., Bob L., Jaime J., Robert P., Judit P., Michelle T., Jill L. Participants not pictured here asked to remain anonymous.

Life really is like a dream. And there are dreams within dreams. This dream lasted a whole week. High up in those beautiful mountains, it felt like we were a little closer to heaven. Was it like that for you, too? We shared something special, didn't we?

What we witnessed and created together will never happen again, at least not in the same way. I miss it. Do you remember? Oh, friends, how bittersweet it is to share moments like those and then to have to let them go. Such is time. Let us reminisce a little longer now, shall we?

But then we must go our separate ways, for there's even more to discover in this life and, perhaps, the next. Just let me say one more time before you go, from the bottom of my heart, thank you.

- Sean

For Dad.

THIS LIFE AND THE NEXT

Here I sit writing the first sentence of the first draft of this book on the one-year anniversary of my father's death. He died of heart failure while using his walker. My mom found him early that morning, and I got the phone call soon after. When I saw him, I noticed the maroon knitted blanket she'd draped over his shoulders after discovering his body, as if he might still catch a chill.

She found him beneath a doorway, which seemed strangely appropriate since he was indeed moving from one place, or state of existence, to another. He'd collapsed onto his knees, and his body remained upright because the walker's handles caught him under his arms. His head was bowed down as if in prayer, lips already an inky purple from the blood pooling beneath the skin.

He probably died instantly, as if in a faint, with just a moment of awareness left to realize what was happening before blacking out. He'd been under hospice care for quite a while, so it wouldn't have been a complete surprise. And if he had more than a moment to think about it, bowing his head in prayer is exactly what he would've done.

Thirty-five years or so before, I overheard him on the phone speaking to his mother in Florida. The nurse on the other end held the receiver to her ear so Granny could listen to her son's final goodbyes. She was probably already unconscious with little time left, but Dad believed she could still hear him, at least on some level. "Bye-bye, Mom. I love you. I know I'll see you and Dad and Mike and Danny again. I'll see you all in Heaven."

Mike was his older brother and best friend who'd died in his thirties of melanoma. Danny was one of his younger brothers. He died of bad luck on the highway when the tire of a vehicle traveling in the opposite direction came off, ejected into the air, and crashed straight through the roof of Danny's car. It killed him instantly. A few years later, sister Peggy would die of cancer. A year ago, his brother Bobby died of a particularly fast and aggressive liver disease. And while working on a subsequent draft of this book, my last surviving uncle, Billy, died from Lewy Body Dementia.

In remembering them, I recall a powerful statement[1] used by Buddhists to reflect on the nature of this existence.

> Death is real.
> It comes without warning.
> This body will be a corpse.

It's a day of mourning for my family and me. I have been sad, nostalgic, and have felt many other emotions since drifting into a fitful sleep last night while thinking of Dad. I almost expected to wake up in the middle of the night, stirred by the distinct odor of my father's skin blended with his preferred body spray's scent filling the room. It wouldn't have been the first time he woke me up that way since he died. Yes, death is real. Yet I can almost hear Dad's voice somewhere far, far away, repeating his favorite infomercial line to break the tension. "But wait, there's more!"

Given the circumstances, one might think today is a terrible day for me to begin writing. But I believe it's the perfect day to start. I didn't purposefully schedule this for today. It just turned out that in the weeks since I finished leading the week-long Mind Possible Psychic Training Intensive, which this book is based on, today is the first opportunity I've had to sit down and start.

---

[1] This contemplation on impermanence is one of the "Four Reminders" or "Four Thoughts That Turn the Mind to the Dharma" in Buddhism. The other three concern the spiritual advantages of having a human life, the cause-and-effect nature of phenomena, and the futility of seeking lasting happiness in the temporary. The concept of impermanence is not solely applied to the human lifespan but is inherent in all aspects of reality. In physics, this is known as entropy.

It's the perfect day to begin because while death and its often-unexpected arrival are certain, contemplating them inevitably makes us take pause and wonder about things that are not as certain.

Is death the complete extinction of one's whole being? Or just the body? And if only the body goes, what remains? *How* does whatever that is abide? *Where* does it abide? And for *how long*?

Like the first in a row of dominoes flicked by a finger, one question of mortality tumbles into the next, then another, and so on. What does it mean to be alive, to exist? What is the mind? Is it only the brain, or something else, too? What does it all mean, and does it matter? Do I matter? Do you matter? Who are we, really?

For some of us so concretely identified with our physical forms, the answers to these questions seem shrouded in a great mystery. Some folks don't mind, though, and barely think on it as they go on with their days, content to live and die as naturally as a deer in the forest.

Others, though, harbor some degree of existential dread. Some of them use life's pleasures and dramas to distract themselves in the endless pursuit of some kind of worldly happiness.

If successful, these people won't have to think about their mortality until that fateful day, hopefully very far down the road, when they get the bad news in the doctor's office during a routine checkup. Or when their left arm goes numb in the middle of a staff meeting. Or when they start choking on that fat piece of meat at dinner. Or when old age is just too much and they yearn for the end.

You, the reader, are taking a different route. You may or may not feel a certain angst about your personal shelf life. Regardless, you've chosen to read a book about telepathy and other psychic abilities. You've chosen to read a book based on the hypothesis and evidence that a person can *send* thoughts from their own mind into another person's. Or the reverse, that a person can *receive* the thoughts originating in another's mind. Instead of distracting yourself, you're deeply investigating the nature of our existence.

A subtle, but perhaps more accurate, definition of telepathy is when two or more people access the same non-physical field of information, a field that permeates space, time, and mind.

Let us consider that a person's mental identity, or selfhood, is composed of ideas, preferences, emotions, feelings (body sensations), aesthetics, intentions, hopes, fears, beliefs, observations, and more. Naturally, physical identity is derived from the body (even though it's composed of around 38 trillion bacterial cells, and only around 30 trillion human cells)[2]. Ultimately, one's whole identity while physically alive is the combination of mind and body.

So, what does telepathy have to do with your approaching death and possible continuation afterward?

Well, if an aspect of one person's mind, such as a thought (as an aspect of selfhood), can travel outside the physical brain while still living, who's to say the thought doesn't carry on even after the brain is dead?

Humans began transmitting audio signals via radio waves around a hundred years ago. Decades later, we started transmitting video as television. And the equipment, the transmitters and receivers used to send and receive those sounds and images is today lost to destruction, deterioration, or at best, encased in museum glass. Those machines are all dead.

But those radio signals are still out there, around 200 light-years away, flying through the dark emptiness of space.

As transmitters and receivers, our nervous systems and the rest of our bodies will also reach their demise. Instead of being encased in museum glass, some of us will be inserted in wooden boxes and placed underground. Or buried au natural in the spirit of ecological conservation. The rest of us might be burned, our ashes scattered by the wind or kept in an urn on the fireplace mantel.

But what of our thoughts? Our memories? And the knowledge we've accumulated? And what about the feelings that arise when

---

[2] https://pmc.ncbi.nlm.nih.gov/articles/PMC4991899/

we're in the presence of someone we love? Perhaps most importantly, what of that aspect of mind we can refer to as *self-reflective awareness*, the capacity to know, "This is me, and I know it?"

Will those most subtle parts of our selves be 200 light-years away someday, flying through the darkness of empty space? Or will they find another radio to enter, another temporary form?

Whether that new radio is an Earth-based human, animal, plant, or fungi, or something in another solar system, or on a whole other plane of existence, is a discussion too far beyond the scope of this book. And this analogy of a radio is severely limited, so please don't overthink it.

The word telepathy typically conjures up a situation involving two people, both alive, each knowing what the other is thinking. In my experience, personal anecdotes most often describe it as a spontaneous occurrence. However, telepathy also occurs in other, stranger ways.

When I arrived at my parents' split-level home after receiving the phone call, I saw police vehicles and another car parked in front. I walked in, already feeling shaky, and climbed the stairs to see several officers upstairs standing around. I found my mom in the kitchen, hugged her, and asked where Dad was. "He's downstairs."

I turned to head back down the stairs when an officer stopped me. He asked me to wait until they'd completed the investigation. They needed to do their routine paperwork. Extremely irritated, I waited. Meanwhile, a plain clothed investigator offered me his condolences. He shook my hand slowly and kindly. His hand was big and soft, and he reminded me of my Grandpa. The moment helped me calm down.

After a while, the police gave the all-clear, and I was allowed downstairs where I found Dad as I described at the start of this chapter. I remember the hospice nurse arriving soon afterward. I remember lifting him off his walker to lay him on the ground so the guys with the stretcher would have an easier time with his body when they arrived. His body looked like he'd shrunk to two-thirds his normal size, but it felt as if he weighed a ton. It took all my strength to gracefully pry him from the walker and lay him down on his back.

For I don't know how long, I rested my hand on his chest, then stroked his forehead. Back and forth, chest, forehead. Slowly trying to memorize the feel of his body. I never touched him that way when he was alive, so this was my last chance. I told him I loved him, thanked him for everything, and told him I hoped he was someplace better now. I could never speak to him that way when he was alive. This was my only chance.

The rest of the day begins to blur. I do remember that at some point, we decided we needed a break, so my wife Cierra and I took my mom to a nearby café for a late brunch, including mimosas for toasting Dad and sending him good wishes. We didn't really need the mimosas, though. We were already in an altered state. I can't even remember how the rest of the day went.

But I do remember that night.

I didn't want Mom to sleep alone in that house. "She might want to talk about it," I thought. "She might want a shoulder to cry on. She just shouldn't be alone." But she seemed oddly fine and didn't have that much to say. She told me she was tired and headed off to her bedroom. I kicked off my shoes and settled down on the upstairs living room sofa.

My childhood bedroom was downstairs, and I could've slept in the bed there. I must admit I was not very comfortable with the idea of sleeping so close to the spot where Dad's heart stopped beating. Things go bump in the night all the time, and it never bothers me. But I knew it might that night. So, I slept upstairs within earshot of my mom in case she needed anything.

But falling asleep wouldn't be easy. I lay on my side, facing the top of the staircase. Through the darkness, I could feel the empty space of the passageway leading down to where I'd laid his body.

I was restless.

After a long while, I decided to help myself sleep by using my headphones to listen to some soothing duduk music[3]. I eventually calmed down enough to remember there was something else I could do too: loving-kindness meditation. In this practice, one generates feelings of loving-kindness and mentally *sends* them to a recipient. In this case, my dad.

Whenever I've done this technique before, I did it silently, without the conditioning effects of music. But since I had my headphones in, I chose a song to help me along. It was Tom Petty's "Wildflowers."[4] The lyrics perfectly matched the sentiment I felt toward my dad that night, so it was a good companion for the meditation technique. I replayed it several times as I sent subtle waves of tender, sad, love out to the Great Mystery. I hoped they'd reach him somehow.

After a while, my experience of the space around me changed. Whatever foreboding I'd projected into the house, especially the room downstairs, dissolved. The emotional warmth of the meditation technique softened everything, inside and outside of me. It was enough to settle me down and finally fall asleep.

Sometime later, perhaps in the early hours before dawn, I became conscious. I didn't wake up, though. I had entered what may have been a lucid dream. I knew my body was asleep on the sofa, but I was looking up at the sky. High above, in a stationary position, was a classic UFO. I call it *classic* because it had a saucer shape with a dome on top. Until the last couple of decades or so, this had been the most recognizable shape of a UFO. It was a flying saucer.

Two things stood out during those few moments before I faded back to sleep. First, it felt like more than a dream. And it felt like the UFO knew that I saw it. Perhaps it wanted me to see it.

---

[3] You can listen to it by searching for "Soothing Echoes of Duduk N1" on the YouTube "Sarkamler." Or go to https://youtu.be/FKvs3Rx__x8?si=HAq91nPQes2ckeYT.

[4] Petty, Tom. (1994). *Wildflowers*. Home recording. Search "Wildflowers" on YouTube or go to https://youtu.be/m2OFxeg4spU?si=o_z8CORPO6SPKh0n.

Given that it was the first night after my father's passing, I wondered if the presence of the saucer had anything to do with him.

Secondly, the scene itself wasn't in true-to-life color. The craft and the sky had a sepia tone to them, as if photographed with a camera from the 1800's. This didn't bother me too much since I was quite familiar with out of body experiences. My perception of colors in the out-of-body state was usually quite different from how they appeared while wide awake using my physical eyes and brain. Could this, then, have been an out of body experience?

If it was, I certainly didn't initiate it voluntarily. Did whatever consciousness that was connected to that UFO initiate it for me? If there were any way to know for sure, I would be fully prepared to accept that idea. And I would accept it, but not without discomfort.

Several months before that night, I'd had a similar nighttime occurrence. I hadn't initiated that one either. When I became conscious that time, I found myself sitting near the edge of a tree line. I noticed other people sitting on either side of me. They were quiet and seemed to be in a collective fugue. I had a clear view of the sky before us.

Instead of a classically shaped UFO, a tremendous, glowing orb appeared to the left, up above. It slowly and silently moved across the sky until it was centered in our field of vision. Simultaneously filled with awe and wariness, I looked directly at it.

Without warning, the orb flashed a blinding white light at us. I blacked out instantly. Upon reflection, it seemed to me that the orb had done it on purpose. I think it wanted to turn my perception off, because that's the last thing I remembered that night.

This frustrated me. I didn't like the notion that mysterious forces could control me that way, that they could shut me down. But if this had been the only time in my life this happened, I could've probably downplayed it, brushing it off as fear-based imagination.

Except, it wasn't the first time I'd been shut down.

In 2022, I ran a series of experiments on psychic perception involving psychedelics. During the first six months, a control group and an experimental group of participants took various psychic tests weekly. The experimental group was on a psilocybin microdosing protocol. The goal of this phase was to see if the experimental group would score significantly better than the control group because of psilocybin's influence on their brains. The test designs, their scores & transcripts, and my conclusions are included in my other book *Dewdrops of Infinity: Psychedelics, Psychic Abilities, UFOs, and the Puharich Project.*[5]

The book also includes transcripts of what happened during the second six months. I was the only subject in these experiments. During this period, I took not microdoses, but large doses with the intention to experience the full psychedelic effects of each substance.

I experimented with psilocybin, Amanita muscaria (the famous mushroom with the red cap dotted in white), LSA (from Hawaiian Baby Woodrose seeds), DMT, and LSD.

As with the other substances, the LSD test session yielded good and provocative results. I was tested on remote viewing and telepathy. It was during the final telepathy test with LSD when I felt like someone or something stopped me from going further.

For each telepathy test, I sat alone at our dining room table with several blank sheets of paper in front of me. Cierra was in another room and out of sight, focusing on a simple line drawing with the intention of *sending* me the information. To help her focus, she slowly traced each line of the drawing with her fingertip.

My primary goal was to *receive* the information from her and put it to paper. This way, we could compare my perceptions with the target afterward. My secondary goal was to sustain enough focus, clarity, and self-control to pay attention to the experiment. Since I was on LSD, it was a significant challenge not to lie down, close my eyes, and surrender to the myriad visions emerging from within.

Another challenge was ignoring the *body load*, the physical side effects such as muscle trembling, chills, and nausea. It took everything

---

[5] McNamara, S. (2023). *Dewdrops of Infinity: Psychedelics, Psychic Abilities, UFOs, and the Puharich Project.* Mind Possible.

I had to remain steady enough to discern the subtle psychic impressions arising within the deepest, darkest regions of my mind.

That evening's first telepathy test yielded good, but not great, results. Instead of calling it quits for the day out of sheer exhaustion, I asked Cierra to choose one more target.

I pulled myself together and drew on every internal resource still available to me. The first thing that came to mind was a pattern of dotted curves. In the video recording, I can hear myself using the word "doily" to describe its lace-like appearance. After drawing it, I turned the paper over and pushed it away to start on a fresh sheet.

I filled the paper with a set of gently curving parallel lines to which I said, "This is nonsense." I set that paper aside and reached for another.

The video then shows me resting my forehead on my clasped hands as if in prayer. Time passes without me moving. I'm concentrating. I'm looking within. I'm waiting. Then I pick up the pen and draw two shapes, one right beneath the other.

The first shape is of a right-pointing triangle, except that the top line is slightly curved. It might vaguely resemble a pennant moving in the wind. It could also be a slice of pizza.

The second shape is of a cross. A shorter horizontal line bisected by a longer vertical one. I run my pen over all the lines to make them thicker and darker, but don't add any more details.

The video shows that I completed the first lines of both drawings in 13 seconds. Another 7 seconds were spent darkening them. After the initial period of silence and stillness preceding my drawing, it was as if I had suddenly gained access to information that had been hidden. I'd opened a door.

The video records me saying, "It's just a triangle-thing floating in the sky." I sigh and gasp, as if straining for more. Then I say, "This doesn't feel like telepathy." I groan, then "This is something…" I squint and lower my head as if to dig deeper. I want more.

Exasperated, I turn and face the camera while waving my palm toward my face a couple of times, mimicking something coming at me forcefully. I remember the feeling when I did that; it was as if someone else was getting involved in my process. Like an invisible hand pressing down on my mind… to suppress me.

It's time to close the door.

Then I say, "Something is… It's so intense." I pause to organize my thoughts. "I'm probably going off into paranoia. It's as if something is stopping… me… from going any further with this." I was too sheepish at the time to say out loud who or what I thought might be involved. I suspected it wasn't human.

You've gone far enough.

I then call out to my wife, "Ok, sweety, do you want to just stop and bring it over?" I was asking her to bring the target so we could compare it to my transcript. I wanted to move on and forget about it.

It turned out to be one of the most accurate telepathy tests of my life. But like so many of the experiments I've done and watched others do, too, and like many of the transcripts you'll find in this book, they produce few, if any, answers, and too many new questions.

As an aside, I want this book to focus on the work done by the participants of the 2025 Psychic Training Intensive, not my own, so I won't use up more space by printing the results here. If you'd like to see the target and transcript from my LSD experiment, or watch the video, see the footnote.[6]

In a roundabout way, the experiences I just shared with you serve to expand the definition of telepathy. Telepathy is broader than human-to-human communication. A person may receive information from, and be influenced by, something that is *not* human, or, said more conservatively, unknown. Or, daringly put… alien.

---

[6] If you'd like to **watch the video**, see the **QR code in Appendix 4**, or search for "DMT, LSD & ESP: Remote Viewing, Telepathy, Clairvoyance psychic psychedelics with Sean McNamara 3/3" on YouTube. This specific test begins at the 18 minutes 27 second mark. The link is https://youtu.be/h0wIwNUKkuA. It's always possible for YouTube to remove the video, so the link may not work in the future. And if you'd like to see the **transcript and target**, they're inside my other book, *Dewdrops of Infinity*.

Of course, it's possible that one day we'll discover that humans from the present or even from the future are indeed responsible for the UFO/UAP[7] phenomena. We can also recall that there exists evidence that animals and humans can also communicate psychically.[8] Ask any large group of pet owners, and you'll probably hear enough anecdotes to at least soften your disbelief.

And what about another expansion of the definition? What about an embodied (physically alive) human being communicating with a disembodied (deceased) one? To answer that question, please allow me to share one more experience of my father with you.

One week had passed since his death. On the final evening of that week, I stayed up later than usual to tinker in my office while Cierra slept. Undistracted, my thoughts naturally turned to my dad. Of course, I was still mourning him. Though I'd gotten used to it, I was intrigued by the state of mind that had become normal for me.

I drove my car slower than usual and could easily ignore or at least forgive the near-collisions and stupid decisions made by more aggressive drivers. I didn't mind the long line for the cashier at the grocery store. I didn't worry as much about the news, and I felt less inclined to browse social media. It's curious to me how similar this state resembled the way I usually feel in the days following a meditation retreat or a psychedelic journey. And just as with psychedelics, I was more sensitive to music.

That night in my home office, I grabbed my guitar and sat on the floor. With my legs crossed and my back against the wall, I plucked and strummed my guitar quietly so I wouldn't wake Cierra. As I played, I thought of my dad. Memories, hopes, regrets, and apologies flowed through me as I lost myself to the strings' vibrations. Then I went to bed and fell asleep.

---

[7] UAP is the acronym for Unidentified Aerial Phenomena and can be used interchangeably with UFO, Unidentified Flying Object, when stricter definitions are unnecessary.

[8] Sheldrake, R. (2011). *Dogs That Know When Their Owners Are Coming Home: Fully Updated and Revised.* Crown.

Like my previous more-than-just-a-dream experiences, I became conscious while remaining physically asleep. And I was with him.

We were hiking the mountains together. The trail curved as we ascended and descended it, and Dad walked at a pace faster than I'd ever seen him move. He was full of energy. He wore jeans and a white sweater which accentuated the vibrancy he emanated. He was in a joyful state and appeared to be in his thirties, not his eighties.

The scene shifted from the mountains to my parents' neighborhood. Dad led me up the street and back to the house. He opened the door and had me follow him up the stairs. He turned right at the top. I assumed he was headed for his old bedroom even though he'd spent his final months sleeping downstairs in his recliner.

Instead, he opened another door, a door that I know is always locked. It's a door I hadn't walked through in years. We call it my mom's "junk room." The last time I saw it, it was mostly filled with papers and folders scattered about. Mom kept every other room in the house clean and tidy. But not this one. This was her space where she could allow chaos to take over. Afraid of what anyone might think if they saw it, she always kept it locked.

But Dad just turned the doorknob and walked right in. I followed. Since I was fully cognizant that he was dead, I was a bit surprised that of all the rooms in the house that he could've returned to, he chose Mom's junk room.

As I looked around, I saw piles of things scattered around, mostly boxes, clothes, and papers. It had the feeling of someone packing up to move out. Dad stood by the closet, looking straight at me with a smile on his face. His left arm was extended to the side with his hand gripping a guitar by the neck.

With that, the experience faded out, and I opened my eyes in bed. Although it felt like more than just a dream, I brushed it off as pre-sleep conditioning since I'd been playing guitar and thinking of him right before going to bed. I closed my eyes and slept through the morning.

As the next day went on, something kept nagging at me. I couldn't stop thinking about my nighttime experience. It was strange to see him so happy, happier than I'd ever seen him alive. I also felt relieved because maybe he really was somewhere else now, somewhere freed from his age, from his physical pain and limitations, and freed from our criticism and opinions about his health, lifestyle choices, and his particular brand of humor.

I decided to visit my mom that afternoon and drove to the house. I walked up the path to the front door, remembering last night's scene of following Dad inside. I headed up the stairs to greet my mom in the kitchen. As we chatted, my attention kept turning to the hallway and to the locked room I hadn't entered in years.

Mom noticed my distraction, so I told her about my dream. Then I asked her if I could go inside the room to look around. She wasn't excited about someone else entering her junk room, but she kindly unlocked it for me anyway.

It was as messy as I expected, but the mess was different. There were more boxes lying around. I remembered that my dad had stood by the closet, so I browsed that side of the room. I caught my breath, surprised.

There, against the wall where my dad had stood, jutting out from a pile of boxes, was the neck of a guitar. I photographed it with my phone before doing anything else, so I could show Cierra how I found it. Then, I pulled the guitar out of the pile and held it up so I could see the whole instrument. I'd never seen this guitar before in my life. And here I stood, guitar in my hand, just as my dad had stood last night, holding the guitar in his.

I called out to my mom for her to come see. I asked her about the guitar's provenance. She said she'd gotten it years ago for one of my nieces or nephews to play with when they visited her. At some point, probably due to disuse, it was relegated to the junk room.

One could argue that I'd simply had a *precognitive* dream, that I'd caught a glimpse of the future. Or that it was *clairvoyance*, and my mind had used the dream state to introduce hidden knowledge (the guitar's existence) into my conscious awareness.

But I believe Dad used my *association* with guitars to create a telepathic moment. I believe he initiated the experience from his new vantage point, one where he had far more awareness of life's intersections and connections than any of us do while we're fully embodied. He saw an opportunity, and he took it.

The point of this story is to illustrate telepathy between an embodied and a disembodied agent. The crucial factor for success? A meaningful connection. A heart connection. Love.

May this book be a bridge for those seeking to understand what it means to be alive, to die, and the depth of our connection within the Great Mystery. I cannot claim to offer answers here, only clues. And, perhaps, hope.

I expect this first chapter has piqued your interest. But please be patient and suppress the temptation to skip the next few chapters and go directly to the transcripts. Reviewing them without context might only cause a person to raise an eyebrow and utter "Hmmm, that's interesting." But with the context provided in the following pages, those transcripts may transform your understanding of reality and enhance your appreciation for the miracle called life.

This chapter discussed what may be the fundamental reason people are interested in telepathy and other psychic phenomena. It's the question of our very existence.

As you already learned in the first sentence, this was the first chapter I wrote when I began working on this book[9]. As readers of my other books already know, I write in a personal way, by sharing poignant events to make the narrative more relatable.

If, while reviewing the transcripts, you find yourself wondering why these scribbles and sketches are so important, I hope you remember the meaning of it all as discussed in this chapter.

---

[9] Other writers will understand and relate to the notion that first drafts are not necessarily begun with a book's first chapter. Sometimes, the author starts in the middle, or even with the conclusion.

The next chapter, *Typical and Divergent, Together*, acknowledges the recent cultural phenomenon known as "The Telepathy Tapes," including evidence that a segment of humanity is significantly more psychic than the rest of us. And though I'm not exactly sure how, I believe there is a way for us[10] and them to come together for the benefit of our whole species.

After that, the two chapters, *Transmission* and *Establishing Set and Setting,* will be especially helpful to those who are or want to serve as teachers. Whether of telepathy or any other consciousness-related topic doesn't matter. There are many ways to teach, and what I present here is one way, the way I've come to do it after much trial and error and based on my experience as a student in various contexts. I hope you can use some of what I offer here and build on it, eventually developing a better way, your unique way, of doing things.

It will be clear that I regard the teaching of psychic abilities as a sacred process. A good teacher must keep their ego in check, convey a sense of presence, and respect their students as much as the material itself.

In *A Note to Scientists*, I set expectations for applying critical thinking to this book and the events it describes. The 2025 Psychic Training Intensive was **not** a scientific study. It was a training program. But this book does offer ideas for scientists developing new experiments to investigate consciousness.

I considered writing a chapter called, *A Note to Pseudo-skeptics* but realized the futility of communicating with people unwilling to change their beliefs even when presented with opposing evidence. True skeptics, which is what many (but not all) scientists are, remain ever-open to new data and are willing to change their opinions based on it.

Part 2 includes a special invitation to the reader through a dream that came to my friend Cheryl, who was also a participant at the intensive. Part 2 also includes the main telepathy instructions,

[10] By "us" I mean the portion of the population that can be reasonably classified as *neurotypical.*

including a transcript of a hypnotic induction I created for improving conscious sensitivity to psychic impressions.

In *Observed Attributes of Telepathy*, I share several insights gained from reviewing the transcripts from the intensive. These observations help us understand not just that telepathy is real, but how the minds of senders and receivers operate to produce it. This is not Hollywood telepathy. It's the real thing, which is, frankly, less flashy. Sometimes, a trained eye is needed to even identify it.

This book cannot include all the transcripts from the intensive due to size restrictions, but the most significant ones are here in Part 3. From them, a small but significant list of attributes has been created. I hope future research by others will, in time, contribute many more attributes to help us understand the associative aspect of psychic functioning.

Also, due to the book's size restriction, I did not include our experiences with psychometry[11] and psychokinesis via spoon-bending.

I believe the participants' overall psychic performance improved over the course of the week-long intensive because of the cross-training. I encourage you to review their transcripts chronologically to watch their progression. However, if you find the first ones too boring, you can always start with the last one on page 321 and work your way backward.

The final chapter, *The Closing Circle*, contains a message I've wanted to share publicly for a long time. It would've seemed out of place here if it weren't for the fact that this book is as spiritual as it is parapsychological. After over ten years of intense psychic exploration, my relationship to psi[12] has changed.

In the final chapter, I'll tell you why.

---

[11] *psychometry* is the practice of using touch (by holding) to psychically determine an object's history, especially information about its owner, who may be living or deceased.

[12] *psi* (pronounced "sigh") is the Greek letter used to represent psychic phenomena in parapsychology.

Below, the guitar exactly as I found it in Mom's junk room.

Below, the guitar replaced on the pile after taking the first photograph.

TYPICAL AND DIVERGENT, TOGETHER

Neurotypical (adjective): *not* affected with a disorder or condition (such as autism spectrum disorder, attention deficit hyperactivity disorder, dyslexia, or obsessive-compulsive disorder) that impacts the way the brain processes information: exhibiting or characteristic of typical neurological development[13]

Neurodivergent (adjective): having or relating to a disorder or condition (such as autism spectrum disorder, attention deficit hyperactivity disorder, dyslexia, or obsessive-compulsive disorder) that impacts the way the brain processes information : exhibiting or characteristic of variations in typical neurological development[14]

- Merriam-Webster's Online Dictionary

Before we go any proceed, it is important for me to address the book's subtitle and its implied audience: *Telepathy Training for Neurotypicals*. As you read on, please know that I make several *generalizations* about the groups I discuss. By definition, they do not apply to all the group members. There are always exceptions.

[13] https://www.merriam-webster.com/dictionary/neurotypical

[14] https://www.merriam-webster.com/dictionary/neurodivergent

It's safe to say that before September 9, 2024, I could've easily left "for Neurotypicals" out of the book's title under the assumption that any person could benefit from these instructions and no qualification was needed.

But on that date, the first episode of an unusual audio series was released via the online streaming service Spotify. The episode was titled "Unveiling the Hidden World of Telepathic Communication in a Silenced Community." Today, many people around the world are familiar with the name of the series, *The Telepathy Tapes*, its creator, Ky Dickens, and researcher Dr. Diane Hennacy Powell.[15]

Dickens' and Powell's hard work and persistence have led to the public's growing awareness that a segment of our population possesses near-perfect psychic perception. These are children diagnosed with autism and who are non-speaking. In the context of the children featured in The Telepathy Tapes, *non-speaking* means that although they are completely (or partially in some cases) non-verbal, they can communicate. They do so through facial gestures, other body movements, non-word vocalization, and tools such as letterboards using protocols like Rapid Prompting Method (RPM).

I can't remember exactly how I found out about The Telepathy Tapes, but I vaguely remember someone recommending it to me. That sort of recommendation wouldn't have been out of the ordinary.

Searching my digital calendar for the word *telepathy*, I see that I held my first public telepathy class in March of 2018. It was a one-day event that I named "Psychic Olympics." I held it at Cierra's meditation center, Mayu Sanctuary.[16] Scrolling more through my calendar, I see numerous telepathy classes I taught in person at local New Age bookstores and more often over Zoom in the years since. So, of course, I was excited to listen to a new podcast called The Telepathy Tapes.

---

[15] https://open.spotify.com/show/1zigaPaUWO4G9SiFV0Kf1c The series is also available to listen to on YouTube.

[16] Sadly, Mayu Sanctuary was forced into permanent closure during the Covid lockdown.

It was so good, I listened to it twice. The second time, I listened non-stop during a long road trip from Nebraska to Colorado with Cierra. There were a few times during the drive when I had to wipe tears off my cheeks and noticed tears on hers too. Although much of the podcast discusses incredible demonstrations of extreme telepathy between an autistic child and their parent or caretaker, the overall message is a profoundly spiritual one. It's about our connection to each other in this world and beyond, and our connection to divinity itself.

The point is, neurodivergent people such as the autistic children featured in the podcast are naturally highly telepathic. They have no need whatsoever for this book. It's for the rest of us who might label ourselves *neurotypical* or normally functioning.

It is unfortunate that the current definition of neurodivergent has a negative slant in using the phrase "disorder or condition." Perhaps one day, with credit to Ky Dickens, Dr. Diane Hennacy Powell, the families they interviewed, and everyone else involved, we'll open the dictionary to find a new definition for *neurodivergent,* including the following:

> ...exhibiting or characteristic of **variations** in typical neurological development ***such as advanced abilities*** *including telepathy, clairvoyance, precognition, past-life knowledge, and communication with non-physical spiritual beings.*[17]

I would only do the podcast a disservice by describing it further here. Since it's easily accessible online, I leave it to you to listen to it yourself or watch the documentary. I highly recommend that you do.

---

[17] I admit this hypothetical definition is problematic for various reason, one being that other kinds of people, for example those with limited brain function due to dementia or those with apraxia due to stroke or injury may also exhibit extreme psychic functioning at times.

These children have helped, and continue to help, people around the world develop a new understanding of love, divinity, and the sacredness of our human existence.

But for the context of this book, there is one aspect of The Telepathy Tapes I must discuss here: The Hill.

As we learned in the podcast, The Hill is a non-physical meeting place where the children can visit, play, learn, and relate to each other. Note the phrase "non-physical." This isn't a material place. It's a realm of consciousness. It's a psychic group chat. And they can "go there," for lack of a better phrase, anytime they want.

In the weeks following my second listening of the podcast, I felt a growing sense of inspiration. I was touched by the children's struggles as well as their wisdom and compassion. I felt compelled to help them. But how?

I had no connection with the autistic community. As a clinical mental health counselor, my client base is composed of neurotypicals. As of this writing, I have no experience working with neurodivergent people, aside from the occasional client with ADHD. So, what to do?

Late one night while lying in bed, I realized I could try asking for guidance. A couple of months had passed since my father died, and I remembered my nighttime communication with him. What if something like that could happen again? What if I could contact those whom I was interested in helping? What if a neurotypical person like me could use whatever telepathic capacity I had to visit The Hill?

Night after night, lying in our bed, I would spend the final minutes of consciousness sending my message to The Hill before fading into sleep. Some nights, I could swear I perceived an energetic response to my effort. Have you ever dipped your feet into a pond or stream with minnows in it? Imagine several tiny fish suddenly darting through the water to investigate your feet, perhaps to nibble the dead skin from your toes.

That's how it felt. Like several lovely, vibrant energies had rushed into my mental space. Or had I entered theirs? But not much else happened, and I gave up the practice.

Then one morning, I logged into my Facebook account and saw a new message request waiting for me. It had been sent the night before, and it was from someone I'd never met.

Her name was Dalia Burgoin.

January 12, 2025, 8:59 PM

Hi Sean, this is very unusual for me to reach out, but spirit has been nudging me to do so with you. Since you're promoting the telepathy tapes so much, I wondered if you'd like to interview my daughter. My daughter is extremely telepathic and uses RPM to communicate. she can do basically everything they mentioned in the tapes and more. She's 14 and has been spelling since she was 11. It makes me nervous to put my daughter out there, but she keeps telling me it's time. She has been on the news 5 times in 2024 simply advocating spelling to communicate but we never expected to talk about her spiritual gifts outside of spiritual groups. she said she is ready for it. I have a large spiritual background and have taken her to many classes, and she always ends up teaching the classes lol.

I didn't know what to think. Half of me was excited. I wanted to believe that my message had gotten through and made its way to Dalia. But the other half of me refused to believe this was what it appeared to be. If anything, it was just an interesting synchronicity. Besides, I thought, Dalia's not autistic; her daughter is. So, why wasn't her daughter the one who initiated the contact?

Fortunately, I knew better than to yield to my materialistic side. Years of psychic exploration alone and with others had taught me there is more to this world if we're willing to take a chance and look.

I replied right away.

January 13, 2025, 9:14 AM

Hi Migdalia,[18] thanks for reaching out. Recently I've found myself lying in bed at night trying to telepathically tune in to "The Hill," while repeating the message that I'd like to help somehow, and that I'd also be interested in knowing if they could teach me something that I could use to help people (including myself) become more telepathic.[19] I'm not especially psychic myself, but I'm skilled at helping others experience whatever ability they already have inside them.

Another thing I do while trying to connect to The Hill is repeat my name and phone number over and over again while inviting the kids to give it to their caretaker so they can call me if they feel it would be useful to them. That hasn't happened, but it's interesting to me that you reached out last night (I just saw your message this morning).

You offered for me to interview your daughter, but I'm not sure if you meant "interview" as in just me talking to her, or "interview" as in me recording it and putting it online. I'm not a podcaster (I usually get interviewed on other people's channels), and I don't have a massive audience, but I know I should be open minded at this point.

It might be good if the next step was just for you and me to chat about all this a little bit more. I know this is sensitive stuff and I want

[18] I didn't know yet that she goes by "Dalia."

[19] At the time, I was leading the first ever Mind Possible Teacher Training program and had my trainees in mind.

to be as delicate and respectful as possible, especially since a child is concerned. How about if we set up a Zoom call so we could chat?

Dalia agreed, and on January 18th, she, her daughter Lidu, and I met over Zoom. I was nervous. I felt intimidated by the prospect of meeting someone who presumably could perceive exactly what I was thinking and feeling. I was also excited. Hadn't I asked for something like this to happen during those nights in bed, projecting my message into the ether in the hope of reaching The Hill?

There was nothing to fear, though. On my computer screen, I saw only earnestness on Dalia's face, and perhaps the same awkwardness that I felt. After all, this was an unusual meeting.

In Lidu, I saw an innocence lost on most of the teenagers (and adults) I've met. This was not an immature type of innocence, though. Rather, she projected a clarity of mind unencumbered by pretense.

Perhaps she was comfortable just as she was. Or maybe it took so much energy and focus for her to control her body that she had nothing left for projecting a false version of herself, the way the rest of us tend to do, even after our teenage years.

I knew this might be an important conversation, so I took notes. I'm glad I did because without them, I don't think I could've accurately recalled such an important exchange.

It was unique not only because of the topics we discussed, but also in how Lidu responded. First, at that time, Lidu was less verbal than she is as of this book's release, and so she and Dalia used a letterboard. I would pose a question for Lidu, and Dalia transcribed the letters Lidu indicated on the board to form words, which then formed phrases. Each one took several minutes to complete.

The process was erratic. Sometimes Lidu's body would cooperate with her will. Sometimes it wouldn't, and I could tell when that occurred because her frustration was obvious. She moaned and groaned when it was extra difficult to get her message out. When she did, I became nervous that our conversation would end too soon. But Dalia knew better and gave Lidu the space and time she needed to refocus and try again.

The second reason the conversation was unusual was that they told me that Lidu's answers were based on what her angels were telling her in response to my questions. When they told me that, I realized our conversation might be part of something bigger. Perhaps this was a small piece of some cosmic plan. It also dawned on me that another type of telepathy was occurring, one between a physical person and divine beings.

My notes don't include everything that was said, so I will try to recreate the pertinent aspects of the conversation here. I will place an asterisk (*) at the end of any sentence you can find in the scanned image of my original notes, which you'll find in Appendix 1 on pages 327 and 328. I may remember some portions a bit differently from how they occurred, but hopefully those differences are inconsequential.

One of the first questions was from Dalia and me to Lidu. Dalia wondered why she had felt compelled to contact me through Facebook. Lidu's response, transcribed from the letterboard, was, "In hill, he was on telepathic elevated frequency."*

I was excited by this. It seemed that somehow, I'd successfully projected my thoughts to The Hill and at least one person perceived them. Dalia asked Lidu for more information, and it turned out that Lidu had psychically influenced Dalia to contact me.

My next question was about how I might help other people develop their telepathic abilities. Lidu responded, "Everyone who wants to *hear* should each ask their angels to help. Team of angels always with you, will help but only interfere when asked."* At some point Dalia clarified that the word "hear" in Lidu's response meant *to be telepathic*.

Although I'd hoped for a practical technique such as focusing a certain way, or using a special meditation, this response made sense. I was aware that Lidu's angels were offering this advice at that very moment, so what more could I ask for? Their suggested technique was so simple that a child could understand it: Just ask for help.

Written beneath these responses in my notes, you'll see a single word, "catacombs." This was from a moment when Dalia and Lidu wanted to demonstrate Lidu's telepathy during our call. Dalia thought of a word and wrote it down without Lidu seeing. Then she asked Lidu to use the letterboard to report what word she perceived. She spelled it out perfectly, "catacombs."

The next paragraph of notes is prefaced with two words I used as a placeholder, "other religions." This was a reminder for me to ask a burning question I'd held since listening to The Telepathy Tapes. In the podcast, the word "angels" is often used, lending a distinctly Judeo-Christian religiosity to the children's otherworldly experiences.

But since my early childhood, I've lived in and traveled to numerous countries in Asia, Europe, and Central and South America. I've seen the many ways humanity expresses its spirituality in religious contexts. Though Christianity, Judaism, and Islam have a majority following, there are many other religions, each followed by many millions of people. And many of those religions bear little or no similarity at all to the Abrahamic, monotheistic traditions prominent in the Americas [20], Europe, and the Middle East.

I'm a citizen of my country, but in my heart, I'm a citizen of the world, and I respect the idea that there is at least some truth within every religion. I also believe that no single religion is completely correct or able to claim ultimate authority over spiritual matters. Therefore, I was concerned about the possibility that the children's accounts might be used by religious zealots to say, "See! They're talking about angels and God and heaven. That means *our* religion is right and everybody else's is wrong!"

If another program like The Telepathy Tapes were to include children raised in Hindu families in India, in shamanic families in

[20] I'm referring to post-colonial North, Central, and South America, following the displacement and genocide of millions of indigenous peoples.

Mongolia, in Buddhist families in Japan, or families in a Hopi pueblo, what would they have to say? How would they describe divinity and the non-physical beings that reside in it?

I knew this might be my only chance to put this question to rest, so I asked Lidu about it. She, and her angels through her, responded, "The angels are the same beings across spiritual categories but with different names that are used. They want him [Sean] to know that his view is a healthy one in his etymology, viewpoint. But it eventually will evolve to include a love for expressing the spiritual religious interpretations as well. They [Lidu's angels] are showing me that he will evolve to help the spiritual teachers of all religions, especially the secret ones out there that help psychics emerge their ability (to) eavesdrop."

Dalia explained that to Lidu, the word *eavesdrop,* like the word *hear* from earlier, means to perceive telepathically.

I deeply appreciated the angels' response, specifically indicating the difference in terminology used by different groups. This made sense to me. And it supported the notion that access to the sacred is not reserved for only two or three major world religions.

But I didn't know how to respond to the angel's comment that I will "evolve to help spiritual teachers of all religions…emerge their ability to eavesdrop." My life is quite limited and focused on helping a small number of people, such as my therapy clients and meditation students. So, I don't fit the angels' description.

But there is this book. It can do things that I can't. Thanks to the internet, it can easily be found by those spiritual teachers actively seeking new resources. And it can travel globally. I hope this is what the angels meant.

Let's continue with my notes. The next line reads, "With dad, not energetically aligned." These were my short notes about Lidu's response when I asked her if she could be telepathic with her father the way she was with Dalia.

The next section starts with my question, "What about private stuff?" I'm aware of my thoughts enough to be very uncomfortable about the idea that a super psychic could perceive them and get to know my anger, my bias, my ignorance, my arrogance, my fears, my regrets, my desires, and my fantasies.

She responded, "I telepathically can see everything that you experience, but I easily can turn my attention elsewhere." I listened to her answer, simultaneously realizing that someone like Lidu probably has much better things to focus on than my faults or what I do in the bedroom or the bathroom. And I suspected someone like Lidu wouldn't judge me if she did. Her perspective, I grew to realize, was far wider and more universal than that of ordinary people, and far more compassionate.

My next note is self-explanatory and reads, "More to Lidu's mission?" She responded, "We are in telepathic teams to bring a paradigm shift to the world." Even after all the psychic experiences I've had and witnessed over the years, Lidu, together with Dalia, were causing a paradigm shift in me. And this was just a single, brief conversation. The idea of telepathic teams was intriguing, but not surprising because the profound connection between non-speaking children with autism is a repeated theme in The Telepathy Tapes.

The next line is my transcription of Dalia posing a question to Lidu for me. "How can he help?" After all, this was my motivation for attempting to contact The Hill night after night. To help.

"He can help by asking non-speakers to telepathically tell their story on his networks on TV then have them see then spell." This was confusing for me because I'm not on TV and I'm not associated with any TV networks. I interpreted "have them see then spell" to mean demonstrating their abilities in conjunction with using a letterboard or other device to share their perceptions.

I wouldn't be surprised to one day see Dalia, Lidu, and others like them, on mainstream TV networks changing the paradigm on a grand scale.

In fact, Dalia and Lidu are already leading their own workshops to help people discover their psychic potential. If you would like to learn more about them, you can find the QR codes for their websites[21] and see their photos in Appendix 5 on page 333 (or see the footnote below).

Maybe one of this book's readers has a connection to a TV network and will suddenly realize a special opportunity. Maybe that's how this book will help, by connecting people like Dalia and Lidu with certain readers for a greater purpose.

The last note reads, "Can I say I am pleased with his desire to help, and his channel will grow exponentially with early expressions of telepathy using the letterboard and telling others the teachings."

Maybe that's where it all starts for each of us, by asking the simple question, "How can I help?" After all, we don't need to know the answer before asking the question.

* * * *

I hope you understand that neurotypical people have something in common with neurodivergent people. We are all conscious beings, capable of love, and so deeply connected that we can communicate through mind alone. You'll see that evidence here.

Some neurotypical readers might hope to one day become as psychic as non-speaking people with autism. Please consider that their extreme abilities are possibly due to *apraxia*, their limited voluntary control over their bodies.

Based on what I heard in The Telepathy Tapes and through my own out-of-body experiences[22], it seems to me that some of these individuals are in a mostly out-of-body state, all the time. From that perspective, it's understandable they can barely manage their bodies. Because for the most part, they're not even inside their bodies. Their

---

[21] www.DaliaBurgoin.com and www.Extra-Ordinaries.com

[22] See my other book "Renegade Mystic" (2nd edition) for instructions for having an out-of-body experience and for my personal accounts.

minds abide largely unhindered by flesh and blood, free to explore the space of the soul, the universal field of consciousness.

I hope the neurotypical reader can appreciate the tradeoff. Although this book will teach you how to access your telepathic ability, it can't help you become super psychic like some neurodivergent people are.

Instead, you get to have completely voluntary control of your body. You can walk, run, climb, and jump. You can sculpt clay, play musical instruments, paint with oil on canvas, and dance ballet. You can deliver important speeches to large groups or easily whisper "I love you" into someone's ear. You can make love. You can ask for chocolate. And you can ask for vanilla instead when your mood changes. You can also say "no" and "stop" to protect yourself. You can ask for help. You can tell the doctor where it hurts inside and how it feels. And you'll get the help you need, easily and without judgment.

Would you really trade all that in for apraxia and the psychic perception that might accompany it?

Being fully embodied is a different kind of freedom, and it's a great opportunity. We neurotypicals may never be as psychic as the children in The Telepathy Tapes, but we get to live our precious physical lives and experience life on planet Earth in the ways fully embodied people can.

If you're still concerned with becoming extremely psychic, don't worry. One day, you'll die. And then, I believe, you'll finally be free to explore the space of the soul unhindered. At least, if it's possible, until you enter a new physical form.

Until then, remember this: Your physical and non-physical life, whether neurotypical or neurodivergent, is sacred. You and I are inherent members of this universe, and as such, we are not separate. Whether you're psychic or not, you matter every bit as much as everyone else.

You are loved.

You are love.

TRANSMISSION

On July 16, 2024, I sent an email to my mailing list composed of people who'd read my books, taken my online or live classes, or who'd signed up on my website for other reasons. Since I'd been collecting names for a long time, I was hopeful that at least a handful of people would reply. I was nervous because deep down inside, I believed how people responded would reveal if any of the work I'd done over the years really mattered.

The subject line read, "Do you want to become a Mind Possible teacher?" The first line in the message's body read, "I think it's time for me to pass the torch and train others to teach what I teach."

I'd had an inkling that my life was entering a new stage and I might not be able to continue teaching the way I had, or as frequently as I had, down the road. This was three and a half months before my father would die. I also didn't know that about a year later, my mom would be diagnosed with Alzheimer's disease.

I had no idea what was coming, just an inkling that it was time for me to pass the torch. I'd also become somewhat bored with teaching and knew that it was a natural, necessary stage of a teacher's evolution to cultivate and train new teachers.

Whenever I concluded a class, I'd encourage the participants to take my techniques and make them their own, improve them, and pass them along to others. After my horrible experiences decades ago with spiritual teachers who withheld knowledge to maintain control over their followers[23], I vowed never to repeat their behaviors.

---

[23] See my other book, *Renegade Mystic*.

But class after class, after encouraging them to use of what they'd learned and teach it to others, I noticed participants breaking eye contact, others sinking down in their chairs just a little bit, and the rest shaking their heads.

Teaching, I realized, is not for everyone. Given that on some lists, public speaking ranks first among people's worst fears, while death ranks not second, but seventh, I shouldn't have been surprised.

And teaching, to me, is about more than delivering a set of instructions. It's about transmission and presence. On the surface, a teacher educates by presenting facts, techniques, and other information. But on a deeper level, a teacher can influence their students through presence. But what is presence?

If you've ever attended a multi-day meditation retreat with a seasoned instructor, you may have felt their presence while sitting silently together hour after hour, day after day. Assuming the instructor had been developing their inner peace for many years, the silence you sensed within them sharply contrasted with the cacophony of thoughts clamoring inside your own head.

But it was the experiencing of that instructor's stillness outside of yourself that allowed you to recognize it within yourself. For a split second at first, if that. But with practice, the stillness endured longer. And with weeks, months, and years of steady meditation training, you realize the instructor's presence has become your own. That is transmission.

But it doesn't always require lengthy periods of cultivation. Sometimes it's immediate and unexpected.

For example, I experienced transmission during my father's memorial service inside a Catholic church. After my sister and I gave our eulogies, it was time for the priest to deliver his sermon. Perhaps it was my mental exhaustion. Perhaps it was that strange way the heart opens more than usual when in a state of grief. But for whatever reason, I noticed a faint white glow surrounding the priest's head.

Rather than standing still at the lectern, the priest slowly paced from one side of the sanctuary to the other. And his halo went with him. More than his halo, though, I recognized he was a genuinely contemplative and prayerful person. I could feel it and hear it in his voice. And listening to him while observing his halo brought me calm. It evoked a sense of sacredness within me that I had been too overwhelmed to tap into on my own that day.

Presence isn't a discrete phenomenon, though. It is experienced variously. It can transmit stillness and peace. It can transmit the absence of craving, desire, or malice. It can also transmit energy as strength, connection, or joy. However way it manifests, one thing is certain. It cannot be forced, and it cannot be faked.

Transmission occurs because the necessary causes and conditions are present. The person transmitting must have a living relationship with that *something deeper*. In the moment, the transmitter must not be distracted or disconnected from it. And the transmitter cannot oblige it to occur. To do so would be an act of the combined arrogance, ignorance, and unearned entitlement that defines the *inflated ego*.

One reliable sign that genuine transmission is occurring is that the transmitter *isn't trying*. Instead, they're just being themselves. They might seem dull or funny, heady or heart-based, logical or instinctual, gregarious or introverted, but it doesn't really matter as long as they have a strong capacity for empathy. To connect.

Sadly, because of the effect of social media, it needs to be said that physical appearance absolutely does not matter. It doesn't matter how much of an influencer you are, how many followers your channel gets, or what your body looks like when you're at the beach. Those are mere appearances.

Simply put, what matters here is authenticity. Real authenticity, not social media authenticity. Not *virtue signaling*. This is not a high school popularity contest. But it certainly feels like it sometimes.

Younger or less experienced spiritual seekers may not spot it when the person labeling themselves teacher, leader, coach, guru, or shaman is putting on an act. But those of us who've been around the block and bear invisible scars from being mistreated by these kinds of people can spot them a mile away.

It's taken a lot of self-work and resilience for me to remember these kinds of teachers are just as much on a journey as I am, and that I've made many of the same mistakes they have in the past. So, I mention this not as a criticism against them, but, humbly, as a caution to vulnerable new travelers on the path. Being a teacher sometimes means serving as a protector, so I share this with you here, now.

Another condition for transmission is that the recipient, or *receiver*, must be psychologically, emotionally, and energetically open to recognizing that *something deeper,* not just within the transmitter, but within themselves. They must have sufficiently healthy self-esteem to understand they mustn't give their power away, and that the teacher is not fundamentally superior to them.

The final condition for transmission is for that *something deeper,* the Great Mystery, to participate. Based on my personal experiences in meditation, psychic exploration, and in using psychedelics, I believe certain events occur because, in those moments, the Great Mystery deems them *meaningful* enough and necessary to occur.

It would take too many pages, and perhaps an entire book, to explain all the reasons I believe this. But I will share one here.

Over years of leading psychic experiments with groups, I've seen successes in sufficient quantity and quality to confirm the reality of psychic phenomena. But I've also witnessed plenty of failures.

Today, I know there is only one question I must ask when a psychic experiment succeeds, "What *meaning* was produced by this event?"

In other words, "How did this event affect the lives of the participants? How did it affect me? How did it affect our understanding of life and consciousness, and what will be the ripple effect of that understanding? What does this mean for the denizens of planet Earth?"

When I contemplate the question, I'm reminded that sometimes the universe allows the apparent violation of physics' laws[24] for our individual benefit. And sometimes it allows those phenomena for the benefit of those around us, or for people we haven't even met yet. During an experiment with consciousness, it could be that the Great Mystery needs to birth a new understanding and, for reasons inconceivable by us, it deems the experiment to be an acceptable matrix[25].

When an experiment fails, I assume the Great Mystery didn't need it to happen. And our lives wouldn't have gained enough from it to justify the apparent violation against physicalism.

For example, in 2019, I led a small group of friends in a series of associative remote viewing exercises with the intention of winning the Colorado Pick 3 lottery. We won it twice, and we learned a tremendous amount in the process. It brought us closer together as friends. It heightened our curiosity about life and consciousness. It contributed to my writing a book about our experiences together, and that book has broadened the minds of readers across the world.[26]

But what about after those two wins? Oh, we've tried. Many times. And I still use lottery prediction as a fun teaching tool for associative remote viewing. But nothing. Zilch. Nada. Jack squat.

The Great Mystery, it seems, has no interest in sanctioning any more ARV[27] lottery wins when I'm involved. I imagine hearing it say (if it had a human voice), "How many times do you need to succeed to get the message? Twice is more than enough. This *meaning* has

---

[24] Of course, through quantum physics we can understand psychic phenomena to be quite natural, albeit rare and difficult to reproduce on demand and in a laboratory.

[25] "something within or from which something else originates, develops, or takes form." See https://www.merriam-webster.com/dictionary/matrix

[26] You can read about the techniques we used and see our remote viewing transcripts and targets in my other book *Signal and Noise*.

[27] ARV – Associative Remote Viewing

already been born into the world. So, move on, because there's more waiting to come to light, but you must let go of the past."

So, I've come to realize that to teach in a profound way is to cultivate *meaning*. People's lives are not enriched by the dissemination of lifeless information. They are enriched through felt experiences, especially when shared with others[28]. And as we've discussed, cultivating deep meaning requires a relationship with, and participation by, the Great Mystery.

But how does a teacher create meaningful experiences? I offer some of my examples from the 2025 Psychic Training Intensive in the next chapter.

---

[28] This statement carries extra weight for me as a mental health counselor. Sadly, I'm no longer surprised when diagnosing someone with major depressive disorder to learn most of their non-work time is spent indoors staring at a flat screen scrolling through social media, watching videos, or otherwise disrupting their neurochemistry in isolation. They are as disconnected from nature as they are from people. As Johann Hari stated in his Ted Talk at TedGlobalLondon, "The opposite of addiction is not sobriety, the opposite of addiction is connection."
https://www.ted.com/talks/johann_hari_everything_you_think_you_know_about_addiction_is_wrong/

ESTABLISHING SET AND SETTING

To describe my approach to teaching during the intensive, I'll use the well-known phrase popularized by Timothy Leary in the 1960's regarding the use of psychedelics: *set and setting*. Of course, we're not dealing with psychedelics here, but psychedelics and psychic exploration are similar in producing some of the most ineffable, transformative, and sacred experiences of mind and spirit.

Set is short for mindset, which includes one's emotional, psychological, and spiritual states before and during the experience. *Setting* refers to the physical and social environment where the experience occurs.

As the teacher, my role in the 2025 intensive was to support each participant's mindset and to create their appropriate setting. In our case, setting also included the participants because who we are surrounded by is as important as our physical environment. Creating the setting began long before the first day of the intensive.

The first step was to establish boundaries. Boundaries do two things.

First, they attract and include the positive forces needed for a good experience, including positively engaged participants. Second, they exclude unhelpful and potentially destructive forces, including inappropriate participants. My boundary setting began after forty people replied to my initial email asking, "Do you want to become a Mind Possible teacher?" The email asked them to complete a survey, which would help me decide which of them would make good candidates for training.

I knew there were some who just enjoyed collecting certifications. I wanted to filter them out. I also knew there were others who were *primarily* motivated by profit. I wanted to filter them out, too.

There's nothing wrong with earning money as a teacher in exchange for one's time, energy, and expertise. But although earning money is one of the benefits of offering classes and workshops (we all have bills to pay), it's not my primary motivation when teaching psychic development. For me, this type of teaching is not just a job, it's a spiritual vocation. And I wanted to train people for whom this could also be a vocation.

Aside from asking them to complete a survey, I used another method to help set the boundary. This one reminds me of how Japanese Shinto and Buddhist temples have *komainu*, statues of fiercely protective lion-dogs, posted outside as the temple's guardians.

Photo credit: Hyppolyte de Saint-Rambert, Wikimedia Commons, https://w.wiki/GNVV

My komainu weren't statues of lion-dogs, though. Mine took the form of language clearly posted on the teacher-training program's description. It listed the qualities that were unwelcome, qualities that could be cause for dismissal. Here are the unwelcome qualities as were listed on the website:

- Narcissism and/or excessive attention seeking.
- Aggressiveness, competitiveness, belittling, or shaming others.
- Dogmatism and/or inability to refrain from inserting one's religious beliefs while teaching these methods. It's okay for you to have your own religion, but you must teach in a secular way whenever you've advertised yourself as a Mind Possible Authorized Teacher.
- Discriminatory behavior toward people based on gender, age, race, sexual orientation, gender identity, religious background, or other personal qualities.
- Sexual impropriety, flirting, or harassment of other participants or the teacher.
- Indications of psychosis, obsession, delusion, or other mental health issues.
- Intentions to use the methods taught in this program to harm others in any way.
- Causing conflict, disruption, insult, or behaving in a threatening manner during or outside of class, toward other participants or the teacher.

When the teacher training program began, the list of forty potential candidates had been reduced to eleven[29]. My komainu had done their job.

Similar komainu would be used on the public registration page for the week-long intensive. I wanted to limit the public registration to only fifteen participants. Like the teacher-trainees, they needed to be the right fit.

Here is how the komainu appeared on the website for public registration for the 2025 Psychic Training Intensive:

Who this program is for:

- People who enjoy having fun in small groups in a healthy, relaxed setting.
- People who seek fun, variety, and innovation in exploring their innate abilities.
- People who are new to psychic development. Beginners welcome! Sean will make sure you feel comfortable and capable with each exercise.
- People who are experienced and looking for extra practice and fun with like-minded people are also welcome.

This program is NOT for:

- Aggressive or overly competitive people.
- Dogmatic people who believe there's only one "right" way to do things.
- People with large egos, such as "stars" who continually demand excess attention from the rest of the group.
- Lurkers. Everyone will participate in the exercises except when needing extra rest or time for self-care.

---

[29] Nine of the candidates successfully completed the program to receive the designation of *Mind Possible Authorized Teacher.*

- Proof-seekers and pseudo-skeptics. Psychic exploration offers evidence, but not proof. And everyone has different levels of ability; therefore, your performance is entirely up to you and cannot be guaranteed. A positive, relaxed, and open attitude is important to success.

I'm happy to say that we did indeed end up with a wonderful group of participants, both in the teacher-trainee and public segments.

I'm also grateful to those participants who allowed me to include their transcripts and anecdotes in this book. They included the teacher-trainees, and from the public segment, those who registered as *research fellows* and received a discount as consideration.

The teacher-trainees would spend nearly a year training with me over Zoom before the week-long intensive since they were in different parts of the world. The final requirement for completion was to join the public segment for the intensive here in the mountains of Colorado.

The teacher-trainees attended the intensive not only to observe me presenting the techniques, but to observe how I responded to the inevitable personal challenges that arise in such intimate settings.

I take a sacred view of the boundaries I set for programs. This means that after the komainu-type interventions have done their job, I regard any challenges that arise once a program has begun not as problems, but as special opportunities for growth.

Sometimes the opportunity is for the participant. And sometimes it's for me to work on myself, whether it's refining a technique, developing patience, or checking my ego. I'm always a student, even in the role of teacher.

Up to this point, we've been discussing *setting* in terms of boundaries and participants. Preparing the rest of the setting was quite simple. I'd selected a lodge to house the participants in the mountains near Estes Park, Colorado. The lodge also had several meeting rooms on the lower level, one of which was reserved for our group.

I'd scheduled the intensive in late September, after the busy summer season, hoping the other meeting rooms would remain vacant. If they were, that would provide the quiet and privacy optimal for our telepathy exercises. Thankfully, it worked out that way.

The rest of the setting was accomplished by Mother Nature. The lodge's property was in a small valley surrounded by mountains sometimes shrouded by low-lying clouds and fog or lightly dusted with snow. They lent an aura of mystery and timelessness to the environment, and that helped us connect to those same qualities within ourselves.

The mountains formed their own boundary to protect us from the "normal" world filled with chaos, pollution, and stress lying beyond. Within their boundary, peace presided, available to any mind stilled and quieted enough to perceive it. The peace and silence, I believed, would help each participant notice the extremely subtle impressions received in their subconscious mind during the telepathy exercises.

The pine, spruce, and fir trees filled the air with an aroma that could release months of stress after just a few slow breaths.

Magpies, eagles, crows, and other birds drew our eyes upward into the pristine sky. Small herds of elk grazed on grass and shrubs nearby. Occasionally, they'd meander across the roadways, reminding drivers and their passengers that it was time to slow down in more ways than one.

That's why I chose this environment, to help settle our bodies and minds. Everything here was conducive to releasing stress and tension, which, again, would help to perceive the subtle perceptions of the psychic mind.

As a teacher, creating an optimal environment includes setting the emotional tone of the event. I did this by reminding myself that I was the host. As a host, I made everyone comfortable by sending email reminders, offering name badges, and giving a presentation about communication, safety, and a description of the whole property, including the location of various facilities such as the cafeteria.

The check-in period and the orientation on the arrival day included playing a popular board game called Blank Slate™, from The OP Games company. The game resembles practicing telepathy by asking players to fill in the blank space to complete a common phrase. Points are made when two or more players fill in their blanks with the same word.

For example, how would you complete this phrase, "_______ rock?"

Did you choose "hard," "volcanic," "acid," or "bed?" Or are you a fan of the actor Dwayne Johnson and filled the blank space with "the" for *The* Rock? How interesting would it be if someone else at the table matched your choice?

Though the game's purpose is not telepathy, it's easy to see how playing it with other participants was a fun and easy way to encourage the spirit of exploration, collaboration, communication, and connection with each other.

During the week, there were several times I needed to help the group 1) relax, 2) connect with each other, 3) connect with their hearts, and 4) take themselves less seriously. To achieve that goal, I would hand out lyric sheets, gather them into a circle, and play a video for us to sing along with. Songs included *Heroes* by David Bowie, *Tubthumping* by Chumbawamba, (Simply) *The Best* by Tina Turner, and others.

Music was valuable in another way. We did two spoon bending sessions that week to practice psychokinesis, so music was used to rouse our energy. I won't describe spoon bending any more here due to this book's space restrictions. But I've included a photo of some of the bent metal on page 46, as well as a photo of participant Blake Farley, who was courageous and confident enough to psychically bend not just a spoon, but a three-foot long steel rod.

Before the program got rolling on the first day, I recalled my conversation with Dalia and Lidu. I'd asked Lidu how I could help others develop their telepathic skills.

Her reply was, "Everyone who wants to hear should each *ask* their angels to help."[30] Following Lidu's guidance, I asked the group to spend a few minutes in silence and to mentally ask their angels, or guides, or higher selves, or divinity, or whatever words worked for each individual, to help them throughout intensive. I also said that anyone who didn't believe in these spiritual type of entities didn't have to engage in this process and could just wait in silence while the rest of us did. I had no desire to change anyone's belief systems. That was up to them.

When the weather allowed, we ended the evenings by relocating to one of the darkest spots in the valley to do some sky watching. Yes, we did witness some interesting phenomena moving through the sky, but those are beyond the scope of this book.

There were also times when I needed to allow for interruptions and changes of plan to suit an individual's needs, if not the whole group's. Due to the highly personal nature of those events, I won't describe them here. But it's important to state the value of being flexible in a community setting.

I did this and all the other tasks of a host and teacher, intending to express kindness, empathy, patience, and compassion in all our activities. For me, this is what it means to teach. To my teacher-trainees who requested a teacher's handbook, the first sentence of this paragraph is what you need to remember the most.

Everything else is just technique.

---

[30] From page 26.

Below: Close-up of some of the participants' results.

Below: Participant Blake Farley holding the steel rod she bent during the spoon bending session. Note how the photo captured a diffuse glow near her head and shoulders.

A NOTE TO SCIENTISTS

If the reader is a scientist or an otherwise academically-oriented reader, it will be important to remember this book's context when being critical.

The results (transcripts, charts, etc.) are measurements taken during skill-building exercises. **This was not a scientific study.** Therefore, arguments about using controls, double-blinding, statistics, participant selection, etc., are misplaced here.

I encourage scientists to take inspiration from this book so that they may design and execute their own experiments using scientific protocols when appropriate.

One question is if the results obtained here would be repeated in a strictly-designed study. After all, replicability[31] is key for determining the validity of an experiment's results.

When replicating our experiments (our training exercises), it will be important to use an experimenter and subjects who possess the same qualities as those at the intensive. For example, I, as the instructor (the *experimenter*):

- believe telepathy is real
- have practiced meditation for years
- have practiced psychic development for years
- encourage my participants while training by accentuating positive results and minimizing negative ones
- imbue the experiments with fun and a sense of discovery
- permit the participants to encourage each other in maintaining a positive mindset and sharing "here's what worked for me"

---

[31] As is *reproducibility*. The two terms are similar but mean different things in science.

- choose settings that support a person's "going within" and reducing stress (such as secluded and quiet mountain settings)

It will also be important to replicate the study using *experimental subjects* who possess qualities like the intensive's participants. They had the following in common. They:

- were personally invested in experiencing psychic phenomena
- were confident, to one degree or another, they would succeed
- had a pre-existing interest in psychic abilities evidenced by having read books, watched videos, taken classes, or worked in the psychic field themselves (as energy workers, mediums, teachers of psychic abilities, etc.)
- dedicated a whole week to training, which suggests a learning curve requiring sufficient time to develop

In the name of fairness and fidelity to the original exercises, when scientists attempt to replicate our experiences, they must take care to include all the personal qualities above in the subjects and the experimenter(s).

Of course, a control group of subjects (and a control experimenter) could and should be used, whether composed of agnostics, non-believers, a random set, or AI robots. I do believe that science, done properly (meaning free of "scientism"[32]) has already helped and will continue to help humanity understand consciousness better.[33]

---

[32] Here, I define *scientism* as a person's improper use of scientific principles to defend their pre-conceived biases and beliefs (typically in physicalism), which, ironically, is un-scientific.

[33] For example, see the Institute of Noetic Science (IONS.org), the Division of Perceptual Studies (DOPS) at the University of Virginia (med.virginia.edu/perceptual-studies/), and the work of William Bengston, PhD (see his book *The Energy Cure*).

CHERYL'S DREAM

Dreams can reveal our subconscious fears. They also show us the hope, joy, and love we've held inside too long, unexpressed or denied. Such feelings serve as the messengers of our mind and, perhaps, our soul. Having received the message, we act.

Sometimes our reaction is obvious and forceful, perhaps a massive course correction in career or relationship. And sometimes the reaction is so small, so subtle, we don't attribute it to its point of origin. It might cause us to ask new questions or pursue a line of thinking we previously thought impossible or foolish. In ways big and small, dreams shape our waking lives.

And since humans are storytellers, a dream's power can be multiplied by sharing it with others. After all, dreams aren't always meant solely for the dreamer. Sometimes they're for the dreamer's community because the Great Mystery (undifferentiated consciousness, Source, God, etc.), deemed it the best way to get its message across. And so, in being retold, a single dream can change us over time by connecting us to the divine, en masse.

Now, I would like to invite you on the special journey described in this book, not by telling you about one of my own dreams, but one shared by my friend Cheryl. She was there in the mountains with us, and the dream came to her when the week-long intensive was already halfway through. She texted it to me at 6:37 am, so it must've been fresh in her mind. I like to believe the Great Mystery sent it to her that day so that I could share it with you now, at this very moment of you reading it.

Her text message has two parts. The first part is her description of her dream. The second part is an AI dream interpretation she prompted afterward. Both parts are as essential to your invitation now as they were for those of us who were in those mountains together that week.

Cheryl's dream as texted to the author:

* * * * * * * * * * *

Thursday, September 25, 6:37 am

The dream began with Sean revealing what was inside his mystery box. I thought it was a pogo stick or another child's toy that has a ball and rope that swings around the leg and you have to jump over the rope each time you swing it around and around. It was so much more cool than that, it was a Tesla Coil! He turned it on and everything turned to tingly static electricity. There were orange orbs forming in the room. Sean reached out to touch one of the little electric orbs and as soon as he touched it his hair grew long and stood on end making him look like a mad scientist. He then began to levitate up in the air! We were all in awe, but then we all began to levitate. We were all flying and dancing with electric lightning bolts and orange orbs and floating around the room!

[AI interpretation]

This dream is filled with vivid, electrifying symbols that speak to profound spiritual energies and experiences. The central image of the mystery box being opened and revealing a Tesla Coil is a powerful metaphor. Boxes often represent hidden potential, mysteries of the self, or spiritual gifts waiting to be unveiled. The

Tesla Coil, an instrument of intense energy, invention, and awe, suggests the sudden and perhaps unexpected emergence of spiritual power in your life.

This is not a mundane or childish plaything, but something wondrous and transformative. The act of Sean turning on the coil and the whole atmosphere shifting to tingly static electricity indicates a shift in spiritual awareness—a field of new possibility and heightened perception.

The orange orbs forming in the room evoke the presence of spiritual forces or beings, perhaps even messengers or manifestations of sacred energy.

Orange is often associated with creativity, vitality, and the sacral chakra, which is the energetic center of joy, connection, and flow. The orbs, combined with the static electricity and lightning imagery, suggest a visitation or stirring of the sacred within your everyday environment.

When Sean touches an orb and his hair grows long and wild, transforming him into a mad scientist, it signals the unleashing of untamed, creative, and perhaps even mystical power. This transformation is both humorous and awe-inspiring—reminding you that spiritual revelation can have an element of playfulness, surprise, and radical change.

The experience of levitating—first Sean, then everyone present—points to the dream's existential questions of freedom, transcendence, and unity. Levitation is a classic symbol of spiritual elevation, release from material constraints, and the lightness of being that comes with awakening.

The fact that this experience is shared collectively suggests a communal aspect to your spiritual journey now, where you are not alone in your awakening or joy, but can dance and float in harmony with others. The dancing with electric bolts and orbs is an image of ecstatic freedom, connection, and the joy of spiritual communion.

Spiritually, this dream reflects a moment in your journey where you are invited to open yourself to hidden powers and let them transform your experience of reality.

The obstacles you may need to address could involve allowing yourself to be surprised by spiritual energies, letting go of expectations, and embracing the unknown with playfulness and awe.

To honor the spiritual power of this dream, you might perform a small symbolic gesture in waking life—perhaps lighting a candle or holding an orange object—to acknowledge the mysterious, joyful energy that is ready to manifest.

Consider also reaching out to others in a spirit of shared discovery and levity and allow yourself to "dance" with the unexpected, trusting that spiritual growth can sometimes arrive as delight and wonder.

* * * * * * * * * * *

TELEPATHY INSTRUCTIONS

How does this book help one learn telepathy? Obviously, it helps by providing you with the instructions in this chapter. But after years of teaching psychic development, I've learned that successful psychic exercises and experiments occur because of several causes and conditions coming together properly.

Briefly, these include:

- feeling optimistic, relaxed, and confident
- being in a hospitable environment
- having sufficient time
- using appropriate and reasonable targets
- knowing how to look within one's own mind
- enjoying and valuing the inner contents & processes of own's mind (not everyone does)
- receiving emotional and intellectual support from the others involved in the same experience

This book also helps one learn telepathy by exposing the reader to the many transcripts contained herein, completed by the intensive's participants. Seeing what actual telepathic information looks like makes it easier for a beginner to ***identify and trust*** **the subtle impressions** that will arise in their own minds once they begin their training.

This is all to say, there is no single "trick" to making telepathy happen. Still, there are instructions. Here, I will share mine, which I've used many times successfully with various groups over the years.

In the following pages, I will share the actual transcript of the audio recording[34] I made while teaching telepathy on the first day of the intensive. I believe that only presenting a numbered list of dry instructions, which I admittedly do on the following page for easy reference, would leave too much out.

There are two parts to the instructions. The first part is the "work." The second part is "the reward" or "the dessert," which are much better terms than "the test."

I give **full permission** for any reader to use these instructions, including the special induction in the second part, when working with a partner, a group of friends, a paid class, and even at large conferences[35]. You could even make it the text for your next metaphysical study group or paranormal book club.

However, **permission is *not* granted** to publish them in commercial paper or electronic media without my express written consent. Using a reasonably limited portion in papers by degree-seeking students is permitted.

Know that the instructions for **receiving** information telepathically were used in several exercises at the intensive and are applicable to:

- Basic clairvoyance – At the intensive, this was done by perceiving colors, colored shapes, and objects.
- Remote viewing – When using a coordinate to help set one's intention.
- Psychometry - Done at the intensive but not discussed in this book due to space limitations.

[34] The transcript has been edited for readability.

[35] Appropriate credit should be given when using this material at paid events.

Also, know that the instructions for **sending** information telepathically are applicable to:

- Remote viewing – As autotelepathy during the feedback period, when sending information about the target back in time to the initial viewing period.
- Psychokinesis – When affecting physical matter, such as a Random Event Generator.
- Direct Mental Interaction with Living Systems (DMILS) – For example, energy healing, and the Heart Rate Telepathy discussed in this book.

For easy reference, here are the **basic principles of receiving**:

1. Relax the body and clear the mind.

2. Set your intention in an undistracted and focused way. Concentrate only on what you want to perceive.

3. Fully release the mental activity involved in forming the intention. Let go. Relax. Go blank.

4. Wait passively for perceptions to enter your awareness.

5. Record your impressions on paper (or audio recording, or by telling them to a co-participant).

6. Re-establish your intention.

7. Let go, relax, and wait for more information to come.

And here are the **basic principles of sending**:

1. Focus on what you would like to transmit to your receiver(s).

2. Do not relax in an open-minded way, as if receiving. Rather, become one-pointed, filling your mind only with the target.

3. Do not become distracted by other thoughts. Regular meditation practice helps develop the capacity for non-distraction.

4. If the target is a fundamental shape, concentrate on its specific qualities, as well as on the motion of your hand and arm as you trace over the lines.

5. If the target is a complex image (like a photo), imbue your imagination with aspects that would stimulate all 5 physical senses. Imagine smelling, tasting, hearing, and touching/feeling the target or scene along with perceiving it visually. Bring the image to life in your imagination as you focus on it. Feel and intensify emotions appropriate to the target/scene.

6. While focusing on the target, *intend* for the information to be shared by the receiver(s). Periodically look directly at them to strengthen the sense of connection. *Want* to share your mind with theirs. *Imagine* them receiving the impressions inside their minds. *Imagine* them writing down accurate impressions on their transcripts.

The transcription of the verbal instructions I gave at the intensive begins on the following page. It has been edited for readability and ease of use, and it preserves my casual style of speaking to the group.

For those who plan to train others with these instructions, please know that the order of shapes used in the training (horizontal line, then circle, then vertical line, etc.) is important for providing sufficient perceptual contrast to help the mind differentiate them.

Transcript of the Telepathy Instructions Given at the 2025 Psychic Training Intensive

Part 1: The Work

It's okay for the energy to drop now, because we're going to sort of move inward and into each other. [The group had just finished the first spoon bending session.]

For most of this training, you'll be tapping into me, but then at the end, you'll be sending and receiving to each other. Last night [at the orientation], I mentioned mental models, that they're *just* models. They might not explain how this actually happens, but they give us a structure to work with. Please take what I say here with a grain of salt.

When I teach telepathy, especially what we're doing this morning with line drawings, I use the model that says the subconscious mind is the receiver of the psychic information, and it has to talk to the conscious mind.

They have to be in communication with each other, so they must build a language that they both understand. And the subconscious mind's messages are so subtle, so soft, like a whisper compared to our noisy, everyday-talking mind. How do we hear that whisper?

Part of this mental model is that we need to develop a vocabulary that both the subconscious and conscious parts of our mind understand.

Some of you are mediums, I know that. And some of you have watched mediums on TV or gone to gallery readings. Sometimes you'll notice a medium saying, "Ah, I see a whiskey bottle," or "I see a wine bottle, and that tells me there was alcoholism involved," or "Oh, I see a red rose. That tells me this is a romantic connection. This is a spouse who's passed over," or "I see books, like this person is very intelligent," right?

These mediums have developed their own *vocabulary.* A perceived symbol means something specific about the person that they're connecting with. So, we're going to do that for the first part of this training. We're going to build our own vocabulary.

We're going to do for the next 40 minutes or so. It's probably the most boring and it's a little bit of a chore, but we're going to develop that language because every line drawing (and these are basic cartoony-type line drawings) can be composed of a straight line, a curved line, or a corner somewhere in it.

Can we train the subconscious mind and conscious mind, working together, to understand what a vertical line *feels* like? Or a horizontal line, or what a triangle feels like, or what that looks like? Can we build that vocabulary between both parts of the mind?

That's what we're going to do first. Then we'll take a quick break for the restroom, and then we're going to sing a song together, just to help us connect and loosen up even more, so that we can really let go of any of our hesitation or any performance anxiety or expectation. We're just going to open our hearts that way.

And then we'll get into dessert [Part 2], where I'll be sending images, and you're going to pick them up telepathically based off the work we do right now. You'll pick up aspects of the image that I'm sending, and then you'll draw it on paper, and then I'll show you the target image.

You'll look at what you wrote down and see how much of it matches. So, first is the work, and then there's the dessert at the end, which is a lot more fun. Again, we're just building vocabulary here.

We'll go nice and slow, so don't make any fast moves. A lot of people get caught up in how we do this training in the first part, because they think they're cheating, because I'm going to *tell you* right now, ahead of time, that I am drawing a horizontal line. We're not doing telepathy yet. We're building vocabulary first.

I'm going to set my timer for four minutes. And you can put on your blindfold for this. I'm just going to be going back and forth with my pen over this **horizontal line**. You know it's a horizontal line. And it's good that you know it's a horizontal line, because now your *conscious* mind knows, "Ah, horizontal line."

But at the same time, you want to try and just open up, because I'm going to be *sending* horizontal line.

This is not telepathy yet. We're just developing the language. So, you're not cheating. This isn't anything to do with that.

I would recommend that you have your paper and pen in front of you. But for most of this, you could just kick back, relax and just tap into my mind. Set an intention to tap into my mind, then let go and relax.

At any point, if you perceive the horizontal line, the one I'm drawing on my paper, even a little piece of it in your mind, go ahead and draw it on your paper. Then you'll know we're in synch.

As I'm drawing, you're drawing too, but only when you pick it up [mentally]. If you're getting nothing, that means you should just exhale, relax, let go and trust that a deeper part of you is picking up horizontal line. But again, if you actually think you're perceiving it, go ahead and start drawing it on your paper. If you disconnect, stop drawing and just relax.

Also, see if you can feel my arm moving as I draw the horizontal line and feel it in your own arm.

Regarding keeping your eyes open or closed behind the blindfold, do whatever is most relaxing for you.

You might not even pick up anything visual, but just *a sense* of a horizontal line, perhaps the most boring type of line drawing that exists. It's just a flat line.

I'll turn on my timer now. I'm going to do this for four minutes now. So just kick back, relax and see what comes through as I trace over my own horizontal line while *sending* it out to you.

This is so simple that trying too hard gets in the way. Just let go.

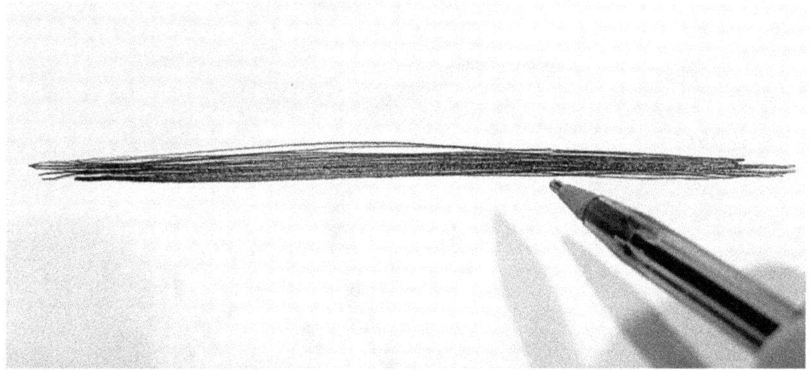

Above: Sean's line after 4 minutes of moving the pen back and forth while *sending*.

[After four minutes, Sean and the group have brief discussion then move on to the next shape.]

The next shape that I'm going to be doing for four minutes is the **circle**. We're going to be focusing on circles. So, whatever you're feeling, whatever you're picking up on some subconscious level, is circle.

A straight line or horizontal line is quite boring. Circle can come across with a certain emotion or some other type of quality to it. Some people say circle feels feminine to them. But it doesn't have to for you. It could feel masculine too. It's unique to you. It could be representative of something. It could be a happy shape or a sad shape or angry shape.

It's not just about the shape, but what comes with it.

Sometimes circle can feel soft, or it can feel like movement.

So, open yourself up to feeling more than just a line on a paper, sort of like feeling the vibe of the shape.

[After four minutes, Sean and the group have brief discussion then move on to the next shape.]

Thanks for hanging in there, folks. I know this is not the most exciting thing, but it's the work we must do in order to have dessert later on. Now we're going to do four minutes of the oh-so-exciting **vertical line**, just up and down, up and down again.

Know that the subconscious mind will draw on your life experience. It'll draw on things you've seen and felt and heard since birth, especially things that you're accustomed to all the time, it'll rely on that to get your attention. That'll happen with telepathy and later with remote viewing and other stuff.

A memory will come back from the past and you might wonder, "What does this have to do with anything? And then you find out that some part of it is related to the target in some way. Whatever is in your memory is going to be drawn upon as a resource.

Now we're going to do vertical line, boredom 2.0, but it's got a *feel* to it. A certain "altitude" quality.

[After four minutes, Sean and the group have brief discussion then move on to the next shape.]

The next shape is taking us out of the Stone Age and into the Iron Age, and it's a **square**. Square is interesting because it incorporates two shapes we've already done, horizontal line and vertical line.

There might be that familiar feeling, but it also incorporates corners, and corners are sharp. They're like this, you know, 90-degree turn. So, there's a sharpness to it, that interruption, the change of direction, which implies movement, sort of like how circle does. But it's sharper in a way, with four corners and then two horizontal and two vertical lines.

For some people, this might have a masculine quality, but it doesn't necessarily have to.

[After four minutes, Sean and the group have brief discussion then move on to the next shape.]

Now we're going to do a **loopdeeloop**, which is really a combination of vertical lines and then half circles. It's that combination of something strong and tall with something round and maybe has a soft quality.

It definitely feels like movement, sort of like a roller coaster.

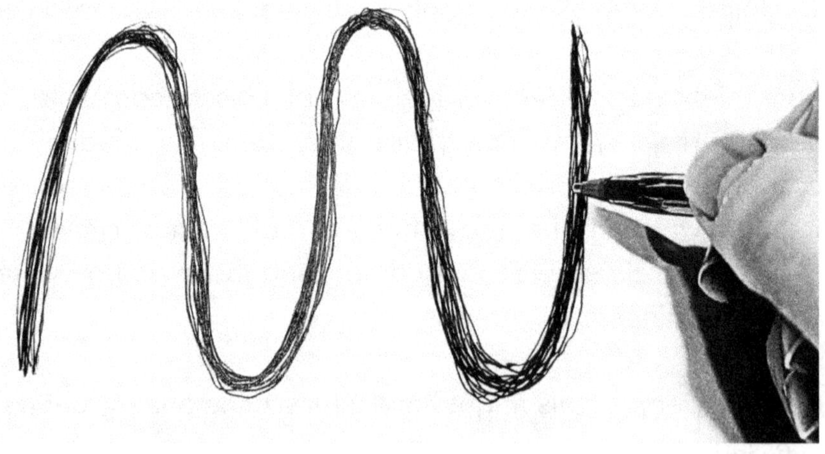

[After four minutes, Sean and the group have brief discussion then move on to the next shape.]

Okay, the final shape, then, is **triangle**. It's a basic triangle, pointing up.

Like square, it has corners, but it has sharper corners because there's only three of them. And there's the slant of the line, so it's not horizontal, well, there's one horizontal, but the other two are slanted.

There are no verticals, so there's a sense of altitude but it's not as direct as a vertical line, so it's somewhere between soft and hard. But then it's prickly having these sharp corners.

I'm just saying these things in case it helps add a sense of meaning to the shapes. Of course, you should all have your own sense of meaning for these shapes.

This is the last shape, so this torture is almost done. [laughter]

* * * * * * * * * * *

After four minutes of working with triangle, we had some brief discussion then took a break before starting Part 2 of the instructions (on the next page).

Part 2: The Dessert

After Part 1, the group took a break. After the break, I handed out the lyrics to David Bowie's song *Heroes* and played a YouTube video from the channel Choir! Choir! Choir![36] on the screen for the group to sing along with.

I told them, "This is to bring us together on different levels."

* * * * * * * * * * *

Okay, so now we're at the dessert part, and hopefully we're a little bit more connected to each other. I'm going to be the sender for a few targets, and then half the room will be the sender, and the other half will be the receiver, and we'll go back and forth a couple times.

We're going to take our time and move slowly. It'll be about four minutes per target, just like before.

Remember that we're doing simple line drawings [as targets], and after you see the first one, you'll think, "Oh, that's a really simple drawing." It's nothing complicated.

For those of you who've done remote viewing, what I say next will sound similar. The goal *isn't* to see the exact image that I'm going to be drawing in front of me.

Just look for little snippets, like if you feel that up-and-down quality, you might do that shape, or a vertical line. Or if you feel an

[36] Choir! Choir! Choir!. (2019, Jan 13). *Choir! Choir! Choir! sings David Bowie – Heroes.* YouTube. https://www.youtube.com/watch?v=lOYGiyzT2Zk

enclosure, you might draw a circle, and then later on, you might pick up a different shape and put it next to the first one.

Your brain will try to guess what the image is. That's the conscious part of the brain. It *guesses* and thinks, "Cool. I think I know this shape."

For example, this might show up in your mind. [Sean holds up what appears to be a simple line drawing of a bird, two curves joined at the center.]

You might think, "It's the McDonald's logo," or "It's a seagull," when really, it's just an upside-down butt. [laughter]

But that's what the conscious mind is going to try and do. It guesses. That's how it helps us survive in this physical world. It's always guessing, trying to get ahead, trying to survive, identify threats, things like that. It's pattern recognition.

It's what the conscious mind does very well when receiving from the subconscious mind. But in this case, we *don't* want to guess. We want to avoid guesswork.

We're really tuning in to very subtle sensations with telepathy. So don't worry about capturing what the actual target image is. Just be interested in capturing the little snippets, the little pieces that come to you.

If you do get a full image, you might go ahead and draw it on the corner of your paper. Or if you get a word instead of an image, you can write that word down on the side of the page too, because, what if you're right? Then that'd be super cool.

Some of you already have great training with Mind Sight, Seeing Beyond Eyes, Vision Without Eyes[37], or others systems, and you might see it completely. That's great and you should do that to see if it helps you with telepathy. Experiment with it.

Just do what works for you. But most of all, have fun. Don't worry about getting anything right. Don't worry about it. Focus on having fun. For this experiment, if you could use the markers, that'd be really great because your lines will show up better on your paper [for photographing for this book].

The way I'm going to work these targets [as the sender] is, instead of tracing over the image with a pen, because you can hear that, I'm just going to run my finger silently over the lines, and it works just as well to help me focus and send.

I'm going to hold my target down here [on his lap, behind the desk]. It's best if you don't look at me, because someone could say, "You can see Sean's shoulder movements," or whatever. So, use your blindfold too.

Another thing about the blindfold is that it helps you move inward, into your own mind, so you're not distracted by the outer world, right?

---

[37] These are names of some of the various training systems for extra-ocular vision (seeing while blindfolded). I didn't know at this point that even though someone is skilled in extra-ocular vision, it doesn't necessarily mean they can do telepathy more accurately than other participants.

In Part 1 ["the work"], those line drawings were of fundamental shapes; but I'm doing something a little more complicated now. These targets represent actual things or scenes composed of combinations of the fundamental shapes that we worked on.

Please put your blindfold on and I'm just going to give you a brief induction to help you slow down and move inward. So right now, mentally, you might say to yourself, "I'll give Sean permission to say a few words, and I'll follow his instructions," because I'm going to direct you a little bit here.

[Sean gives the following instructions by using a tone of voice like he uses for guided meditation and hypnosis: slow, soft, and heavy.]

Please notice your position in your chair and check that you're fully comfortable. Make any corrections you need to the placement of your legs and your feet and your hands. Don't worry about using a pen right now. Just get nice and comfortable. Take a nice deep breath in so that you feel your belly extending on the inhale, meaning you're breathing with your diaphragm muscle, then exhale fully and feel that sense of relaxation spread from your torso down your legs, up into your chest and out of your arms.

Begin turning your head slowly from left to right in a way that feels good, and as you do that, feel that wonderful sensation spreading into your jaw, your face, your scalp, down your neck and your shoulders. You can stop turning your head now. Let that feeling of relaxation move downward through your body, all the way down to your feet, one… two… three…

... and notice your body slowing down... feeling a little heavier... feeling yourself sinking into your chair, a little bit more... going deeper and deeper into a state of rest, into a state of stillness and peace... feeling so calm and so comfortable.

Now, scan your body for any part that might still be a little bit tense, and after you've identified it, take a nice deep breath in, and as you exhale, mentally release the tension in that part of the body. And your whole body feels even more relaxed as you continue going deeper and deeper.

Feeling so heavy now... you don't even want to think about getting up out of your chair. You're so comfortable exactly where you're sitting.

Now, we need to tune in to an even quieter place within. So, imagine now that you all your attention is inside your skull, right in that space your brain normally occupies.

See how it's as if you're sitting inside a big, dark cave. There's barely any light inside. It's almost pitch black. Not only is it a cave, but there's a pool of water inside and you're sitting on the edge of that pool. You can barely see the surface of the water in the darkness, but you know it's there, and you can tell it's so still and quiet because it's barely making a ripple.

You look around inside this cave, but you can't find any walls. It's just dark space, and it's so comfortable. You feel so safe inside this space of your mind, so peaceful and still.

You know that this is the space where you can perceive the very subtle impressions of your psychic mind. This space is so quiet, and that water is so calm, that the slightest impression, the slightest psychic vibration, shows up in your awareness clearly.

It's really easy to perceive the psychic impressions inside this space. The slightest impression shows up very clearly here. So, as we continue these exercises for the next 40 minutes or so, know that you can always tune in and hang out on the edge of the water inside your skull, inside this very dark cave. It's so peaceful and so still and quiet, because the slightest ripple really stands out.

This is where you'll perceive your psychic impressions. Anytime you start working too hard, it might make the cave a little noisy, the water might start rippling too much, and you start making waves because you've accidentally slipped into trying way too hard and exerting too much energy, too much effort. That's a sign to just release, let go and relax. As soon as you notice you're trying too hard, you immediately release, relax, and let go, returning to that peaceful space inside your mind.

When you relax by taking a nice deep breath in and out anytime you need to, you'll notice that the water returns to stillness. The surface of the water is almost free of any motion at all. Now it's like glass, perfectly still again.

Anytime you notice you're pushing too hard or forcing it, all you must do is take a deep breath in and out, and you'll see the stillness in the water, and you'll appreciate the stillness inside this dark cave of your mind.

This way, the slightest psychic impression really stands out. This helps your conscious mind pick up on it and draw it on the piece of paper in front of you.

Where does the psychic impression appear? It appears in the same place you see your memories, your daydreams, your ideas. It's not really a place at all, but like a mirage in your mind. So don't go looking for it. Just remain still and quiet, and the impressions will arise on their own just like memories and daydreams. Let them come into your conscious awareness on their own, in their own time. Just wait. Do nothing.

How do the impressions appear? Imagine using a stick to draw a line on the surface of a pond. The line disappears almost as soon as it's drawn. Perceiving it is less about seeing it visually and more about feeling the line, as if you could *feel the shape of the water.*

We're going to remain in this space of your mind as we move forward. One thing to know about with these telepathy exercises is, *don't* reach for the psychic impressions. *Don't* reach for whatever image Sean is focusing on.

Instead, you'll just set an intention. Your intention is *to perceive any aspect of the image that Sean is focusing on*, and then after you set your intention, you'll just release it and wait and be still.

Your only job to do now is wait for the impressions to come to you, because when you *wait*, you can trust that the impression will be accurate.

It's when you reach, when you're in a hurry, when you're pushing, you're trying to force it, or guessing, when instead of picking up on the psychic impressions, your mind plays make-believe instead and comes up with false material.

Remember, you set your intention to perceive and then completely let it go, and be still within that deep, effortless relaxation.

In fact, setting the intention is so relaxing, because you know that as soon as you do it, all you have to do is let go and relax completely and hang out in that dark cave inside of your mind, waiting for the impressions to come.

And when an impression comes, all you have to do is use your marker to write it down on the paper. Feel free to take off your mask if you need to at that point. You cannot be afraid of making a mess. Or you could just make sketches without taking off your blindfold. It's perfectly fine if your transcript is messy. It's totally your choice, because you want to stay completely calm, peaceful and at ease.

I'm going to take 10 seconds to find my target, and I'll let you know when I start focusing on it. Until then, just relax in that quiet space of your mind.

[Sean places a target in his lap.]

I'm going to set my timer for four minutes. Set your intention now, then relax, let go, and let the impressions come to you. Starting now.

[4 minutes pass and Sean notifies the group that time is up.]

Okay, the easiest way to show you what the target is to draw it on something much bigger. [Sean draws an enlarged version of the target on the whiteboard.] Can you see this?

* * * * * * * * * * *

At that point, receivers compared their transcripts to the target, and the group discussed their experience and results for several minutes. Then, we moved on to the next target.

I recommended that in between rounds, everyone should take a moment to clear their minds of the previous impressions as well as of the target. I suggested visualizing their mind's eye as a large whiteboard and imagining erasing it until it was completely clean.

You'll see the targets and transcripts starting on page 83, but it's important for you to read the next chapter, *Observed Attributes of Telepathy,* first.

Before we continue, I would be remiss if I didn't mention one of my inspirations for teaching telepathy the way I did during the intensive by using the hypnotic induction.

Several years ago, I was fortunate to obtain a self-published manuscript titled *How to Develop ESP in Yourself and in Others*[38], by Milan Ryzl (1928-2011). Ryzl was a Czech parapsychologist[39] known, in part, for winning the Czech lottery multiple times by engaging his subjects in ESP.

The induction I used in the intensive and other classes is my own creation, but the fact that I used an induction at all is partly influenced by his book because it includes the inductions he used with his subjects. His record shows that hypnosis for psychic functioning helps. I think our record here will, too.

---

[38] Ryzl. M. (1973). *How to Develop ESP in Yourself and in Others*. Milan Ryzl.

[39] https://www.academia.edu/33307887/In_Memoriam_Milan_Ryzl_1928_2011_

Below: The author *sending* by quietly tracing over the target image held in his lap and behind the desk. These are extra and probably unnecessary precautions since the participants are blindfolded.

Below: The author showing the target after drawing an enlarged version of it on the whiteboard for the whole group to see.

Below: The author passing out individual target images for half the group (on one side of the room), who will act as *senders* for the others.

OBSERVED ATTRIBUTES OF TELEPATHY

Before showing you the participants' transcripts in the next chapter, I want to share the observations I made after reviewing them. I could have concluded what I was seeing was merely the result of limited telepathic ability and left it at that. But that would have been a grave mistake, one I want to help you avoid.

I noticed commonalities in how participants received and recorded their perceptions. I then realized these were valuable clues to how the subconscious and conscious mind cooperate to process psychic information. I decided to call these commonalities *observed attributes*.

I'll briefly describe each attribute below. But you'll develop a better understanding of each one by carefully studying each transcript and getting a *feel* for them.

1. Primary shape recognition: The primary shape present in the target (circle, square, curve, etc.) is strongly indicated in the transcript.

2. Recognition of multiples – symbolic: An image is duplicated on the transcript to indicate that an aspect of the target is also duplicated. The number of duplications and/or the image does not exactly match the target. It's as if the receiver's subconscious is communicating, "I'm seeing there's *more than one of these* here."

3. Recognition of multiples – accurate: An image is duplicated on the transcript to indicate an aspect of the target is also duplicated.

The number of duplications and/or the whole image strongly resembles an aspect of the target.

4. Deconstruction: The receiver's mind has broken a whole target image into individual components and recorded them separately. Whether this is due to how the subconscious mind initially perceives the target or how the conscious mind subsequently receives/interprets the information from the subconscious, I do not know.

5. Reconstruction: The receiver's mind has broken a whole target image into individual components and rearranged them to create a different, yet still coherent, whole image.

6. Analytical overlay (AOL): This term is taken from the field of Remote Viewing. In common parlance, it's ***guessing***. Rather than focusing on and recording *only* the raw information being received using adverbs and adjectives to *describe*, the conscious mind uses nouns and names to *identify and label* the whole target.

For example, if the target is a bicycle with two large wheels, the conscious mind may pick up on two circles and *guess* the target is a pair of eyeglasses. This leads the receiver to erroneously write down the word "eyeglasses," or to actually sketch a pair.

7. AOL with primary shape recognition: In this case, an AOL-sketch strongly resembles the target's primary shape. Though the conscious mind's guess is incorrect, telepathy is still strongly indicated by similarity.

8. Accurate AOL – When a word-based AOL, such as a noun or name, is accurate in describing the target.

9. Precognitive bleed-through: This term is also taken from the field of Remote Viewing. It can occur when a receiver works with several targets within a given period. It is clear from their transcript that their mind had *travelled to the future*[40] and focused on a future target instead of the current one.

10. Thematic similarity: Aspects of the transcript relate to the general theme of the target, even though they may not be visually similar.

11. Psychic soup: This term is taken from Jean Millay's book, *Multidimensional Mind: Remote Viewing in Hyperspace*[41], where she describes it as, "When groups of people participate in remote viewing experiments, parts of the thoughts of many are woven into the responses."

Here, I apply the term *psychic soup* to when the same image appears on two or more different transcripts, including when the image has *no* association with the target[42].

Since it does not resemble the target, we cannot assume the sender originated the image. This leaves us with the questions, "From where or from whom did this thought originate?" and "Why did multiple receivers pick it up?" To explore those questions, we must begin with the assumption that *psychic soup* extends or originates beyond the group's collective field. How far? I do not know.

---

[40] I chose the phrase "travelled to the future" for simplicity. Perceiving future and past events through precognition and retrocognition is a complex topic requiring an exploration of the nature of space, time, gravity, causal determinism, brain processing, non-physical consciousness, and more. Obviously, this is far beyond the scope of this book.

[41] Millay, J. (2000). *Multidimensional Mind: Remote Viewing in Hyperspace*. North Atlantic Books.

[42] Psychic soup appeared several times and is documented in transcripts from my other book, *Dewdrops of Infinity: Psychedelics, Psychic Abilities, UFOs, and the Puharich Project*.

12. Proto-perception: Indicating a nascent or primitive quality, as if in the earliest evolutionary stages of one's psychic perception. As you'll see, the examples of proto-perception resemble a child-artist's first attempt at realism.

To be clear, this attribute's appearance on a receiver's transcript does not necessarily imply their overall psychic ability is primitive (though that could be the case), only that their performance *in this instance* appears primitive.

DAY 1 – INDIVIDUAL TELEPATHY WITH LINE DRAWINGS

In this chapter, you'll see the targets and some of the most accurate transcripts from the first day's telepathy training session. In the earlier chapter, *Telepathy Instructions*, you learned the two stages of how I introduce people to telepathy using line drawings. The first stage is the *work*, and the second stage is like *dessert*; it's the fun part. For targets, I chose Icons[43] from MS Word. The transcripts you see here are the result of the second stage, the fruit of the participants' efforts.

This chapter's title begins with *Individual Telepathy* only to differentiate it from the team-style telepathy discussed later in the book. Telepathy can never be individual since it requires the participation of at least two minds. When only one mind is involved, it's clairvoyance.

I was the only sender for the first two rounds. All twenty-four participants, as the receivers, **intended** to read my mind, then **let go** and **allowed** perceptions to enter their awareness. They recorded their perceptions on paper. At the same time, I focused on my perception of the target while holding the intention to send it out to the whole group.

For the remaining rounds, half the participants, seated on one side of the room, were the senders. I handed them individual printouts of the target for them to silently trace their fingers over and concentrate on while intending to send the image to the other half of the room, the receivers. The two sides of the room switched roles after each round.

As you'll see, I listed each target's *associative features* beneath the target image. I believe association is a core mechanism for how

[43] In MS Word, select Insert from the menu, then select Icons. But any simple line drawing will make a good target, even those you create yourself by hand.

the mind knows itself, knows "other," perceives and understands causality, and generates meaning. Association is also how visual information is transferred from the psychic mind to the subconscious mind, then from the subconscious to the conscious mind.

For highly psychic individuals like the children featured in The Telepathy Tapes, the association is whole, as far as I can tell. But for neurotypicals with limited psychic ability, the association is fragmentary, as you'll see here.

Each target's list of associative features is a compilation of features I gathered while reviewing all the transcripts. The bottom of each transcript will show which from the total list of associative features it included. And if a transcript happens to include one of the *observed attributes* from pages 77-80, those are listed as well.

Because the transcripts were scanned, you will notice most of the images contain artifacts such as paper edges, creases, and shadows. Other artifacts are notes that the receivers wrote on their transcripts *after* seeing the target. Examples are check marks, circles around certain words, or even re-drawing the target.

If, at any point, you doubt the association between a transcript and its target, please remember the target could've been *anything* in the world representable by a simple line drawing. I was the only person with access to the targets before the exercise began.

So, to conclude these transcripts (which were created at the *same* time, in the *same* room, by the *same* group of people) "just happened" to resemble unique aspects of each target due to randomness, would be silly. It would also be obstinate.

If a pseudo-skeptic doesn't want to believe in telepathy, even these images won't convince them it's real. They'll say this whole book is based on my confirmation bias. But this book isn't for them. It's for those who earnestly want to learn telepathy and understand how some of the most subtle aspects of consciousness work.

* * * * * * * * * * *

Remember, the target could've been *anything*.

Telepathy Target 1:

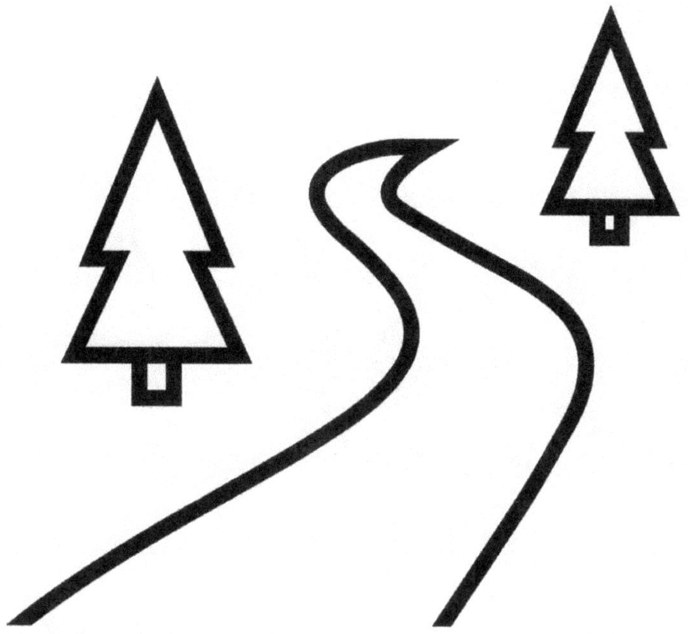

Target: Two trees and a path

Associative features:

- triangle / pointed shapes are dominant
- multiple similar shapes
- pair of long, curved lines
- curved lines resemble a path or river

Target 1: Transcript 1

Participant: Light of Wisdom

Associative feature: "triangle / pointed shapes are dominant"

Observed attribute: Accurate AOL – See the word "tree" on the left.

This transcript is powerful in its simplicity. It reflects the direct effect of working hard at the first stage of the training: building the "vocabulary" to perceive fundamental shapes (starting on page 57).

Target 1: Transcript 2

Participant: Joyful Explorer

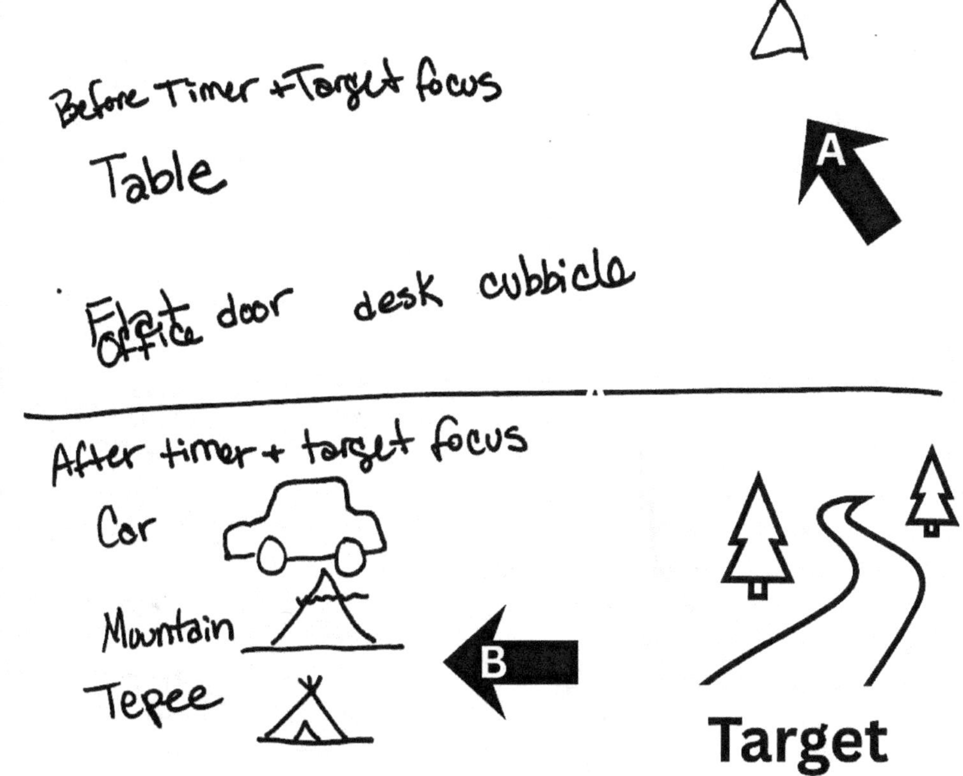

Associative feature: “triangle / pointed shapes are dominant” – (A) and (B)

Target 1: Transcript 3

Participant: Diamond Eyes

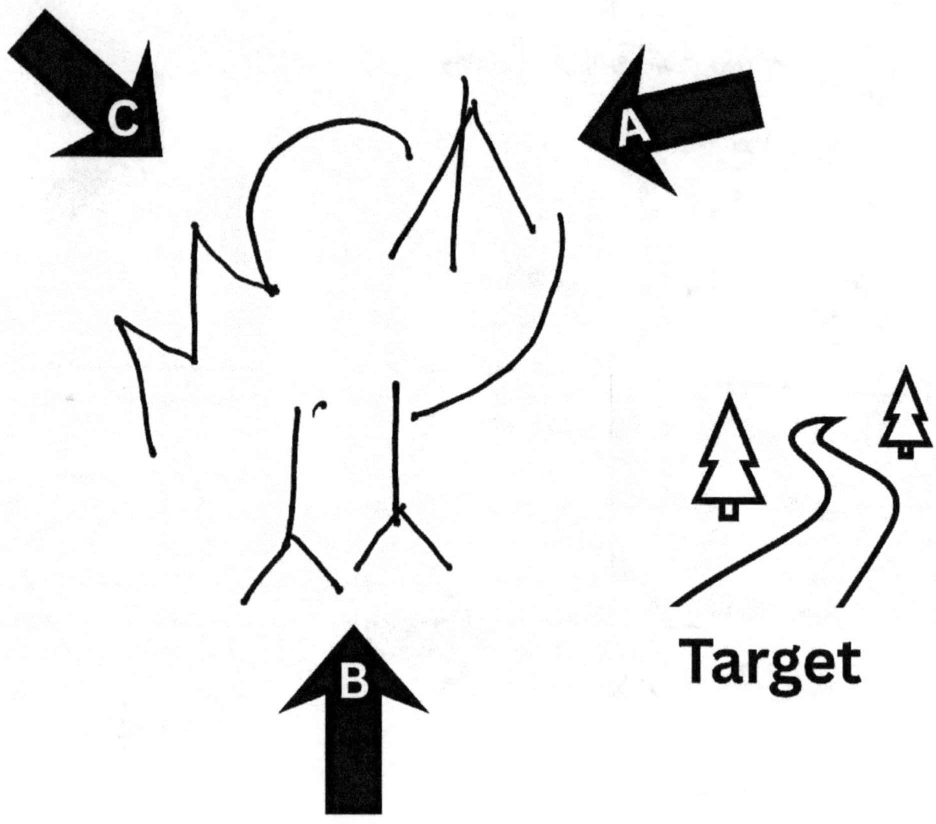

Associative feature: "triangle / pointed shapes are dominant" – (A), (B), (C)

What other similarities do you see?

Target 1: Transcript 4

Participant: Rain of Energy

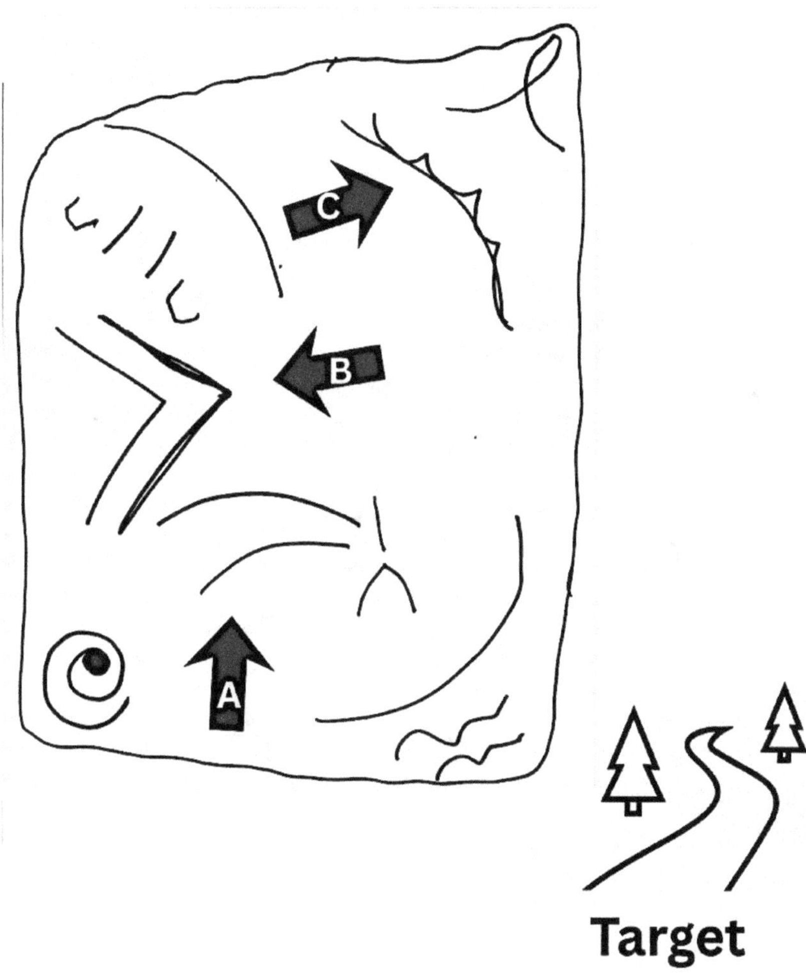

Associative feature: "pair of long, curved lines" – (A)

Associative feature: "triangle / pointed shapes are dominant" – (B), (C)

Observed attribute: Recognition of multiples – accurate. This is a weak instance but the repetition of the angles in (B) may be illustrating this, by indicating the presence of the 2 trees.

Target 1: Transcript 5

Participant: Power of Love

Associative feature: "triangle / *pointed shapes* are dominant" – (A), (B)

Target 1: Transcript 6

Participant: Cosmic Dancer

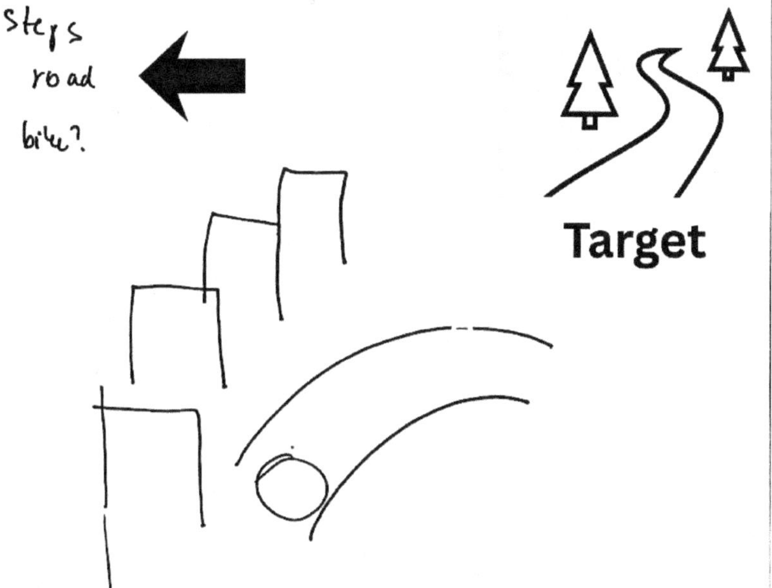

Associative feature: "pair of long, curved lines"

Associative feature: "multiple similar shapes"

Associative feature: "curved lines resemble a path or river"

Observed attribute: Accurate AOL. See the descriptor "road" indicated by the arrow.

Target 1: Transcript 7

Participant: Star Gazer

Associative feature: "triangle / pointed shapes are dominant"

Associative feature: "multiple similar shapes" – The participant made the note after seeing the target. Had she not doubted herself, there would have been 2 triangles.

Target 1: Transcript 8

Participant: Gentle Wolf

Associative feature: "triangle / pointed shapes are dominant" – (A)

Associative feature: "multiple similar shapes" – (A) , (B)

Observed attribute: (C) is indicated as a possible instance of psychic soup (page 79), or precognitive bleed-through (see target on page 107), or a combination of both due to association.

Target 1: Transcript 9

Participant: Insight at Dawn

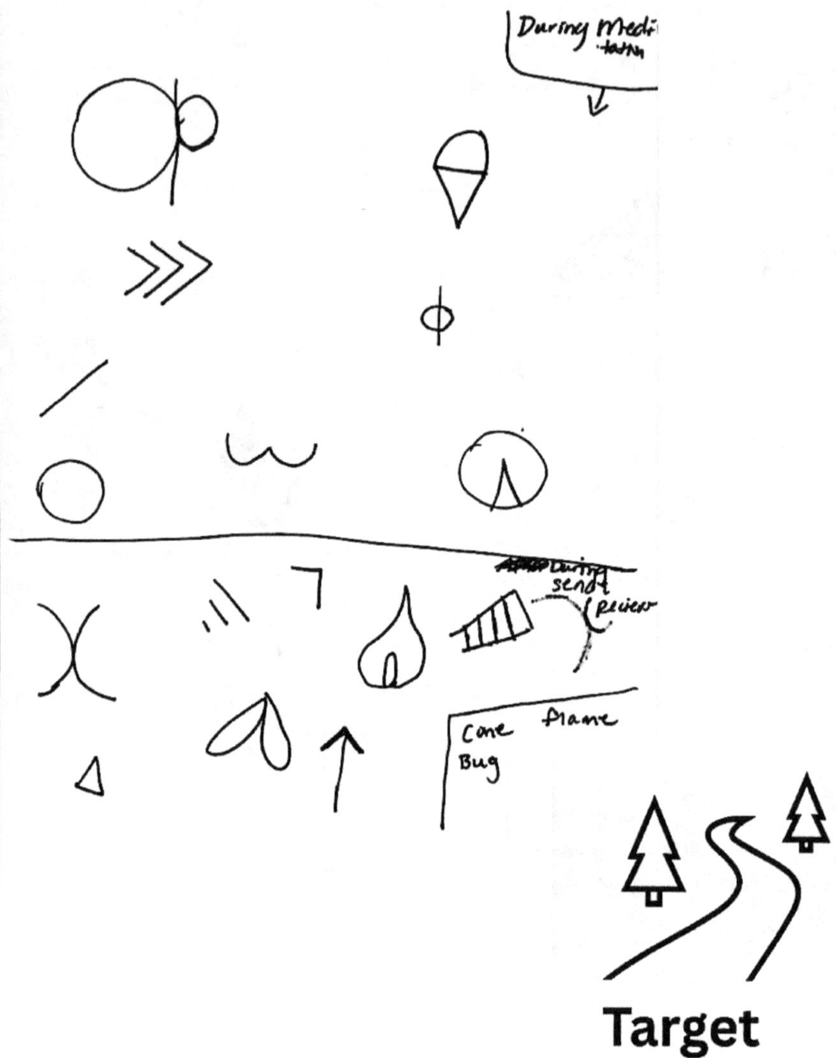

Associative feature: "triangle / pointed shapes are dominant"

Associative feature: "multiple similar shapes"

Observed attribute: Analytical overlay. See how the mind noted "cone" "flame" and "bug").

Target 1: Transcript 10

Participant: Courageous One

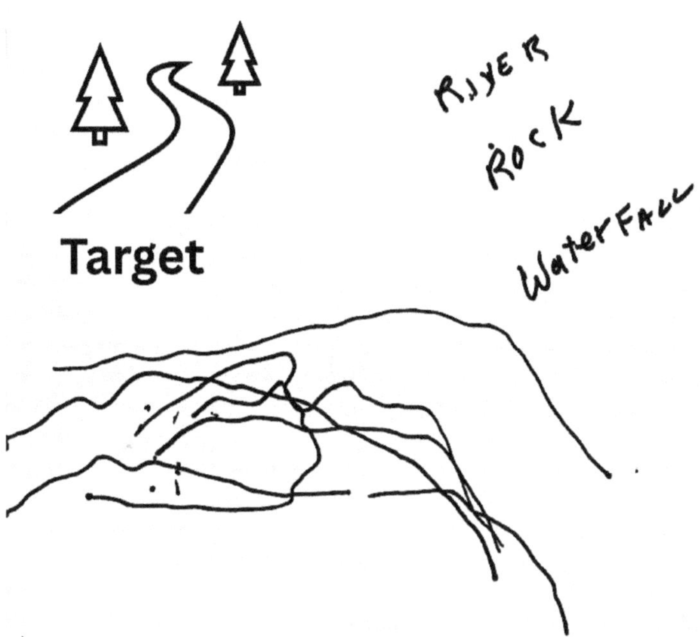

Associative feature: "curved lines resemble a path or river"

Observed attribute: Analytical overlay. "river" "rock" "waterfall"

Observed attribute: Proto-perception (see page 80 for a refresher about this attribute).

Target 1: Transcript 11

Participant: Forest Tantrika

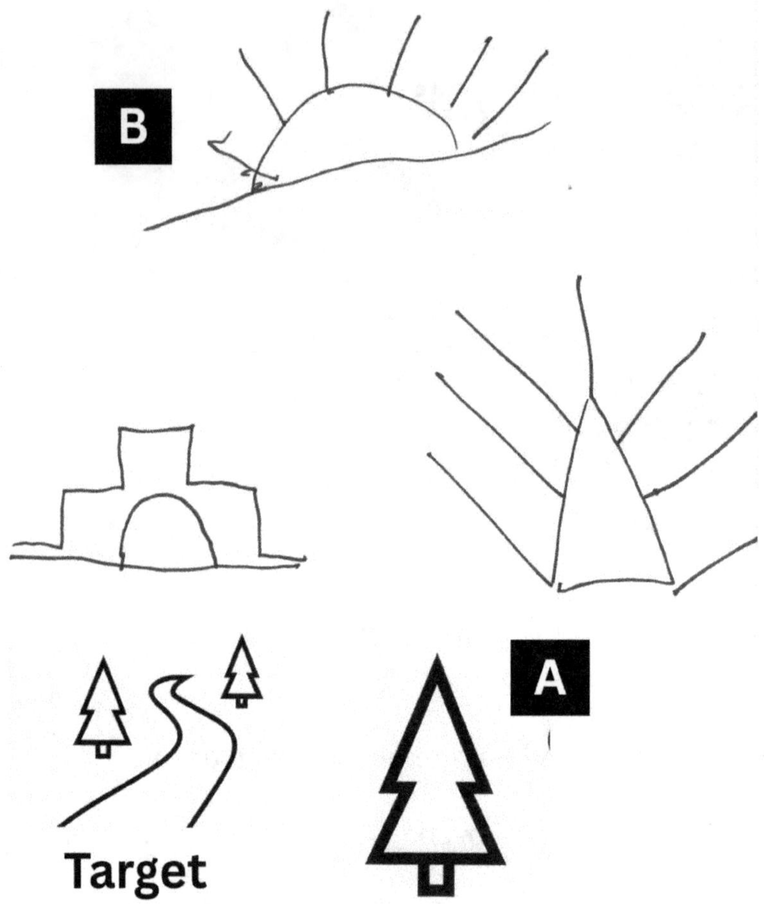

Associative feature: "triangle / pointed shapes are dominant" (A)

Observed attribute: Precognitive bleed-through (B) - See the target on page 107.

Observed attribute: Psychic soup. See how (B) resembles an object on page 91(C) on Gentle Wolf's transcript in this section.

Target 1: Transcript 12

Participant: Kindness Smiling

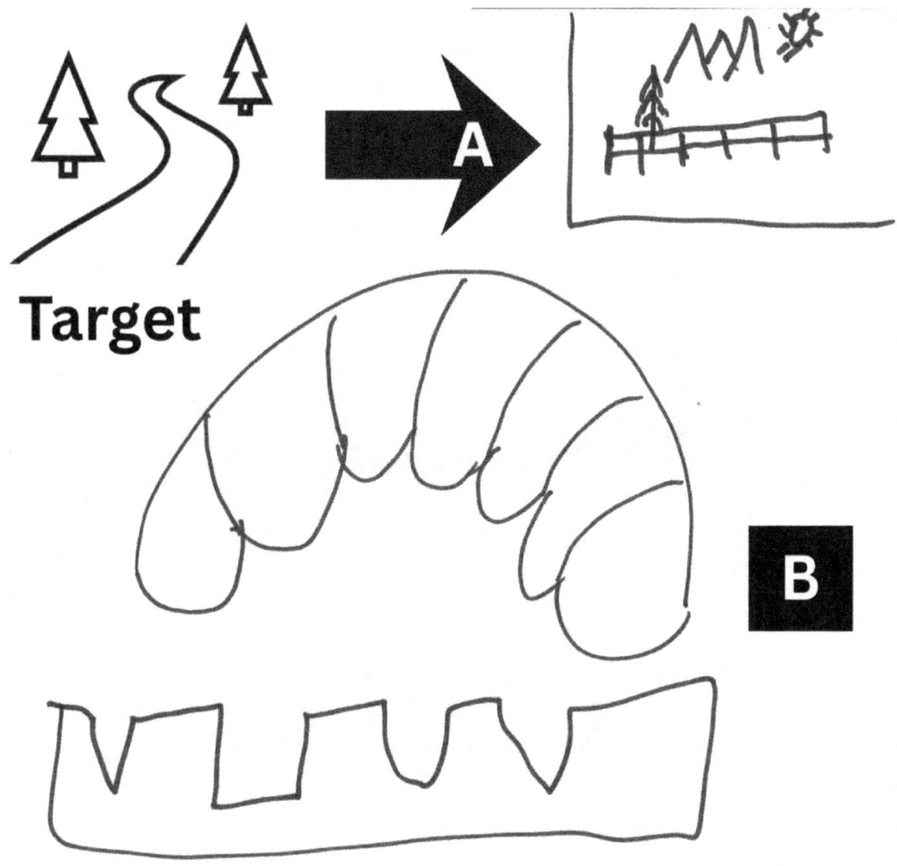

Associative feature: "triangle / pointed shapes are dominant" – The upper-right corner of the transcript may have been where the participant put his first perception, which was quite strong. (A)

Observed attribute: Thematic similarity (A)

Observed attribute: Precognitive bleed-through. Compare (B) with the target on page 96.

Telepathy Target 2: Coliseum with pennants

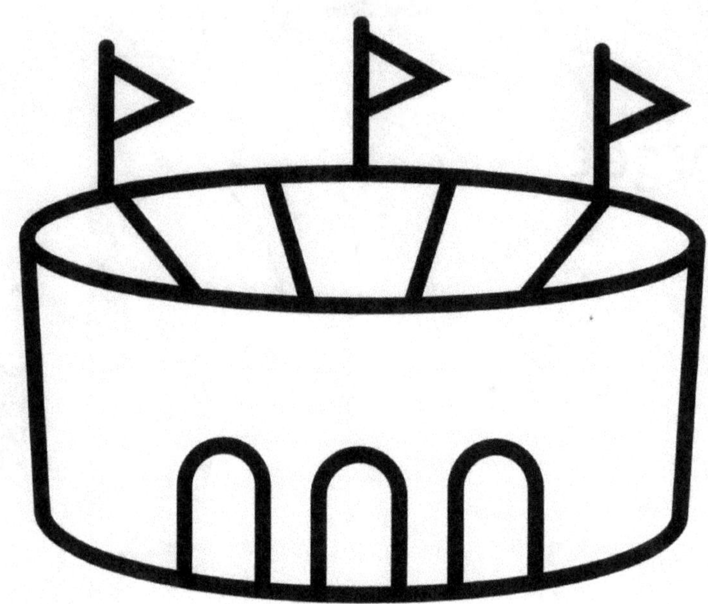

Target: Coliseum with pennants

Associative features:

- triangle shapes are significant (3)
- triangle shapes are at the top
- diagonal lines are significant
- rounded/ovoid shapes (3)
- large, horizontal oval

Target 2: Transcript 1

Participant: Atlantis

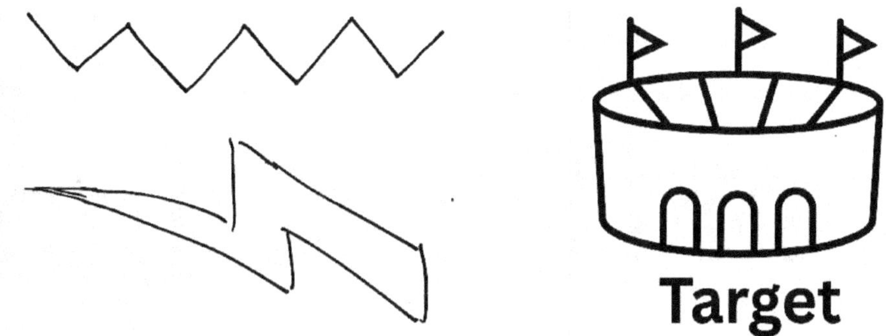

Associative feature: "triangle shapes are significant"

Associative feature: "triangle shapes are at the top"

Associative feature: "diagonal lines are significant"

Target 2: Transcript 2

Participant: Across Dimensions

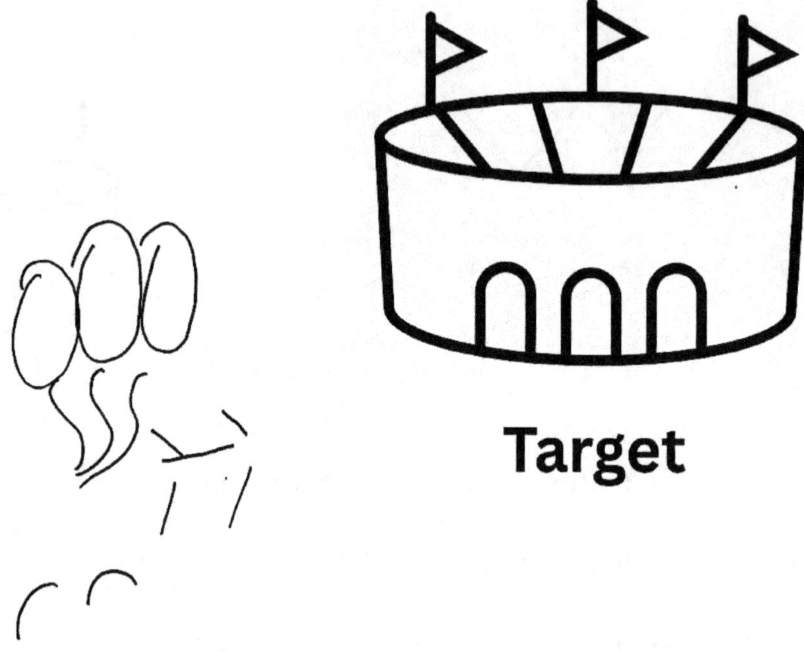

Associative feature: "rounded/ovoid shapes (3)"

Observed attribute: Recognition of multiples – accurate.

Observed attribute: Psychic soup. See the transcript for the same target on page 100 regarding the idea of "balloon" and implied balloon string.

Target 2: Transcript 3

Participant: Star Gazer

Associative feature: "triangle shapes are significant"

Associative feature: "diagonal lines are significant"

Target 2: Transcript 4

Participant: Cosmic Dancer

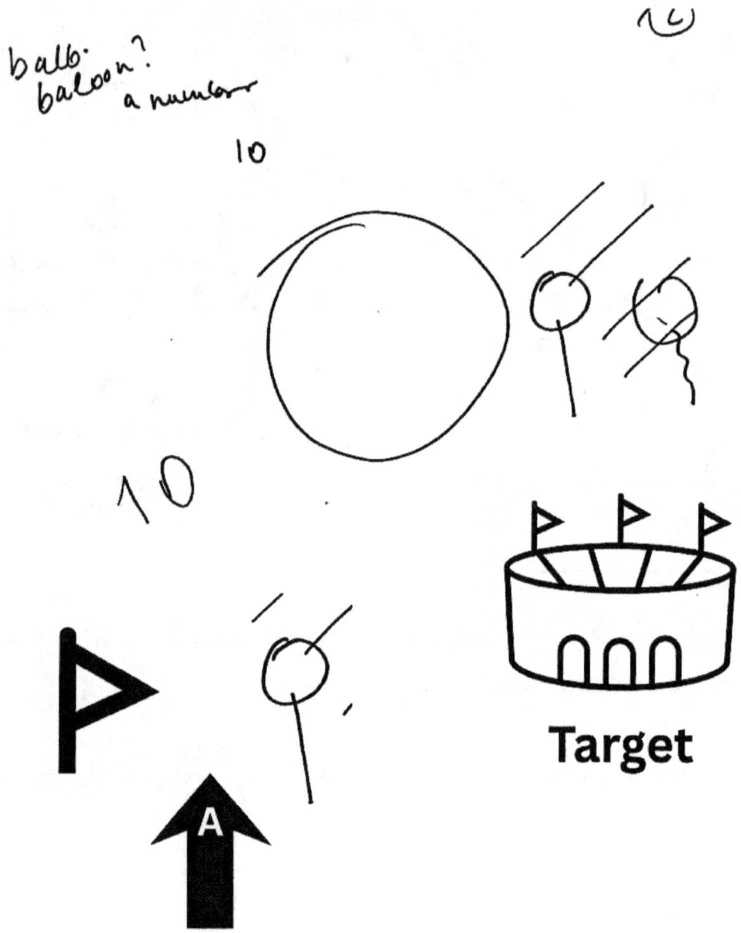

Associative feature: "rounded/ovoid shapes"

Observed attribute: Thematic similarity. The pennants have stems just as the circles in the transcripts do. Compare enlarged portions in (A).

Target 2: Transcript 5

Participant: Code Talker

Associative feature: “large, horizontal oval” – Notice the mouth-like shape.

Associative feature: “triangle shapes are significant” – Look carefully, how many triangles or pointy shapes do you see here?

Observed attribute: Thematic similarity. Note the tower-like structure to the right. It’s a building with openings, as is the coliseum. The receiver even indicated a circle near the bottom with an arrow, associating it with the oval-shaped entries in the target.

Target 2: Transcript 6

Participant: Synchronicity

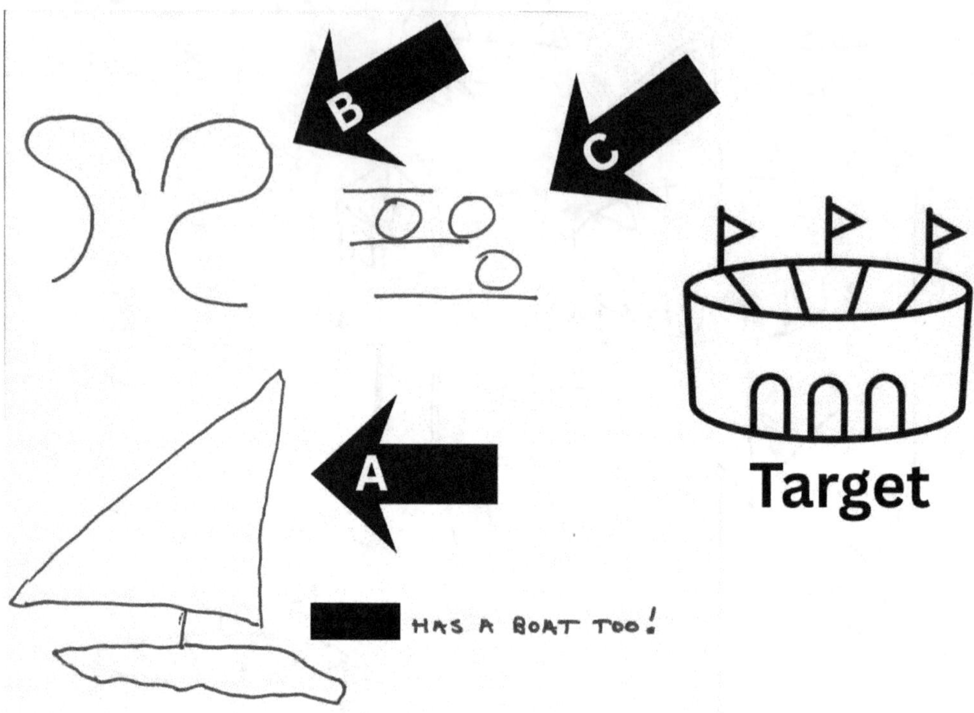

Associative feature: "triangle shapes are significant" – (A)

Associative feature: "rounded/ovoid shapes" – (B), (C)

Observed attribute: Recognition of multiples – accurate. (C)

Observed attribute: Psychic soup. Compare (A) with transcript on the next page.

Target 2: Transcript 7

Participant: Forest Tantrika

Observed attribute: Psychic soup. See the transcript on the previous page. These participants are friends and have done numerous psychic exercises together with the author. The connection is not surprising, but rather to be expected at this point.

Target 2: Transcript 8

Participant: Rain of Energy

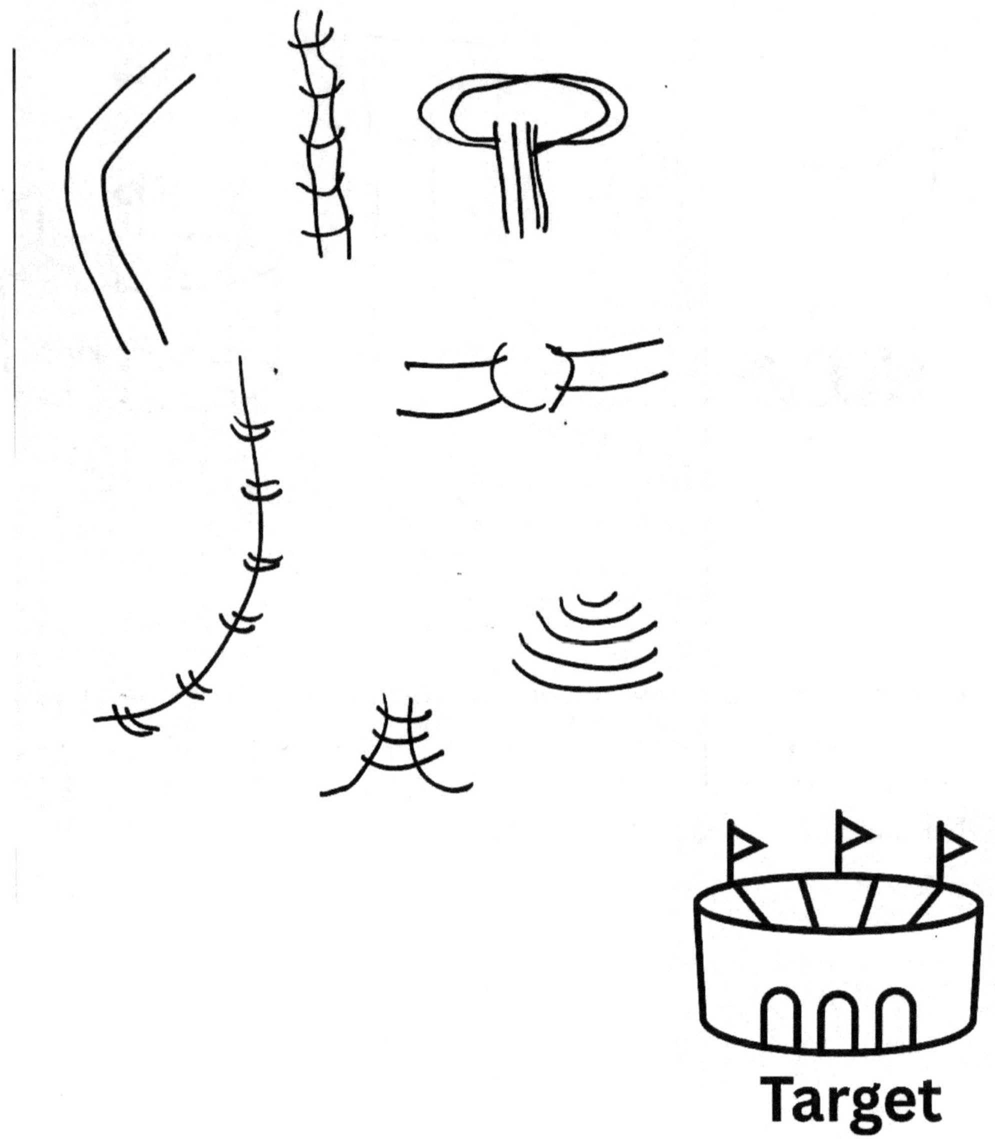

Observed attribute: Primary shape recognition (ovals and curves).

Observed attribute: Recognition of multiples – symbolic.

Target 2: Transcript 9

Participant: All-Seeing

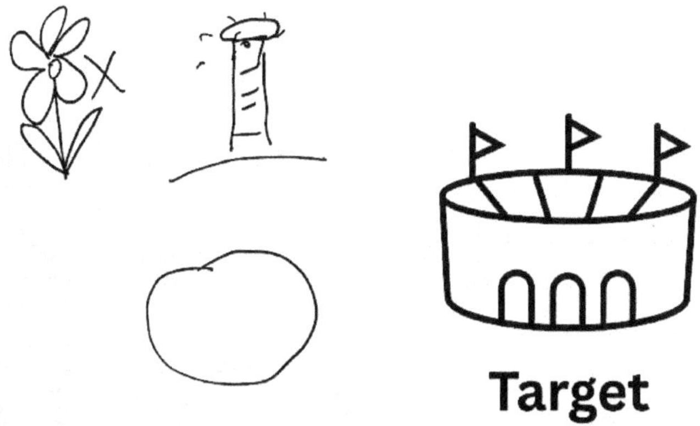

Associative feature: "large, horizontal oval"

Observed attribute: Psychic soup. See transcript 6 for Target #4 on page 122.

Target 2: Transcript 10

Participant: Courageous One

Observed attribute: Proto-perception

Precognitive Bleed-through Example

Transcript for Target #1

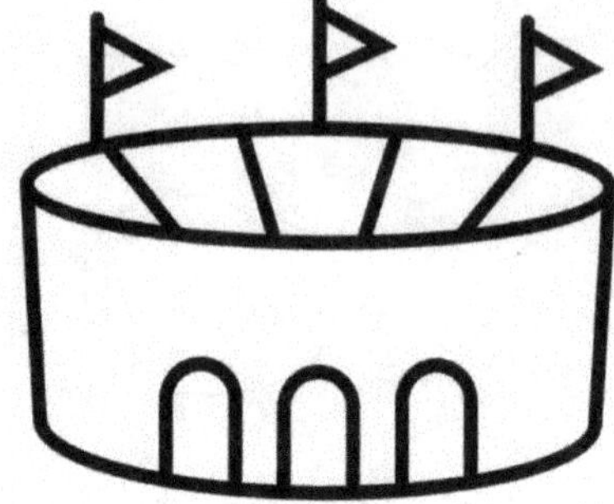

Target #2

Look at the transcript 12 for Target #1 (Two trees and a path) from page 95. This indicates the participant's mind had moved too far into the future and focused on Target #2 instead.

Telepathy Target 3: Sun and ocean waves

Target: Sun and ocean waves

Associative features:

- dominant shape is circular
- circle is incomplete
- dominant shape sits atop horizontal, wavy lines
- multiple wavy lines in parallel
- short, straight lines moving out from a central point
- straight lines appear to originate from the surface of the circle

Target 3: Transcript 1

Participant: All-Seeing

Associative feature: dominant shape is circular (C)

Associative feature: dominant shape sits atop horizontal, wavy lines – In (A), a large shape sits atop a single horizontal line. In (B) a large shape sites atop two curved lines.

Associative feature: multiple wavy lines in parallel – (D)

Observed attribute: Reconstruction - In (B), the waves have been reconstructed to replace the sun rays (straight lines) and also replace the smooth line of the circle to make it resemble a cloud.

Target 3: Transcript 2

Participant: Rain of Energy

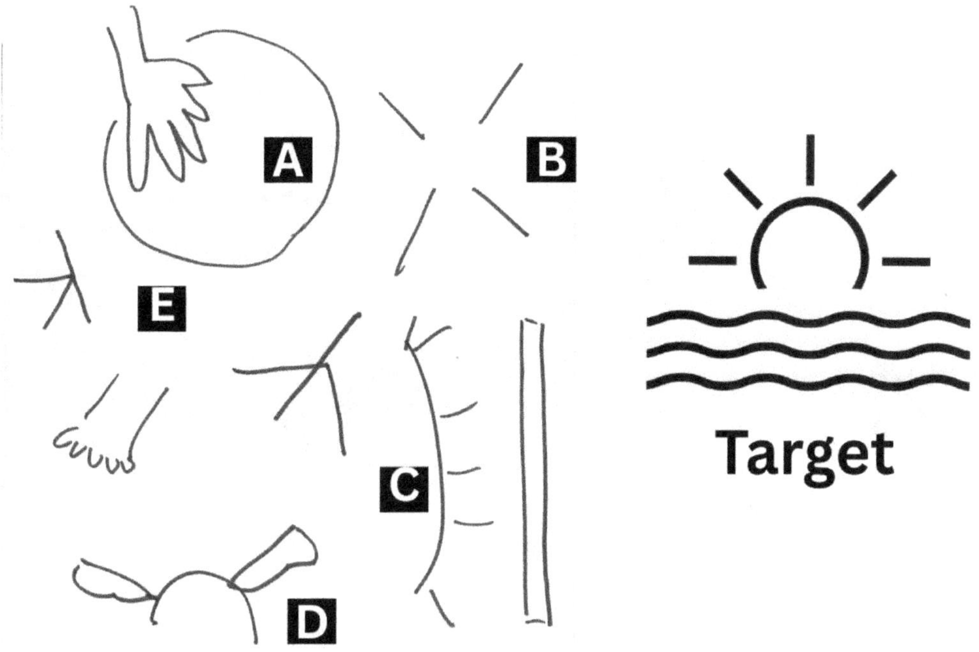

Associative feature: Dominant shape is circular – (A)

Associative feature: short, straight lines moving out from a central point – (B)

Associative feature: straight lines appear to originate from the surface of the circle – (C) & (D)

Observed attribute: Deconstruction – In (C), the sun's surface has been flattened while retaining its rays

Observed Attribute – Recognition of multiples – accurate – In (E), 5 fingers emanate from the palms of both hands. There are 5 sunbeams emanating from the sun.

Target 3: Transcript 3

Participant: Insight at Dawn

Associative feature: dominant shape is circular – (A) & (E)

Associative feature: circle is incomplete – (B)

Observed attribute: Thematic similarity – (A) is sun-like, (C) *might* relate to the waves, (D) *might* relate to the sun rays

Notice the very top of (E), the long curve with a squiggle at the end. Did the mind combine the sun's curve with part of a wave there?

Target 3: Transcript 4

Participant: Forest Tantrika

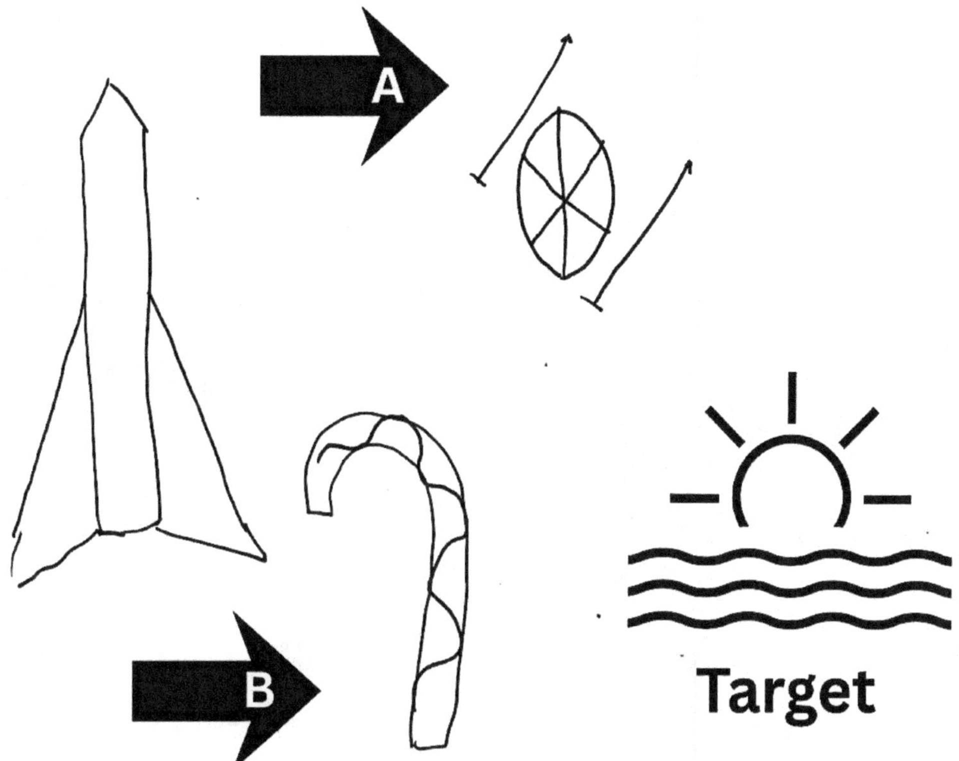

Observed attribute: Reconstruction – (A) The mind placed the shorter straight lines inside the circle and placed two of the longer lines on either side.

Observed attribute: Reconstruction – (B) The mind placed a wave inside a curved shape, although it was not a circle.

Target 3: Transcript 5

Participant: Snow Lion

Associative feature: multiple wavy lines in parallel – In (A), a single wavy line

Associative feature: short, straight lines moving out from a central point – The lines in (B) have a "shortness" resembling the rays in the target but lack the emanation from a central point.

Target 3: Transcript 6

Participant: Cosmic Dancer

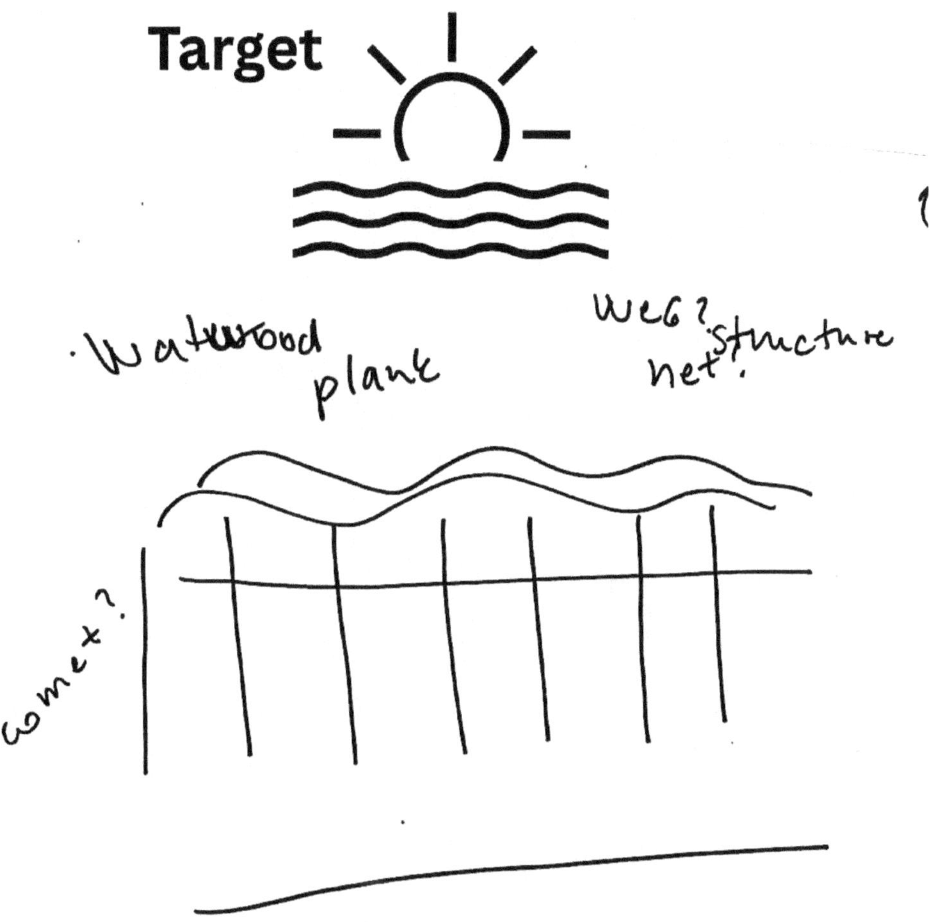

Associative feature: multiple wavy lines in parallel – Not only are top horizontal, wavy lines parallel, but there are multiple verticat lines, also parallel.

Observed attribute: Analytical overly - The participant wrote "web?," "structure," and "net?," all of which are somewhat evocative of the *symmetry* in the target. The participant also wrote "water" (on the left, slightly overwritten with "wood." The target's wavy lines are representative of water.

Target 3: Transcript 7

Participant: Courageous One

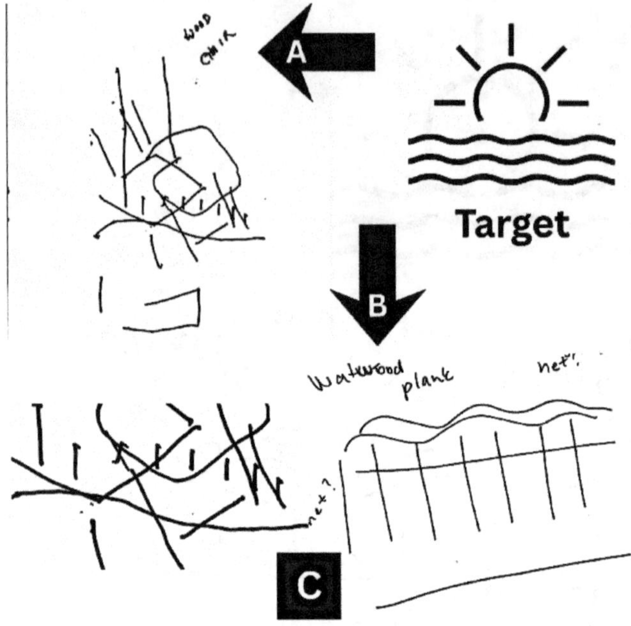

Note: The transcript (A), is magnified at the bottom and placed next to the transcript from the previous page for comparison (C).

Observed attribute: Proto-perception

Observed attribute: Psychic soup. The participant wrote "wood" (B) at the top of the transcript. The other participant also had the word "wood" on their transcript. Also, note the strong overall visual resemblance between the two transcripts. Therefore, the proto-perception is not of the target, but of another participant's *interpretation* of their target.

Observed attribute: Analytical overlay – The participant also wrote "chair," due to the resemblance with what is otherwise an abstract collection of lines.

Target 3: Transcript 8

Participant: Atlantis

Associative feature: dominant shape is circular

Associative feature: straight lines appear to originate from the surface of the circle (sketches to the left)

Observed attribute: Precognitive bleed-through – the sketches to the left resemble the next target more than the current one (next page).

Observed attribute: Analytical overly – The participant wrote "spiderman" and "spiderweb." It seems the AOL was not for the current target but for the next one, a spider.

Telepathy Target 4: Spider

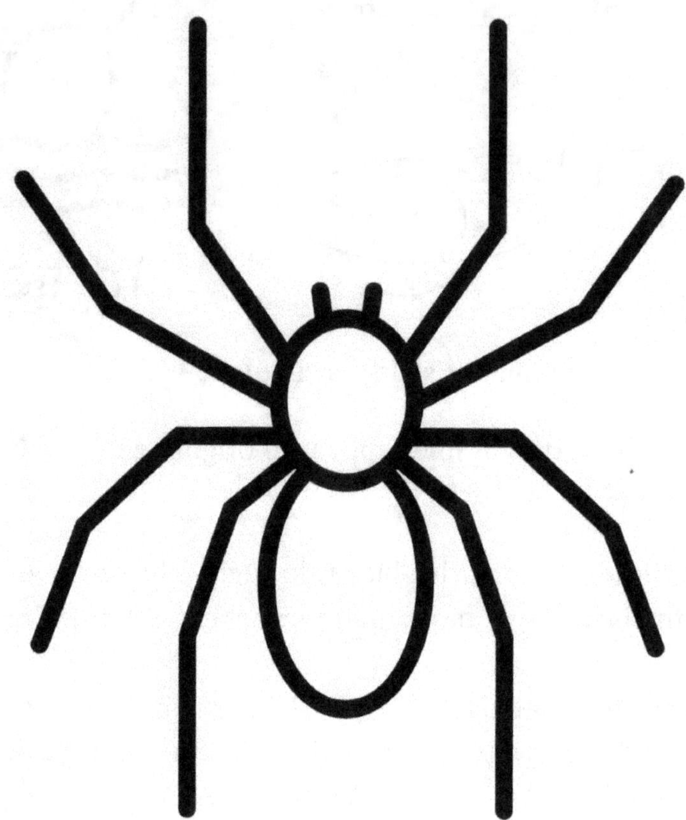

Target: Spider

Associative features:

- multiple straight/bent lines
- central shapes are circular and oval

Target 4: Transcript 1

Participant: Gentle Wolf

Target

Associative feature: multiple straight/bent lines

Observed attribute: Proto-perception

Target 4: Transcript 2

Participant: Diamond Eyes

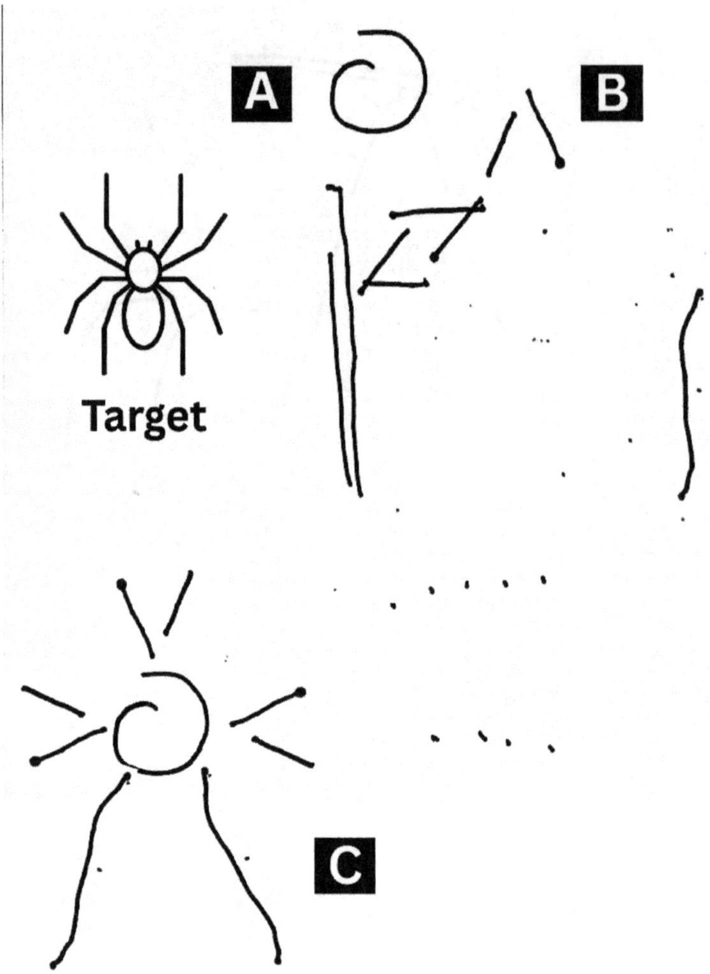

Associative feature: central shapes are circular and oval – (A)

Associative feature: multiple straight/bent lines - (B)

Observed attribute: Deconstruction - (A) and (B) are a deconstruction of the target. To test this, the author rearranged and duplicated some of the parts taken from the transcript to *reconstruct* them into a semblance of the target (C).

Target 4: Transcript 3

Participant: Lord of Water

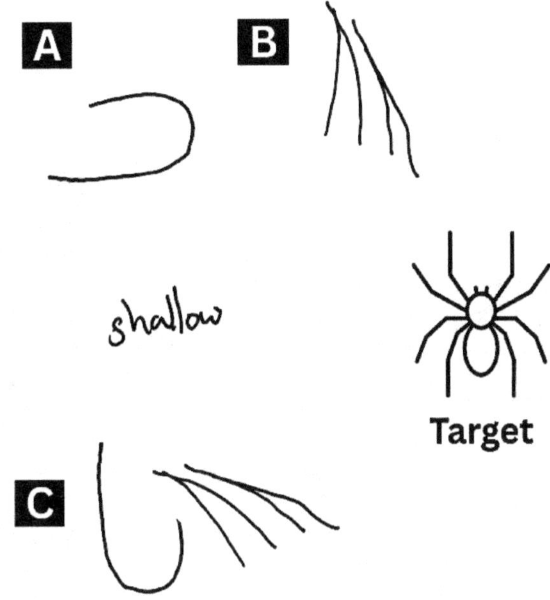

Associative feature: central shapes are circular and oval – Partially accurate

Associative feature: multiple straight/bent lines

Observed attribute: Deconstruction - (A) and (B) are the deconstruction of the target. To test this, the author rearranged and duplicated some of the parts to *reconstruct* them into a semblance of *a portion* of the target, such as the lower-right side of the spider (C).

Target 4: Transcript 4

Participant: Joyful Explorer

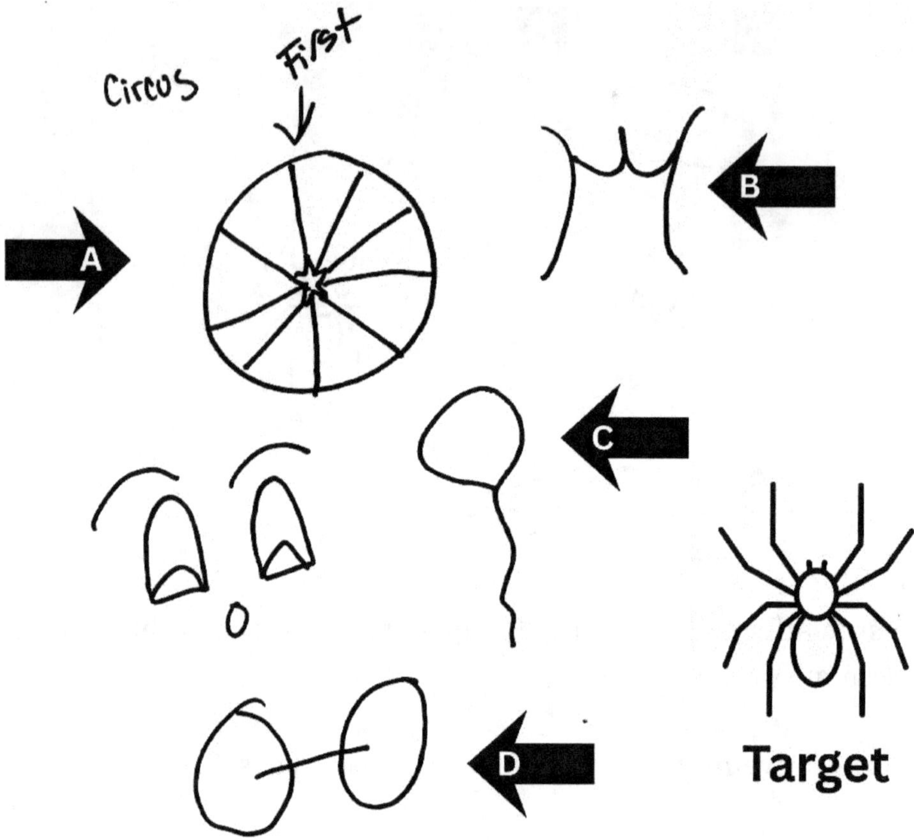

Associative feature: central shapes are circular and oval – (A), (C), (D)

Observed attribute: Reconstruction – (A) The lines (the legs) were moved inside the primary circle to construct a wheel.

Observed attribute: Thematic similarity – (B) resembles an amorphous creature holding up its arms, and is visually similar to the target, albeit in abstract fashion.

Target 4: Transcript 5

Participant: Code Talker

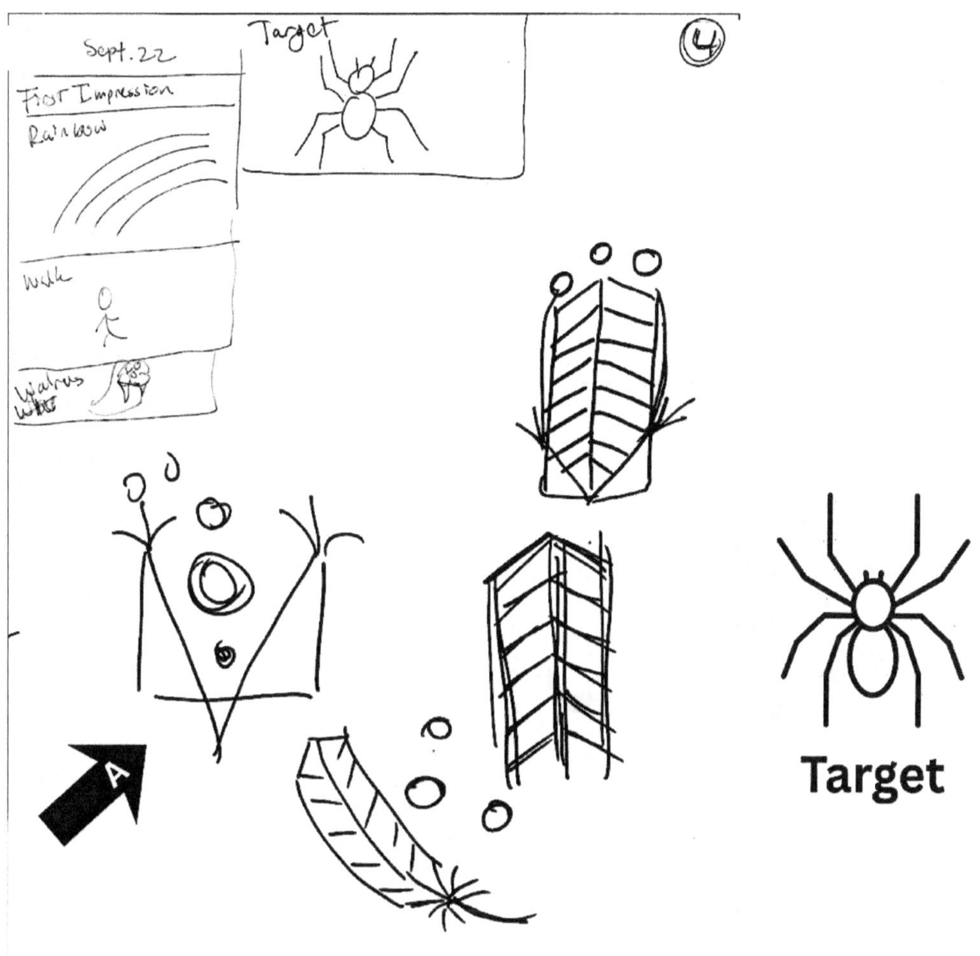

Associative feature: multiple straight/bent lines

Associative feature: central shapes are circular and oval – In the transcript, the circles seem tangential, but their repetition indicates a confidence in the presence of round shapes in the target.

Observed attribute: Deconstruction – (A)

Target 4: Transcript 6

Participant: Star Gazer

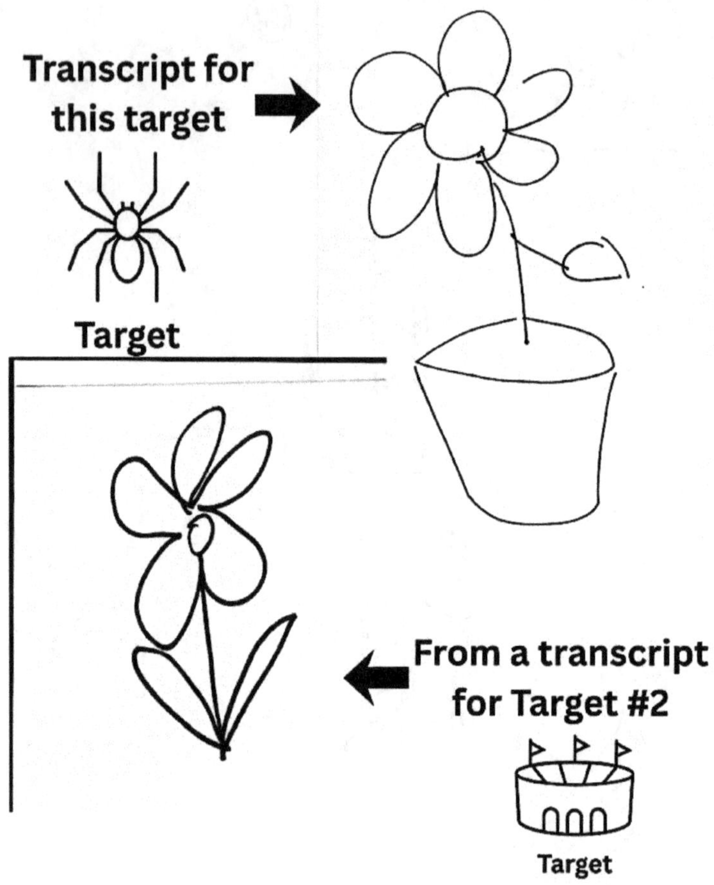

Associative feature: central shapes are circular and oval

Observed attribute: Psychic soup. See All-Seeing's transcript for Target #2 on page 105. It contains the flower pictured on the lower half of the page. The only image Star Gazer put on her transcript for Target #4 was her flower (top of page). Although it does possess an associative feature for this target, it also seems that the flower might be an unrelated object of the mysterious psychic soup we all seem to occupy.

Telepathy Target 5: Two hearts

Target: Two hearts

Associative features:

- 2 objects
- 2 same-shaped objects
- object resembles a [curved] triangle by being pointed on one end and wide on the other
- object possesses a distinct cleft at the top-middle

Target 5: Transcript 1

Participant: Synchronicity

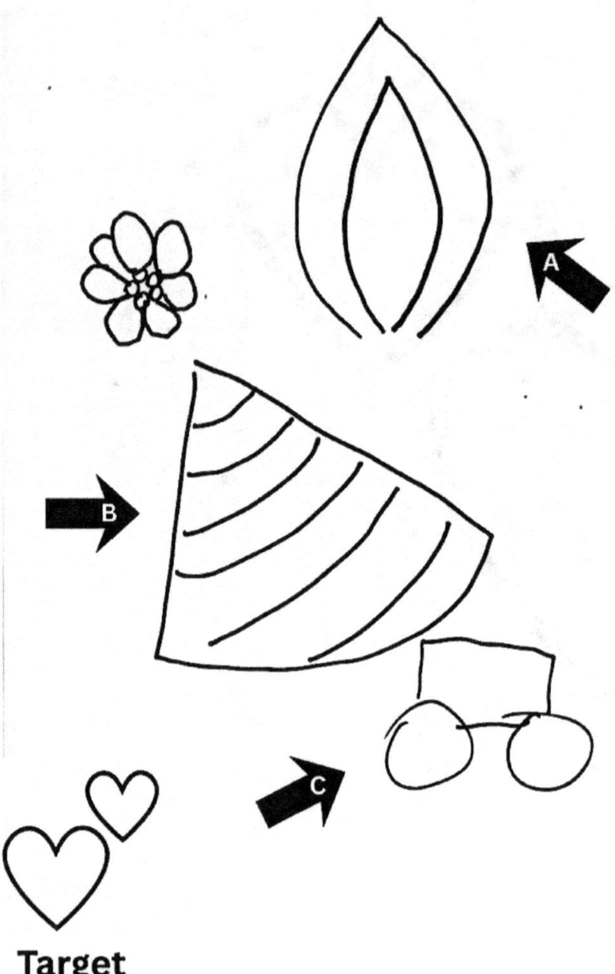

Associative feature: object resembles a [curved] triangle by being pointed on one end and wide on the other (B)

Observed attribute: Recognition of multiples – accurate – (A) and (C) indicate 2 of similarly-shaped objects

Target 5: Transcript 2

Participant: Insight at Dawn

Associative feature: object possesses a distinct cleft at the top-middle - (A), (B), (C)

Observed attribute: Recognition of multiples - symbolic – (C)

What else do you see here?

Target 5: Transcript 3

Participant: Rain of Energy

Associative feature: object resembles a triangle by being pointed on one end and wide on the other (A), (B), (C), (D)

Observed attribute: Recognition of multiples - symbolic – (A), (B), (C), (D)

What do you think about that shape in the center?

Target 5: Transcript 4

Participant: Forest Tantrika

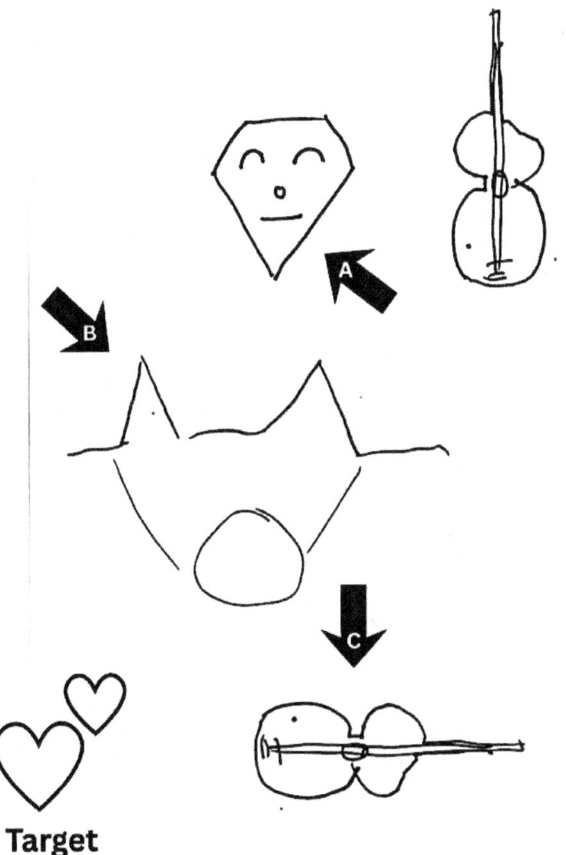

Associative feature: object resembles a triangle by being pointed on one end and wide on the other (A) and *perhaps* (B)

Associative feature: object possesses a distinct cleft at the top-middle – In this case there are 2 clefts, on either side of the musical instrument (C) [original image tilted 90 degrees by the author for visual comparison]

Observed attribute: Recognition of multiples – symbolic – (B) seems to indicate 2 of something.

Telepathy Target 6: Shower head / lamp

Target: Shower head / lamp

Associative features:

- long straight line
- long straight line topped with complex object
- round/semi-circular object
- multiple straight lines longer than the main line

Target 6: Transcript 1

Participant: Star Gazer

Associative feature: long straight line topped with complex object

Observed attribute: Analytical overly – The mind labeled/named their impression "a flag?".

Target 6: Transcript 2

Participant: Kindness Smiling

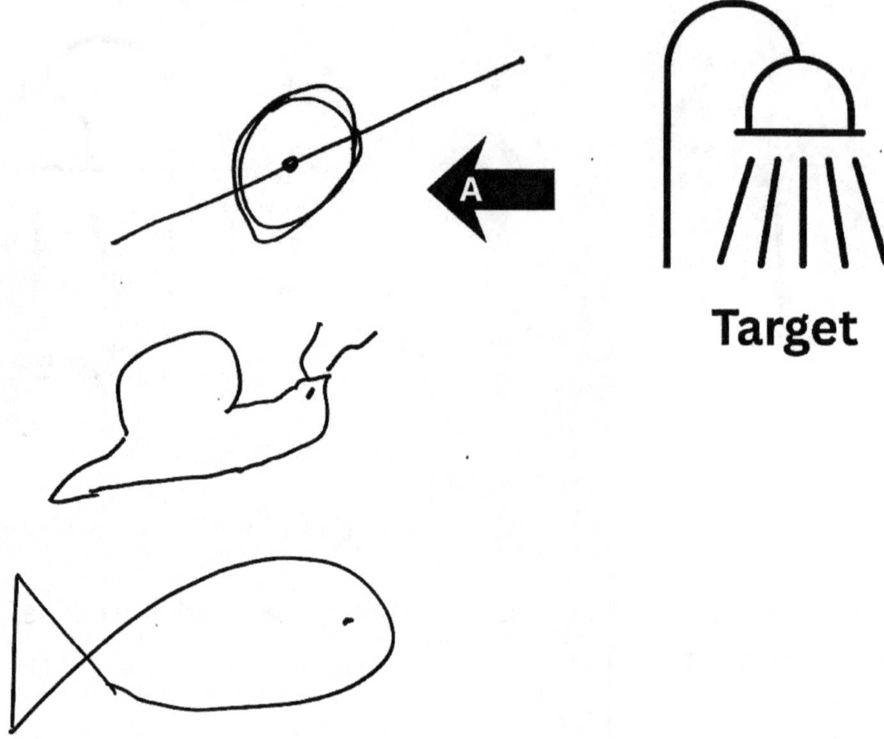

Associative feature: round/semi-circular object + long straight line (A)

Target 6: Transcript 3

Participant: Across Dimensions

Associative feature: round/semi-circular object – (A)

Note: At the bottom, the author copied the bottom of the 3 repeated semi-circles (A) and pasted it atop the line's arch to gauge similarity (C). He then pasted it side-by-side with the shower head/lamp again to gauge similarity with its curve (B).

What do you think? Are they similar? Or were the multiple semi-circles (and one full circle) indicating the two curves in the target?

Target 6: Transcript 4

Participant: Joyful Explorer

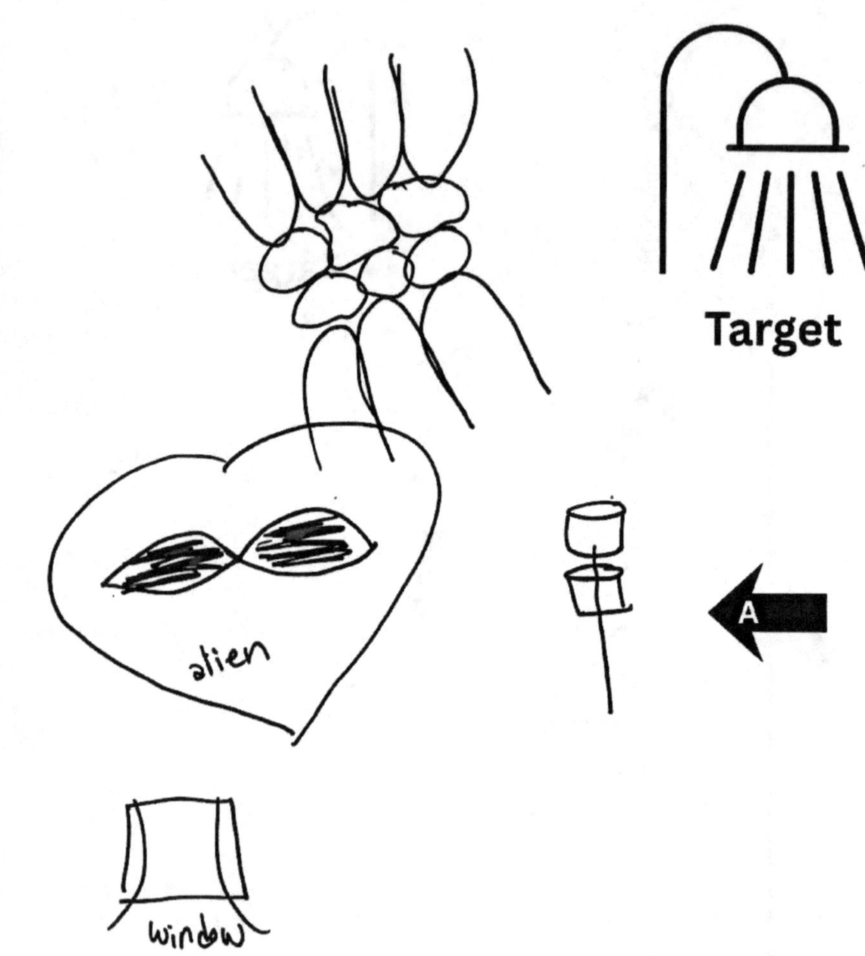

Associative feature: long straight line topped with complex object - (A)

Do you think the shape labeled "alien" resembles the shower head/lamp? Or is it a lingering mental echo of the previous target on page 123 (the two hearts)?

Target 6: Transcript 5

Participant: Lord of Water

Associative feature: long straight line topped with complex object (A)

Associative feature: multiple straight lines longer than the main line (A)

Observed attribute: Reconstruction - This case is subtle in that the mind combined the *verticality* (height) of the target with its *width* (B).

Target 6: Transcript 7

Participant: Sojourner

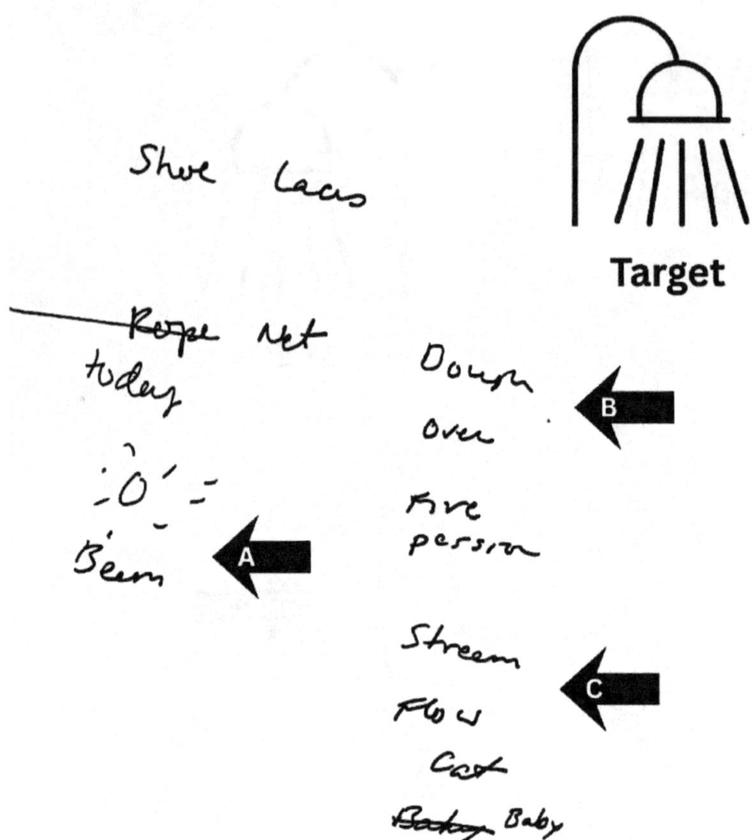

Observed attribute: Deconstruction – See (A), the shower head/lamp deconstructed, which the participant labeled “beam,” which itself is an accurate interpretation of the “beams” descending from the shower head/lamp.

Observed attribute: Thematic Similarity – See the word “Bough” (B). If you’re not sure, do an online image search for “holiday bough” and then decide if there’s some similarity. Also, see “stream” and “flow” (C), which are quite accurate if the mind perceives this as a shower head.

DAY 2 – CLAIRVOYANCE WITH COLORS

On the second day of the intensive, we practiced several types of clairvoyance, beginning with sensing colors. These exercises were intended to serve as cross-training for the mind. My hypothesis is that becoming psychically sensitive to colors engages a part of the psychic mind that black-and-white line drawings don't.

This type of training is covered at length in the first Mind Sight book, *Mind Sight: Training to See Without Eyes*[44]. If you'd like to begin training right away, it's quite easy. All you need is a blindfold and sheets of paper in various colors. Here are the steps I recommend you take:

1. With eyes open (no blindfold), hold one of the papers and look at it for a minute or so. Pay attention to how the color makes you feel. You might even hover your hand close to the paper to "feel" the color's frequency coming off the paper.

2. Put on your blindfold and repeat the process with the same piece of paper. You already know what color it is, so this step isn't about trying to figure that out. It's about associating the most subtle, subconscious perceptions of the paper with the information the conscious mind already possesses. Since you can't see it with your eyes in this step, you must be sensitive to what happens *inside* your mind as you focus on the paper, and as you hover your hand over its surface.

---

[44] McNamara, Sean. (2021). *Mind Sight: Training to See Without Eyes Pilot Program for Adults.* Mind Possible.

3. As you work with the paper while blindfolded, hold it up in front of your face *as if* you were looking at it with your eyes. Keeping your eyes open beneath the mask may help activate the visual cortex in the brain and help it process *not* the signals from the optical nerve, but signals from wherever psychic perceptions are processed in the brain when entering the conscious mind. But if you prefer to keep your eyes closed beneath the blindfold, it's fine. The most important thing is to A) direct your attention toward the paper and B) intend to notice the subtle perceptions occurring inside your mind as you do so.

4. Repeat Step 3 while holding the paper near different parts of your head and body, which we call "windows." Don't be surprised if some areas of your body produce more impressions than the front of your face.

5. Also, see what happens when you slowly wave the paper back and forth. Does that produce more distinct impressions for you? What if you flick it with your finger, or shake it a bit?

6. After several minutes, remove your blindfold and look at the paper again to reinforce the association of its color with whatever perceptions came to you.

7. Then, choose a new color to work with and start over with Step 1.

8. After doing this with at least 2 or 3 colors, prepare a stack of papers with at least 4 sheets of each color in it. While blindfolded, shuffle the papers, set down the stack, and pick up the top sheet.

9. Give yourself some time to work with that paper, being careful to stay in a receptive mindset. Let the impressions come to you in their own time. One of the biggest hurdles to cross is preventing the conscious mind from guessing what the color is. Guessing feels quite different from passively waiting for impressions to come. Guessing

feels like grasping for information or pushing the mind to produce something. Guessing feels like actively thinking. Passively waiting feels like meditating with a wide focus.

10. When you're confident about your perceptions, remove your blindfold to see if you were correct in your association. This is still part of the learning process, so even if you were incorrect, take a minute to repeat Step 1 at this point to improve how your subconscious and conscious minds correlate with this color.

11. Then, put your blindfold back on and draw another paper from the pile, and try again.

12. Avoid boredom. If all you can do is a few minutes before getting distracted, that's fine. Over time, you'll find other colored objects to repeat this exercise with, such as colored cups, toys, balls, scarves, etc. Using different targets in the same training session is a great way to keep it interesting.

13. Have fun, celebrate your successes, and ignore the times when you're incorrect. Stay positive and don't take yourself seriously. This is your chance to feel like a kid again.

Below: Participants hold and move their colored papers near different parts of their heads and bodies to notice how impressions arise inside their minds as they do so.

DAY 2 – CLAIRVOYANCE WITH SMALL OBJECTS

After working with colors, we shifted gears and worked with small, variously colored objects. Physical objects add the dimension of depth to a target. Here, my hypothesis is that becoming psychically sensitive to depth engages a part of the psychic mind that line drawings and colored papers don't.

Here's a sample of the objects we used for this exercise, below.

This was primarily a clairvoyance exercise, but it was quite possible for telepathy to be involved because it was done in pairs. Each receiver sat and waited blindfolded while their partner *quietly* placed several objects on an opened folder in front of them.

The purpose of the folder was to create a bordered workspace, so the participant wouldn't need to scan the entire table looking for their objects.

When the targets were set, each blindfolded participant's task was to lift each object off the folder and set it aside in as few attempts as possible.

It would be too easy for a participant to use sweeping motions with their hand to find the objects, so we created a rule. They had to use one hand like those cranes you see at the arcade, where you push a button at just the right moment to make the moving mechanical arm descend and grab a toy or stuffed animal out of the case.

So, the participant's hand had to come straight down from above, fingers acting like pincers. If they touched nothing but the folder, they had to lift their hand straight back up without sweeping around searching for a nearby target.

The participant could hover their hand over the table and try to sense the objects beneath. They could also hover their face over the table and try to "feel" the mass of the individual objects that way. This only works if the objects are odorless, as ours were.

And of course, they could simply intend to perceive the table surface similarly to how they perceived the colored papers in the previous exercise.

Since their partner was watching, telepathy could've spontaneously occurred by transferring information about the location of the objects from the seeing partner to the blindfolded one.

If you try this at home, be open to *any* perception. Your mind might not produce an accurate visual representation of the object. It might appear as a tiny spark, disappearing as quickly as it appeared, in a flash. Or a gray fuzzy shape. Or a color. Or, the texture of the space at a certain spot might "feel" different than the rest of the folder.

Scan the workspace for a few minutes, and when you think you've located an object, let your hand descend like a crane and find out. When you find one, set it aside and keep going after the rest.

If you don't have a partner to set the objects in place for you, there's a solution. You can use a large box and small, soft objects, such as the small foam dice you can order online. Insert some earplugs and put on your blindfold, then use the box to shake the objects around. Then, flip the box over and onto the table so the objects land randomly but within the boundaries of the box's opening. Otherwise, they could scatter out of reach.

Take measures so that you neither *hear* where the objects land nor *feel* them landing on the table. With or without a partner, this is a particularly fun exercise.

Below, participants practice locating their small objects.

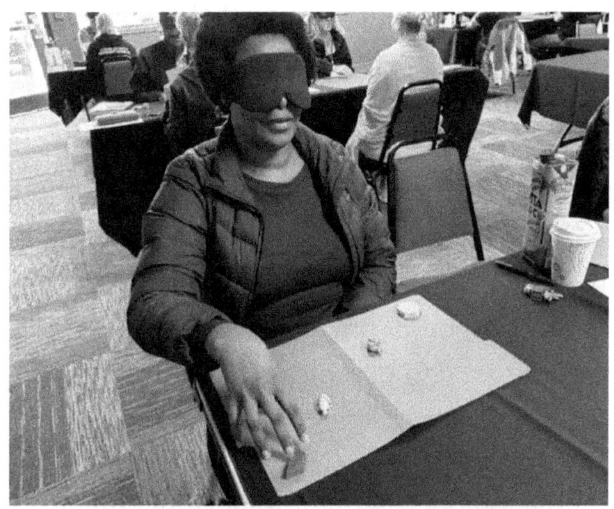

DAY 2 – TELEPATHY WITH COMPLEX IMAGES

This exercise was an opportunity to combine and develop the skills from the earlier ones. By this point, the participants had practiced psychically perceiving line drawings, which is about identifying fundamental two-dimensional shapes. They had also practiced identifying colors.

Then, they moved on to locating physical objects, which increased their sensitivity to three dimensions. Now they were ready to practice telepathically perceiving complex images. Basically, color pictures of real-life scenes.

One might wonder if developing a sensitivity to spatial dimensions (width, height, depth), as was done with the small objects, is truly necessary to psychically perceive a photograph. My hypothesis here is that our imagined perception of an object's three-dimensionality is included in the information shared during telepathy.

For example, below is a two-dimensional image of a baby elephant. But my mind associates the image with mass and a three-dimensional shape. Baby elephants are very thick and very heavy compared to other baby animals. So, the elephant's *thickness* and *heaviness* are associative features that a sender would include when psychically sharing information about the target with their receiver.

The complex images used for this exercise were in the form of cards drawn from the *Send and Receive* telepathy training deck I created years before. The images on each card were hand-selected for their associative features. The cards are also specifically ordered in the deck, so every card is distinct from the card before and after it. This is important because of how one structures their training session.

For example, a sender may start by drawing the first three cards and laying them face down on the table. Then, the sender chooses only one of the three to pick up, focus on, and intend to send to their receiver or receivers.

We allotted three or four minutes for each sender and receiver to attempt to transmit the information about the target card. We broke up into several groups of three, with one sender and two receivers. Everyone took turns. Each round, the receivers were to write down any impressions they received about the target image.

When the time was up, the receivers were to describe their impressions to their sender. Then, the sender was to shuffle the three cards without looking at the two they'd drawn earlier but only laid on the table face down at the start.

After shuffling them, the sender placed all three cards face up on the table so the receivers could look at them and select the one they believed was the target card. At that point, the sender would confirm which card was the target.

There are other ways to use the cards. To reduce the complexity, the sender may draw only two cards instead of three. If that's too easy, the sender could draw four or more cards.

However, when presenting multiple potential target cards, there is always the possibility for the receiver's mind to travel three minutes into the future, see *all* the cards on the table, focus on the card that is *most interesting* to their subconscious mind, and send *that* information back to the receiver (in the present) instead of information about the card the sender actually focused on. In remote viewing terms, this is called *displacement*.

To remove the possibility of displacement, the game can be simplified so the sender only draws one card, the target card. When the allotted time has passed, the receiver reports their impressions to the sender, who then reveals the card as feedback for comparison with the receiver's notes.

Senders can experiment by using their minds in different ways. They can:

- Alter the intensity with which they focus on the target card.
- Mentally repeat or chant a significant descriptor or label while focusing on the image, for example, "Elephant, elephant…"
- Recall and intensify past sensory experiences (memories) that resemble the target, such as how an elephant smells (perhaps from a zoo trip), how it sounds, etc.

Receivers can experiment by:

- Setting an intention to receive visual, auditory, olfactory, gustatory, and tactile impressions about the target, then relaxing and patiently waiting for the impressions to arise in their own time.
- Imagine entering the sender's mind via the skull and "seeing" the target image through the sender's eyes.
- Imagine standing beside or behind the sender to peek at the card.
- Expanding their sense of self beyond the boundary of their body through visualization and relaxation, then extending it toward the sender's energy field (aura) with the intention of *joining* with the sender's consciousness to share in their experience of looking at the card.

It's considered good form for receivers to ask for their sender's permission to use some of these techniques due to their intimate and intrusive nature.

Below, one person is the sender for two receivers. She focuses on the image drawn from the deck, intending to mentally send them the information. Note the two *potential* target cards face down on the table.

To train with a friend at home, order your own deck at www.MindPossible.com/send_and_receive_telepathy.html or use the QR code above.

DAY 2 – REMOTE VIEWING AS AUTOTELEPATHY

Just as the earliest exercises prepared everyone to train using complex images (previous chapter), training with those images prepared them for remote viewing. The difference between the two is not necessarily in the quality of psychic perception. Rather, it's in the use of protocols. If using complex images is simple clairvoyance (when training alone) or simple telepathy, remote viewing could be described as clairvoyance *with a protocol*.

The way I taught it at the program, though, was as telepathy (specifically, autotelepathy) with a protocol. Let us first discuss why I view remote viewing as an autotelepathic exercise as well as a clairvoyant one.

I'd like you to imagine it's 6:00 pm, and you've opened an envelope containing a color printout depicting a scene. It's of a sailboat regatta. Your eyes see several white sailboats racing each other, their colorful sails taut against the blustery wind, ocean spray soaking the crew members who are clearly having the time of their lives. The sky is clear blue, and seagulls fly above.

As you soak in the visuals, you imagine tasting the salt water, smelling the marine odors, and feeling the sun's warmth and cool breeze on your skin. You even remember times in your life when you enjoyed similar experiences on a boat.

And while you bring the scene to life in your imagination, you engage your intention to send the scene *backward in time,* to 10:00 am that same day. Who are you sending the information back in time to? To yourself, because at 10:00 that morning, you sat down to focus on a six-digit coordinate that represented this target.

After setting your intention to receive information about the target, you let go and relaxed, patiently waiting for impressions to arrive. And when they did, you wrote them down on your transcript.

You wrote down the information that your *future self* sent you at 6:00 pm.

In this way, remote viewing is a protocol involving **autotelepathy.** It's a conversation between your past self and your future self.

Because of this, we must let go of the idea that the exercise began at 10:00 that morning and finished at 6:00 that evening. With autotelepathy, the exercise *begins in the future*, and ends in the present, when the remote viewer sits down to receive impressions about the target from their future self.

It's also possible to do remote viewing as only a clairvoyant exercise. I say this because I have heard of professional and military remote viewers who were given a task, did the viewing, and submitted their transcripts to the client. But they were never shown the *feedback* due to the confidential nature of the information. In other words, they never got to see the "picture in the envelope"[45] at the end. In that case, how did the remote viewer obtain information about the target? There are two likely possibilities.

First, it was straightforward clairvoyance.

Or second, it was still telepathy, but with an unknown partner. Even though the remote viewer was never shown their feedback (the target), somebody looked at it eventually, probably their client. And the mind can do so much without our conscious awareness of it. It can peep into the mind of the unknown telepathic partner at a future point when that other person sees the target. But there's no way to consciously verify this is what happened.

Let's move on to discuss the protocol. I will keep it simple for ease of reading. If you're interested in taking a deeper dive, see my other book *Signal and Noise.*[46]

USING A COORDINATE

In the complex image exercises, the receivers simply formed the intention to see the card the sender held in their hand. They knew, "That's my target, right over there, on the other side of that card."

---

[45] "picture in the envelope" is a metaphor. *Feedback* can take various forms, such as digital photos, videos, written descriptions and transcripts, physical objects, and going to the target location in person.

[46] McNamara, S. (2020). *Signal and Noise: Advanced Psychic Training for Remote Viewing, Clairvoyance, and ESP*. Mind Possible.

In remote viewing, the *tasker*, the person who coordinates the exercise, assigns a coordinate to the target. It's a numeric symbol based on the tasker's intention. Through their intention, that coordinate represents the target in that big invisible database in the sky, the larger consciousness system: the Great Mystery.

When I create a task whose targets are digital images, I save them in individual folders on my laptop and name the folders and filenames by their coordinates. When the target is printed out and stuffed inside an envelope, I write the coordinate on the envelope. That's the extent of assigning the coordinate. But how do I create the coordinate? I use an online *random number generator*. They are easy to find online, and many are free to use.

THE VIEWING SESSION

Continuing the example from the start of this chapter, let's say it's 10:00 am. The remote viewer waits at a table, pen and paper ready. The tasker gives them the coordinate assigned to the target.

The viewer then writes the coordinate down on their blank transcript to set their intention. Then, they quiet their mind and wait for impressions to arrive. When they do, the viewer does their best to write them down quickly, before their conscious mind takes over and starts creating false narratives and interpretations about them.

Anytime the viewer feels distracted or disconnected from the process, they may rewrite the coordinate on their paper to reset their intention. Then, they let go again and wait for more.

To prevent their conscious mind from guessing, viewers are instructed to only use adverbs and adjectives to describe their perceptions. They are to avoid using nouns or names, because those are the activity of the conscious mind, the storytelling mind...the guessing mind.

The viewer can also sketch any shape or image that comes to mind, no matter how abstract it may be.

As you read in the chapter *Observed Attributes of Telepathy*, when the mind guesses, identifiable by its use of nouns or names, this is called *analytical overlay* (AOL). AOLs can have a sticky effect and linger in the mind, distracting the viewer and preventing the influx of new information. To help process the AOL and get it out of the way, viewers simply write down or draw their AOL on a dedicated section of their transcript and label it AOL to differentiate it from the other data.

There exist sophisticated protocols that instruct the viewer in accessing and recording their impressions in a certain order. For example, one might start their session by writing down the target's *Gestalt*[47], which can be defined as its *whole impression*.

Gestalt can be a one-word or one-phrase description. It's the remote viewer's first overall "hit" about the target. Examples include, but are not limited to:

- indoors (or outdoors)
- water (or land, or land-water interface)
- natural (or man-made)
- machine
- biological (as in people, or animals, etc.)
- on Earth (or outer space, or in the atmosphere above)
- an overwhelming emotion, feeling, or sensation
- fast/speed/movement (or slow, or still)

After writing down the Gestalt, the viewer might then focus on word-based adjectives and adverbs, such as colors, textures, the size of things, if there's one thing, or multiples of things, etc.

Then, the viewer may shift their intention to receive visual representations of the target and sketch them.

For our intensive, I wanted to make the process easy to learn and organic, so that each person could discover their own strengths. Therefore, I did not describe a specific order for recording their impression. I simply told them to write everything down that came to them while taking care to label their guesswork as AOL.

When the viewer is finished, they close the session by writing "End" or "End of Session" or "EOS" at the bottom.

THE FEEDBACK SESSION

At the predesignated time, the remote viewer is shown their feedback. This is important for training purposes because it helps the viewer develop trust in their impressions.

[47] You'll see the word *Gestalt* used again later in a different context, in the chapter *Team Telepathy Events*.

It's common for new viewers to make remarks like, "I *knew* I should've written that down, but I didn't think it was right, I didn't trust myself," when seeing their feedback.

Aside from building trust, it provides evidence for psychic perception. And the more evidence they see, the more they trust themselves. It also helps the viewer develop accuracy for future sessions. During the feedback session, the viewer compares the target to their transcript to note which of their impressions, and how many, were accurate.

Remember that this is the point in time when the exercise actually begins: in the *future*. At this point, the viewer *intends* to send everything they see, smell, taste, touch, and feel about the target *back in time* to themselves, to when they did their viewing session.

Doing a *complete* feedback session supports a good viewing session. To do a complete feedback session, I recommend using a ***feedback*** *transcript*. On this piece of paper, the viewer first writes down all the *accurate* words and sketches that appeared on their ***viewing*** *transcript*. Doing so is like an affirmation, "I got these right!"

While identifying the accuracies (their "hits") and writing them down again, the viewer sends them back in time to themselves, to their viewing session.

Then, the viewer completes their feedback transcript by writing down as many descriptors (adverbs and adjectives) as they can to describe the target (the feedback photo). They also sketch the significant aspects of the target. And while doing this, they again send that information back to themselves, back to their initial viewing session.

For some reason, perhaps I didn't explain this step well enough, most participants at the intensive didn't produce detailed enough feedback transcripts. But there are a couple of excellent examples here.

On the following pages, you'll see each target (the feedback photo) with its coordinate, followed by 1) each person's *viewing* transcript, and 2) their *feedback* transcript. Pay attention to how information on their feedback transcript appears on their viewing transcript. One might think, "Of course it looks that way. They already know what their viewing transcript looks like, so that's why their feedback transcript looks similar." **But don't forget, their viewing transcript was done with nothing more than a coordinate.**

Visual Description of Autotelepathy in the Feedback Process

In a typical, unidirectional timeline model, we regard the viewer as someone attempting to see an image that they'll be shown in the future. They cast their attention forward in time to perceive it. This may be labeled *clairvoyance*, or specifically, *precognition*.

However, the book's hypothesis is that time is *not* unidirectional[48]. With **autotelepathy**, the future self *initiates* the exercise by seeing their feedback (target) image, then sending the information back to themselves, in the past, who waits in a state of receptivity.

By the way, if the final paragraph on the previous page, especially the last sentence, left you feeling slightly disoriented, it's a sign that *you actually get it* and your brain needs a moment to adjust to this new way of thinking about how time behaves.

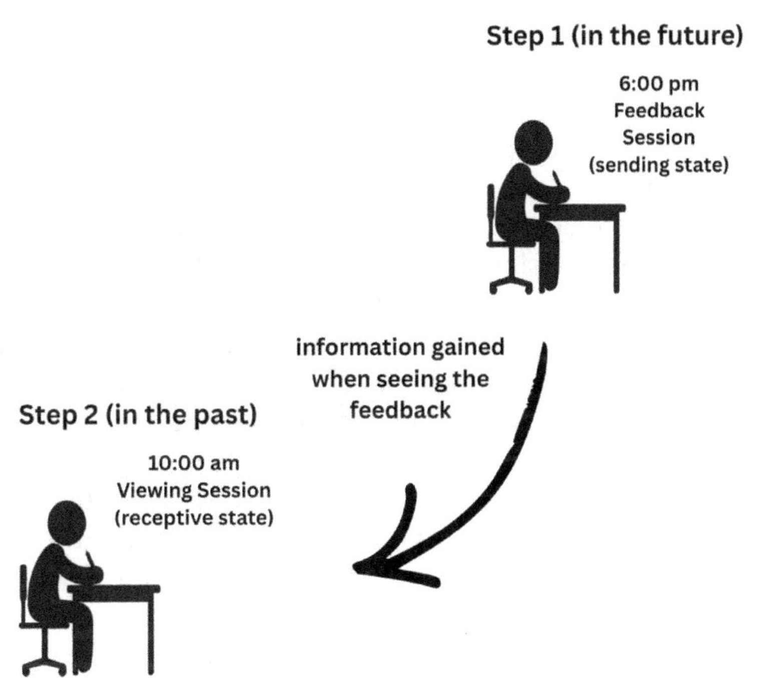

[48] Stating time is bi-directional may still be too limiting. This is a complex topic beyond the scope of this book.

THE LUCKY THREAD OF AUTOTELEPATHY

Have you ever noticed that some people tend to be lucky? Whether it's how they met the love of their life, chose the right career track, or pulled the lever on a winning slot machine?

What do you notice about their personality and communication style? What do you notice about how they respond to unexpected challenges?

When I reflect on the luckiest people I know, I notice they're optimists. And when something good happens to them, or for them, they tend to celebrate. Not necessarily by throwing a party, but at least by verbally acknowledging the goodness of what occurred. Often, they express gratitude to God, the universe, or their lucky stars. I don't think it matters who they express it to, only that they mark the significant and positive events of their life with acknowledgement, gratitude, and especially, an emotional charge.

And when an unforeseen challenge arises, or they make a mistake, or it just doesn't work out, do they complain and blame the universe, God, or their unlucky stars? No. They forge ahead, still with a sense of optimism and trust that things will work out in the end.

What if autotelepathy was the mechanism behind their good luck? What if, while decision-making, their intuition was subconsciously informed by their future selves?

What if you could follow the silent, "lucky" thread of your future self, the *version of you* living a life where a significant percentage of your choices result in desired outcomes?

The only way to find out is to behave like a lucky person. Stay optimistic. When good things happen, celebrate and give thanks. You might even thank *yourself.* And when things don't work out the way you hoped, keep your negative emotions somewhat muted while focusing on optimism that things will improve. Remember that you're also sending messages back to your past self because the lucky thread goes in both directions. Perhaps farther than we can imagine. Then wait quietly. Sense your intuition. Listen to your gut.

It could be your lucky day.

Remote Viewing Coordinate: 271765 (color version in Appendix 3)

Sahrawi tribal men performing fantasia at the Tan-Tan (Moussem) Festival in Tan-Tan, Morocco. Photo by Максим Массалитин (Maxim Massalitin).
Source: https://commons.wikimedia.org/wiki/File:Муссем_(фольклорный_фестиваль)_в_Тан-Тане_(Марокко).jpg

TRANSCRIPT by participant Insight at Dawn

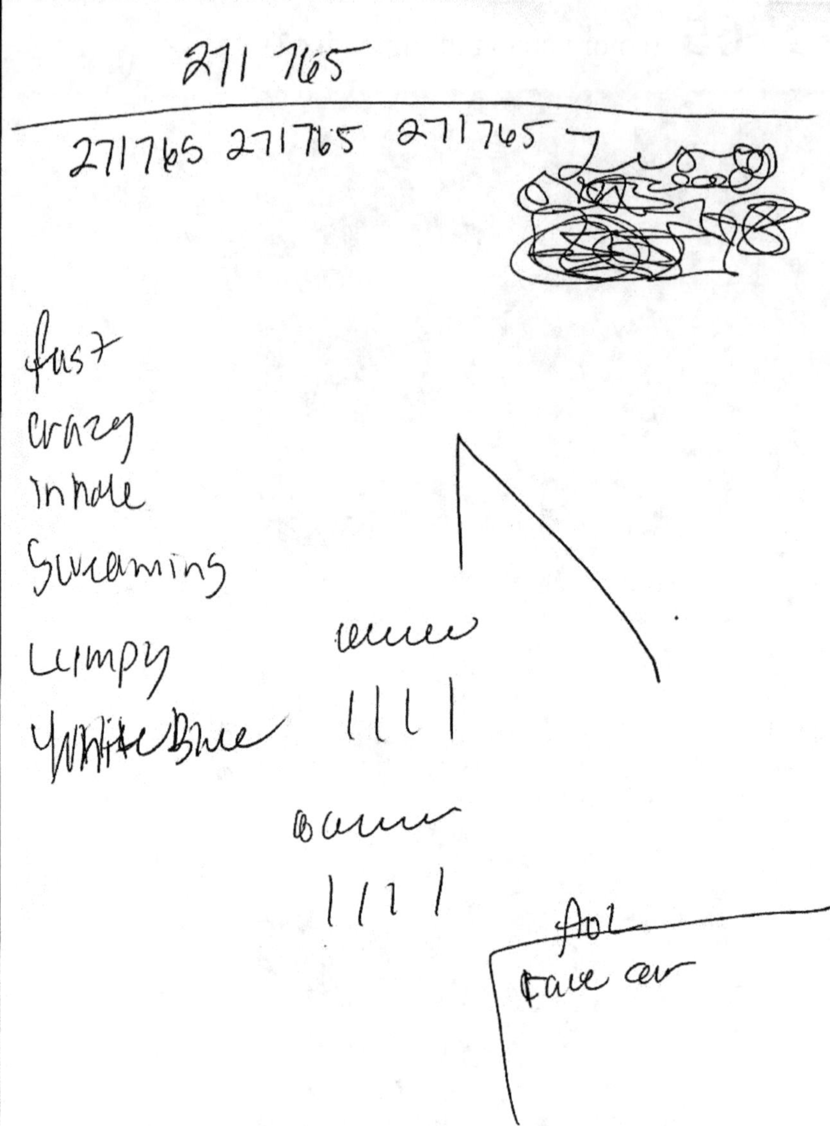

Accurate descriptors: "fast" "crazy" "screaming" "blue"

Accurate AOL: "*race* car" – The target resembles a horse *race*.

Graphic similarity: These resemble the images sent back to self during the feedback session (next page).

FEEDBACK by participant: Insight at Dawn

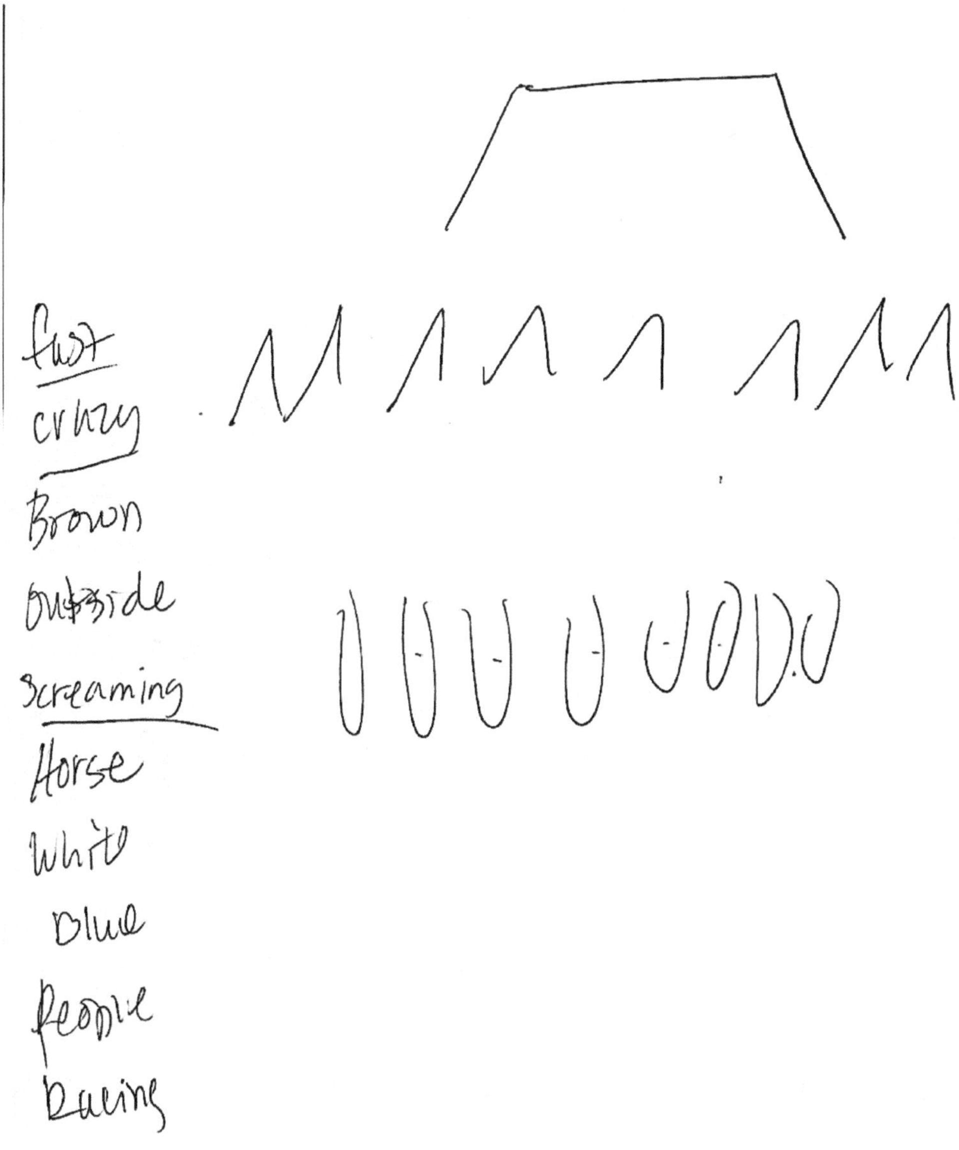

fast
crazy
Brown
outside
screaming
Horse
White
Blue
People
Racing

Feedback descriptors *sent back* that do appear on the viewing transcript: "fast" "crazy" "screaming" "blue"

TRANSCRIPT by participant Rain of Energy

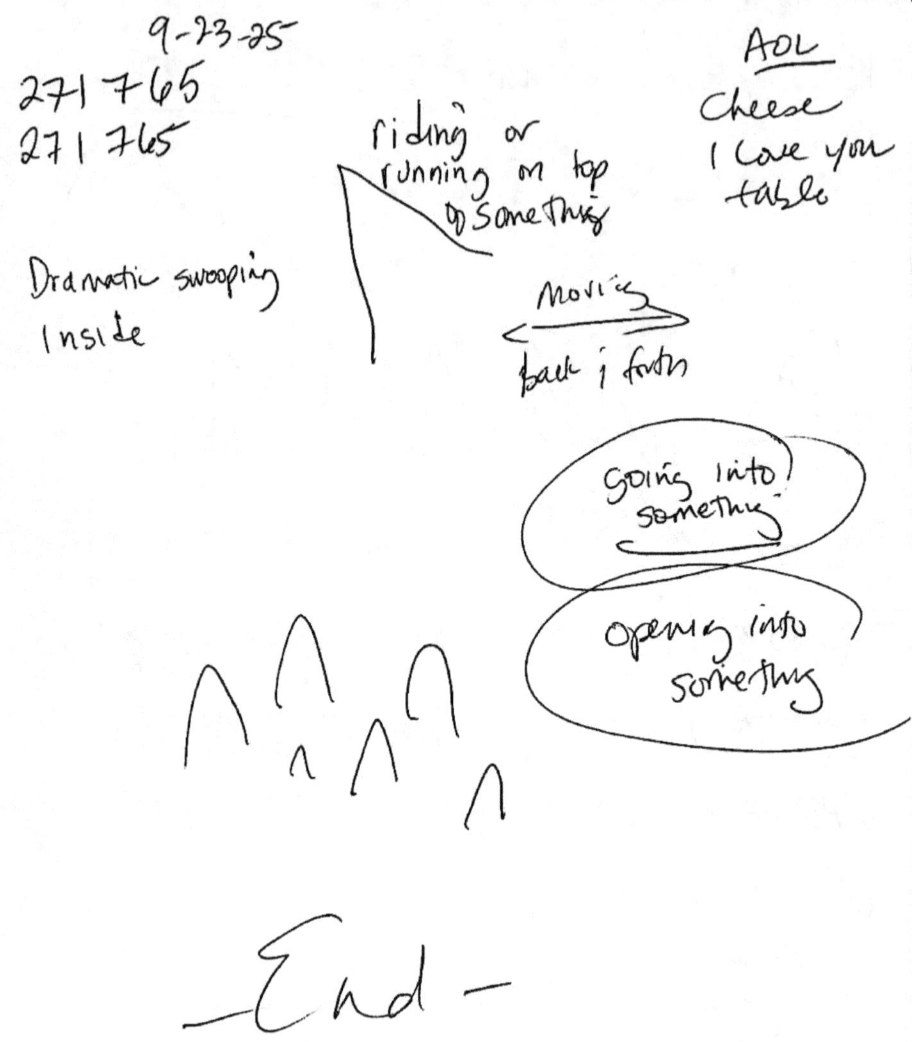

Accurate descriptors: "riding or running on top of something"

Graphic similarity: Compare the multiple mound-like shapes here to the tents in the center of the target photo. Might they also represent the riders? See how the tents were sent back to self during the feedback session (next page).

FEEDBACK by participant: Rain of Energy

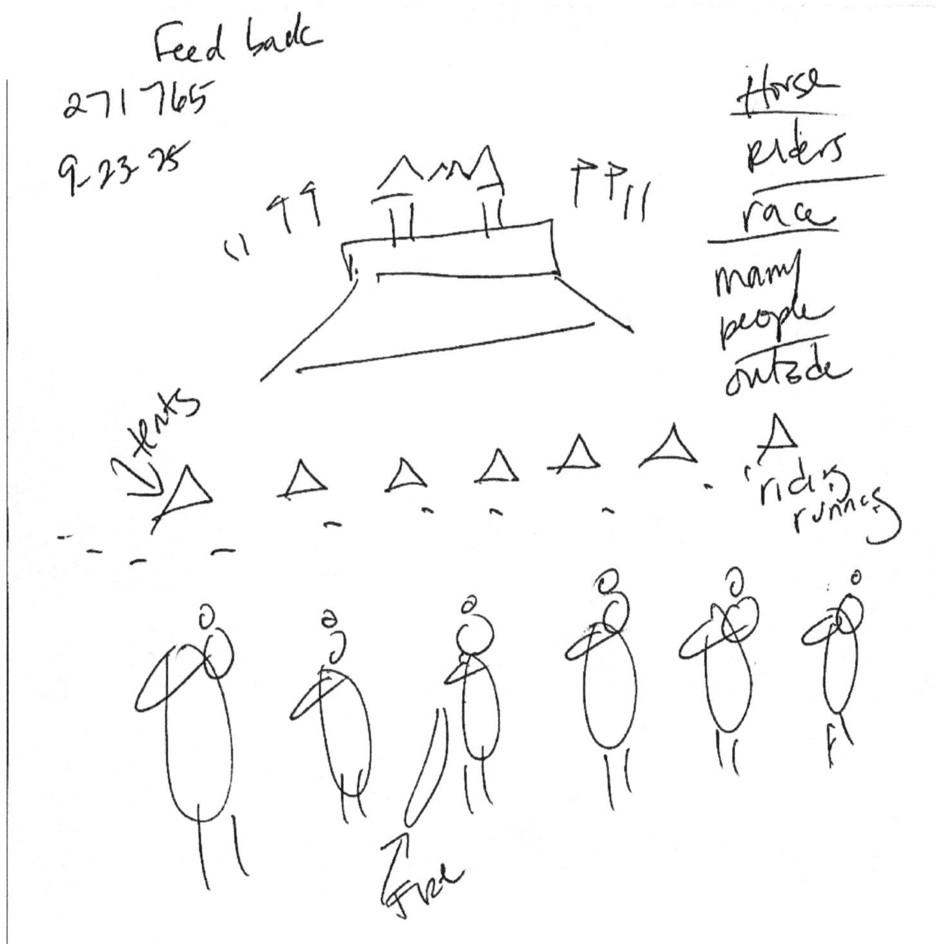

Feedback descriptors *sent back* that do appear on the viewing transcript: “riding” “running”

Note: The words indicated with arrows, “tents” and “fire,” were added *after* the target was revealed to indicate an accurate association.

TRANSCRIPT by participant Across Dimensions

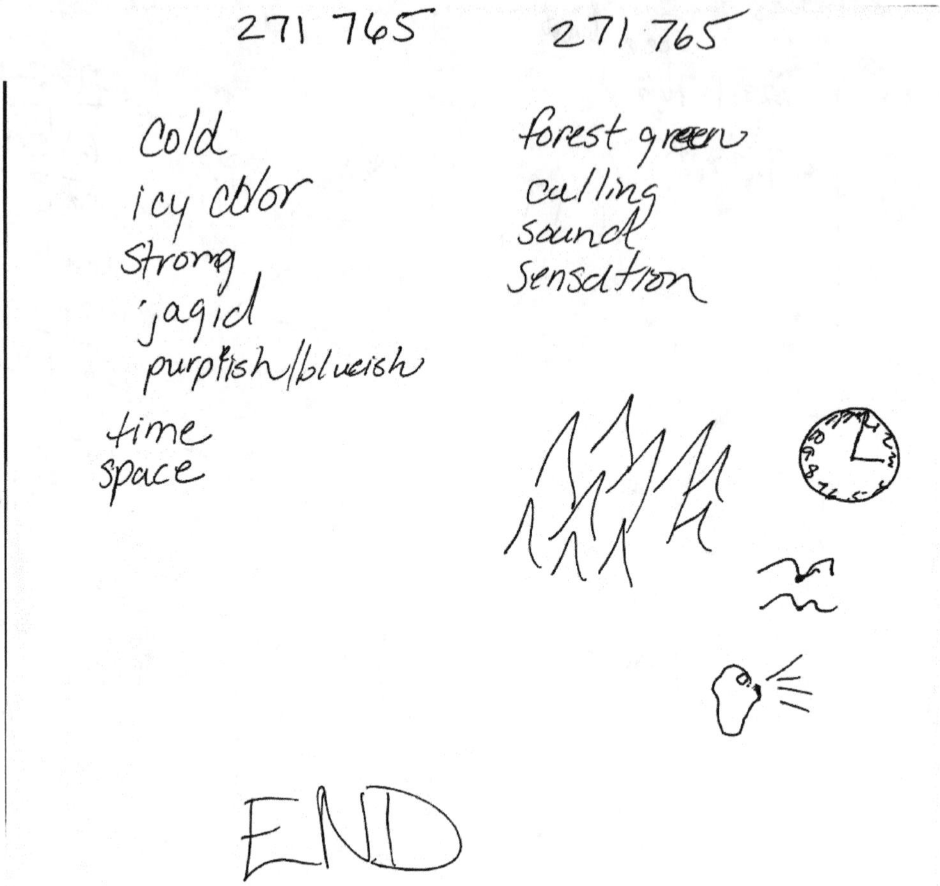

271 765 271 765

Cold
icy color
Strong
jagid
purplish/blueish
time
space

forest green
calling
sound
Sensation

END

Accurate descriptors: "sound"

Graphic similarity: Compare the pointed images in the center to the images sent back during the feedback session (next page).

FEEDBACK by participant: Across Dimensions

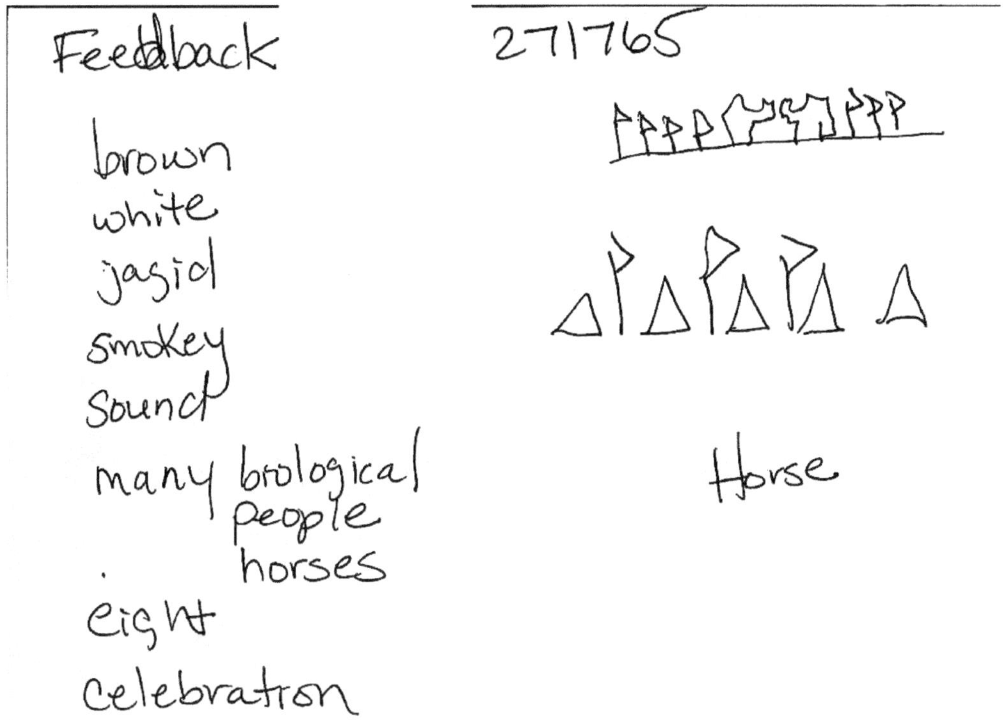

Feedback

271765

brown
white
jasid
smokey
sound
many biological people
horses
eight
celebration

Horse

Feedback descriptors *sent back* that do appear on the viewing transcript: "sound"

TRANSCRIPT by participant Time Traveler

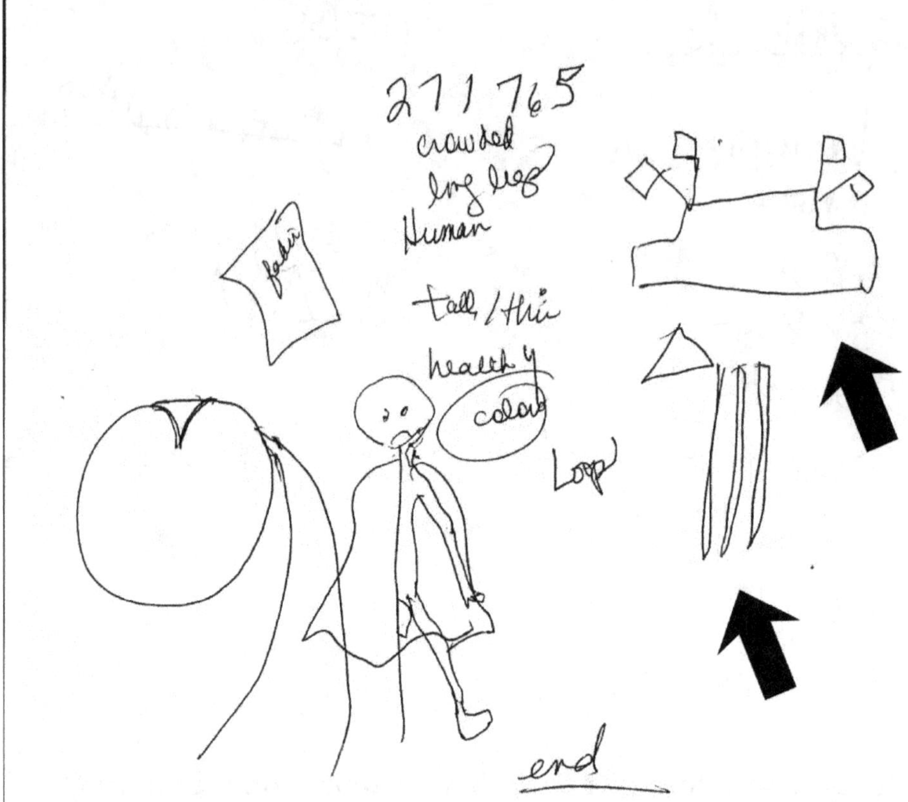

Accurate descriptors: “crowded” “long legs” “human” “tall/thin” [“color” appears, but is too universal to be considered an accurate association]

Graphic similarity: The figure here appears to be wearing a cape just like the riders in the target. Also, **see the images in the upper-right corner** (indicated by arrows) and compare with the images sent back during the feedback session (next page).

FEEDBACK by participant: Time Traveler

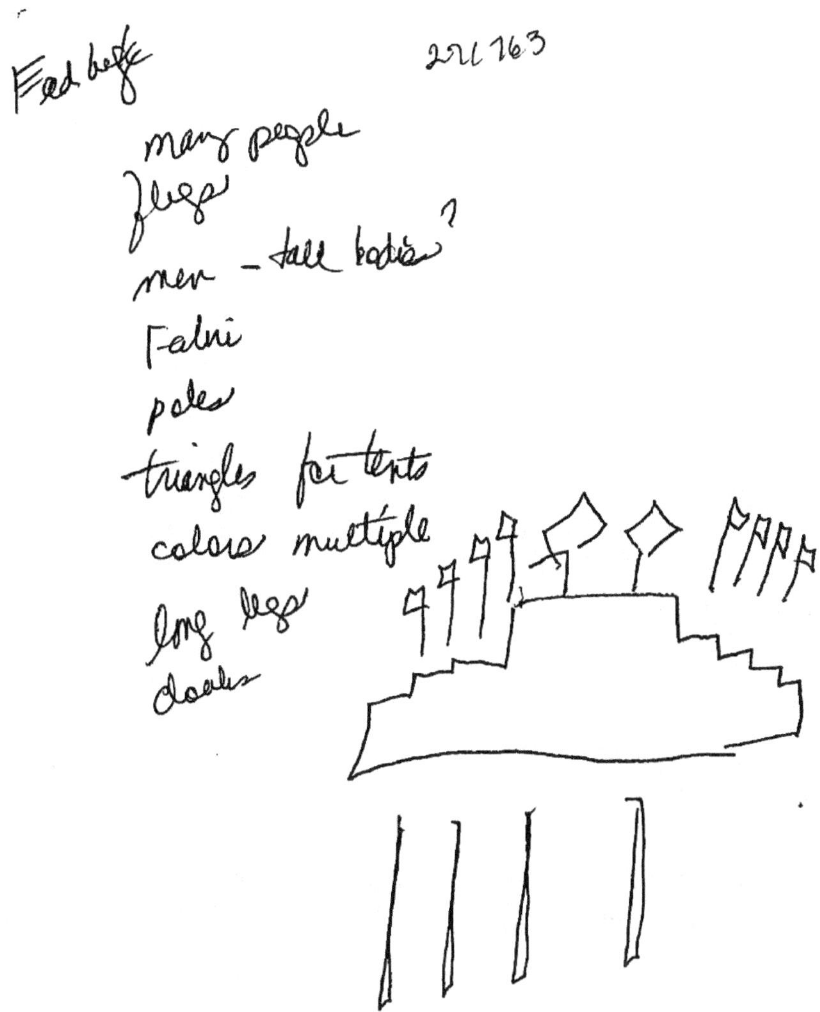

Feedback descriptors *sent back* that do appear on the viewing transcript: “long legs” “tall”

TRANSCRIPT by participant Joyful Explorer

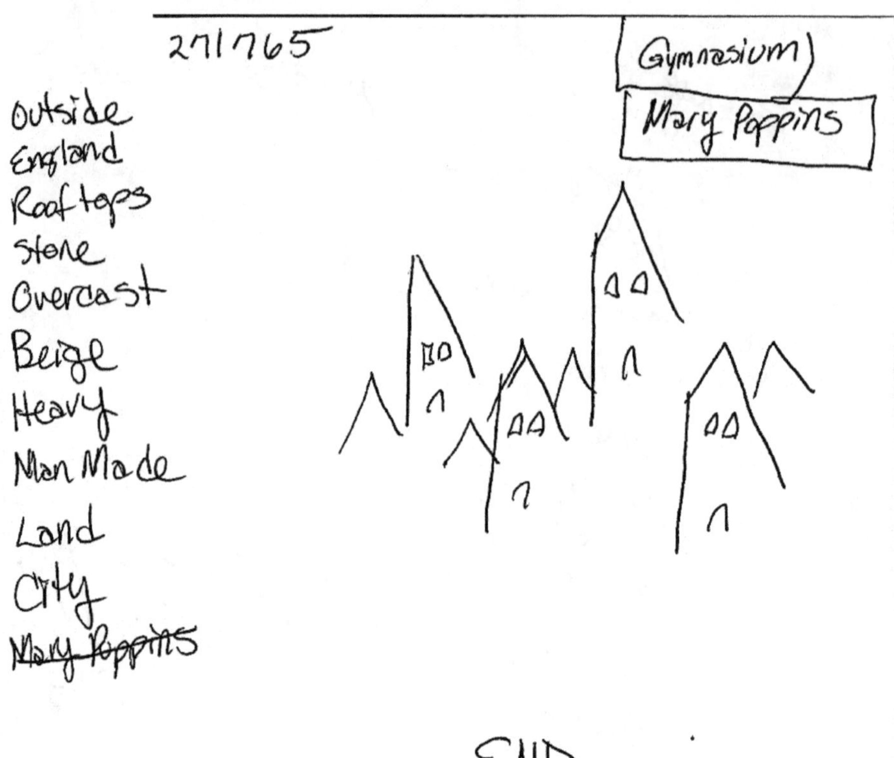

Accurate descriptors: “outside” “stone” “beige” “land”

Graphic similarity: Compare the angles of the images on this transcript to the images sent back during the feedback session (next page).

FEEDBACK by participant: Joyful Explorer

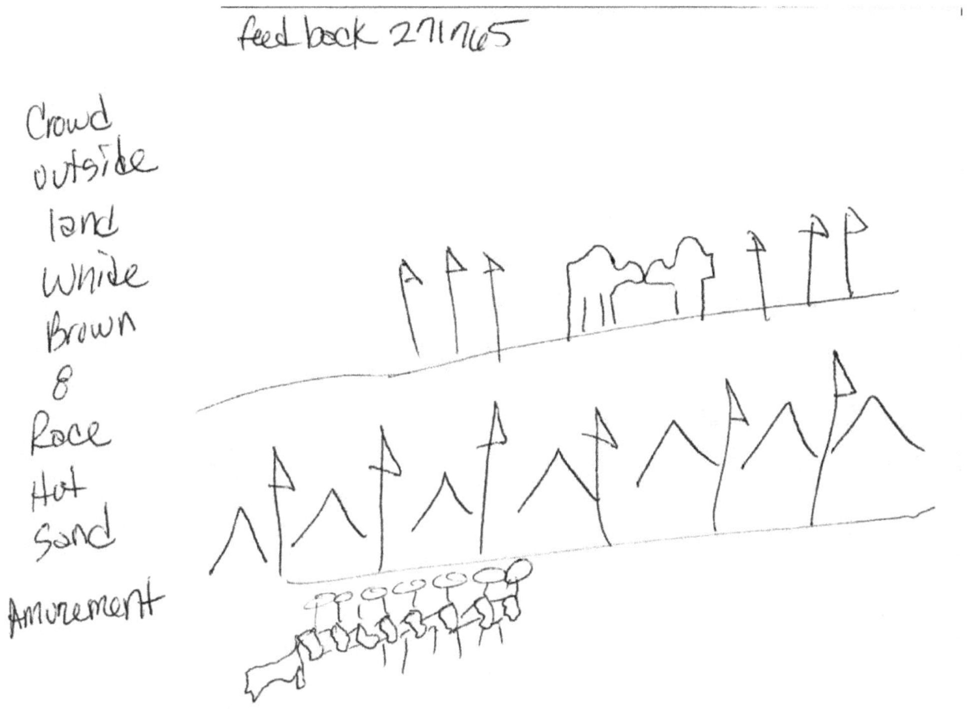

Feedback descriptors *sent back* that do appear on the viewing transcript: "outside"

Note: The word "brown" was sent back, but "beige" was received (see viewing transcript on previous page).

THIS PAGE IS INTENTIONALLY LEFT BLANK TO PLACE THE **VIEWING** TRANSCRIPTS AND **FEEDBACK** TRANSCRIPTS DIRECTLY ASIDE EACH OTHER (IN THE PAPERBACK VERSION) FOR EASE OF COMPARISON.

Remote Viewing Coordinate: 453191 (color version in Appendix 3)

View of Blue Mosque in Istanbul, Turkey. Photo by Moonik. Source: https://commons.wikimedia.org/wiki/File:Exterior_of_Sultan_Ahmed_I_Mosque_in_Istanbul,_Turkey_002.jpg

TRANSCRIPT by participant Cosmic Dancer

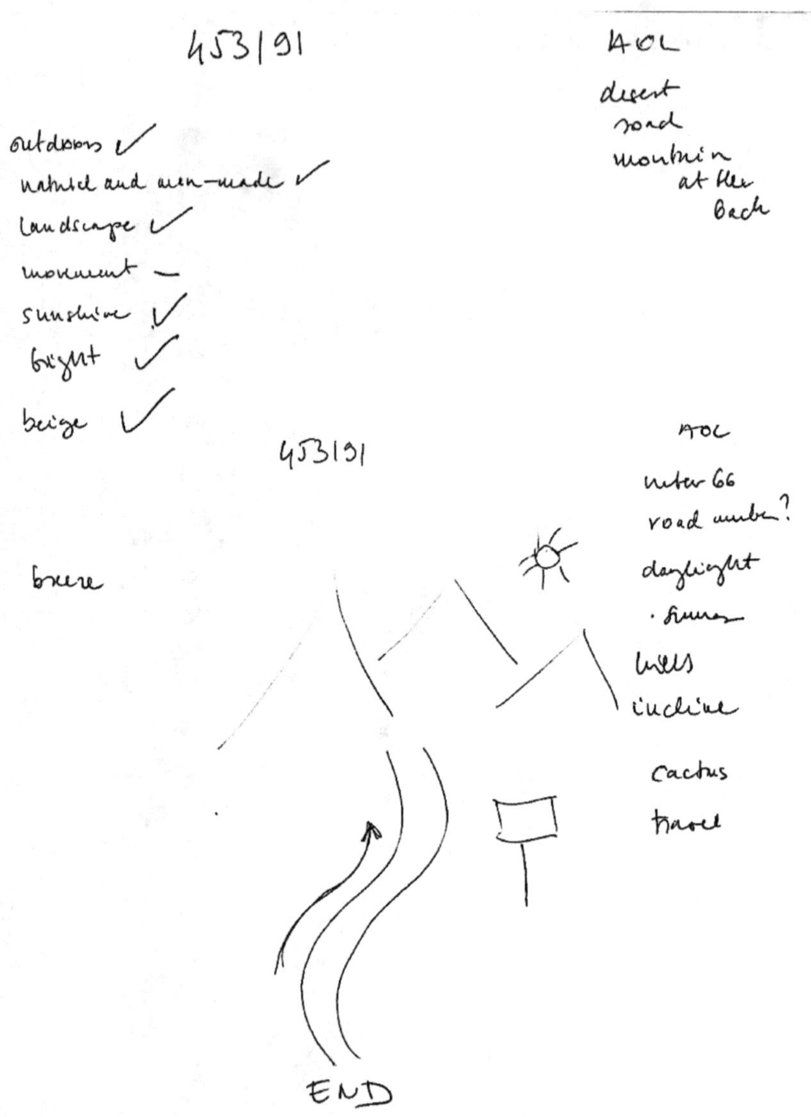

Accurate descriptors: “outdoors” “natural and man-made” “landscape” “sunshine” “bright” “beige” (The participant placed check marks next to their accurate associations.)

Graphic similarity: The peaks in the drawing relate to the Mosque’s minarets.

FEEDBACK by participant: Cosmic Dancer

Feedback descriptors *sent back* that do appear on the viewing transcript: "outdoor" "bright" "man-made"

TRANSCRIPT by participant Forest Tantrika

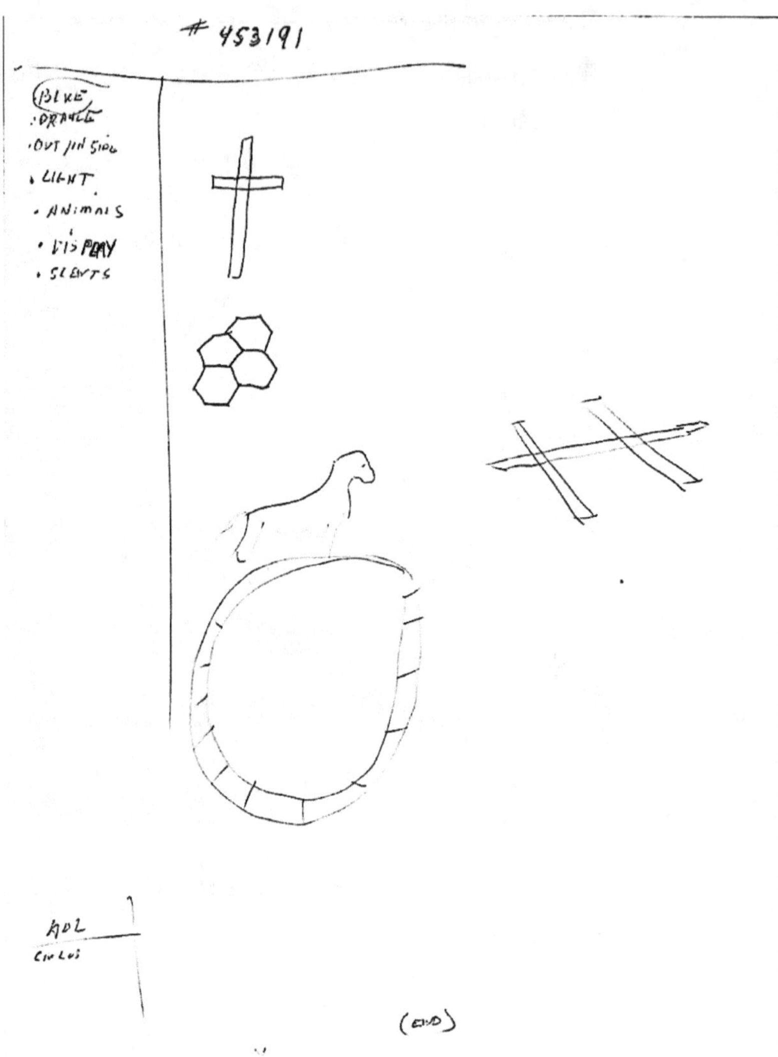

Accurate descriptors: “blue”

Note: The target is named the “Blue Mosque.” Although it’s not actually blue on the outside, the inside has a considerable number of blue tiles and blue stained-glass windows.

Graphic similarity: The drawing features a round shape attributable to the Mosque. Compare the other objects here with the ones drawn in the feedback session (next page), especially the parallel lines.

FEEDBACK by participant: Forest Tantrika

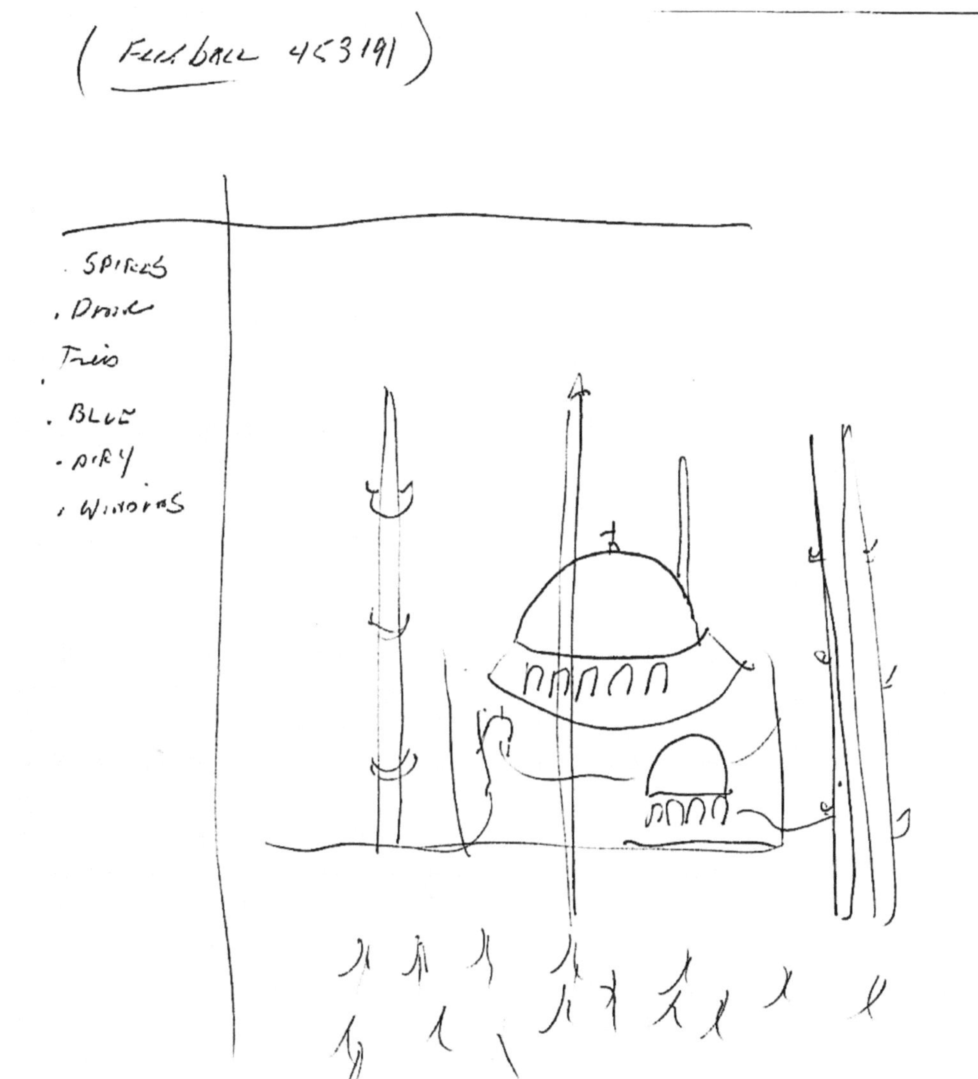

Feedback descriptors *sent back* that do appear on the viewing transcript: "blue"

TRANSCRIPT PAGE 1 by participant: Snow Lion

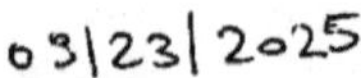

OUTDOOR
ORANGE
AOL: CITYSCAPE AT SUNSET
HARD
ANGULAR
MANMADE
MANY
COMPLEX
HISTORICAL
WHITE
BLUE
BLACK
LIGHT / SHADE
VISIBLE PARTS / HIDDEN PARTS
CONVOLUTED
SECRETIVE
WHITE
COLD
AOL: NARROW PATHS

Accurate descriptors: "outdoor" "hard" "manmade" "many" "complex" "historical" "blue"

Accurate AOL: "cityscape at sunset" (This AOL is written higher up on the transcript, as opposed to the AOL written at the bottom.)

TRANSCRIPT PAGE 2 by participant: Snow Lion

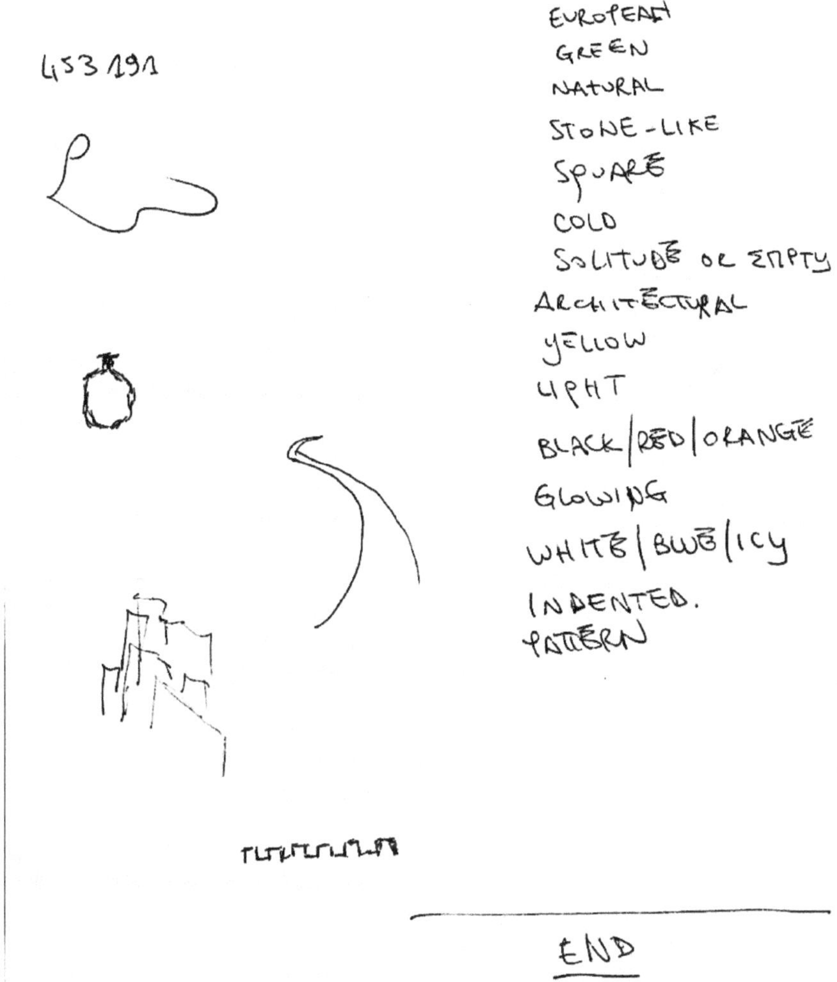

****NOTE** This is the second page of the transcript. The feedback is on the next page.**

Accurate descriptors: "natural" "stone-like" "architectural" "blue" "indented pattern"

Graphic similarity: Compare the drawing on the bottom-left with the one drawn in the feedback session (next page).

FEEDBACK by participant: Snow Lion

FEEDBACK FOR 453191
IS MOSQUE AT DAWN|SUNSET

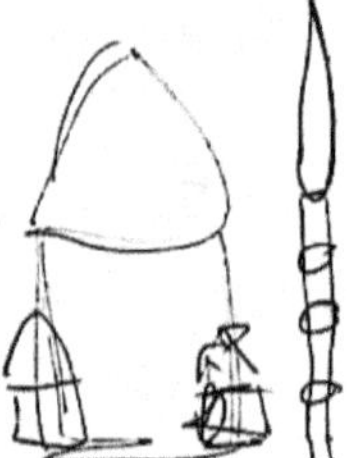

OUTDOOR
ORANGE
AOL: CITYSCAPE AT SUNSET
HARD
ANGULAR
MANMADE
MANY
COMPLEX
HISTORICAL
WHITE
BLUE
BLACK
LIGHT|SHADE
VISIBLE PARTS| HIDDEN PARTS
CONJOINED
SECRETIVE
WHITE
COLD
GREEN
NATURAL
STONE-LIKE
SQUARE
ARCHITECTURAL
YELLOW
INDENTED
PATTERN

Feedback descriptors *sent back* that do appear on the viewing transcript: “outdoor” “cityscape at sunset” “hard” “manmade” “complex” “historical” “blue” “natura” “stone-like” “architectural” “indented pattern”

This is a **great** example of the use of the feedback session to send information back in time to the viewing session.

THIS PAGE IS INTENTIONALLY LEFT BLANK TO PLACE THE **VIEWING** TRANSCRIPTS AND **FEEDBACK** TRANSCRIPTS DIRECTLY ASIDE EACH OTHER (IN THE PAPERBACK VERSION) FOR EASE OF COMPARISON.

TRANSCRIPT by participant Joyful Explorer

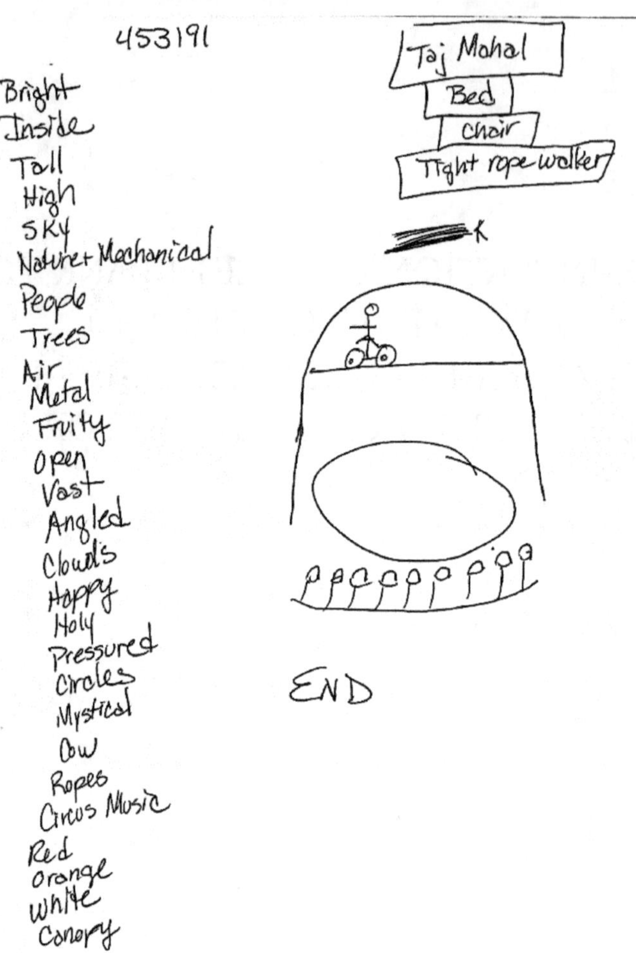

Accurate descriptors: "tall" "high" "trees" "angled" "circles" "mystical"

Accurate AOL: "Taj Mahal" - The Taj Mahal is a different building in another country, but if you do an image search for it online you will understand why this is a good AOL.

Graphic similarity: The main drawing is rounded like the Mosque's dome. The row of circles with "stems" on them resemble another participant's representation of the trees in their feedback on page 167, as well as their own feedback on the next page.

FEEDBACK by participant: Joyful Explorer

Feedback descriptors *sent back* that do appear on the viewing transcript: “tall”

Additionally, “outside” may have been received as “outdoors” in the viewing transcript, and “holy” as “mystical.”

TRANSCRIPT by participant Synchronicity

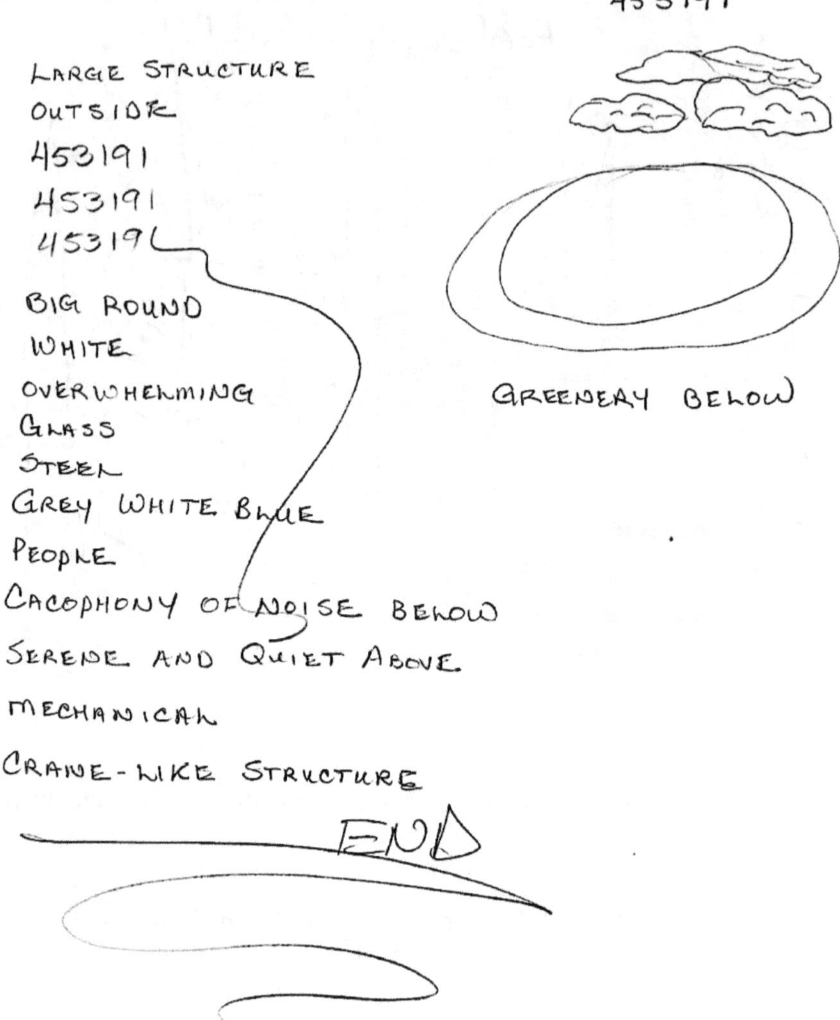

Accurate descriptors: "large structure" "outside" "big round" "overwhelming" "grey" "white" "blue" "serene and quiet above" "crane-like structure" "greenery below"

Graphic similarity: The large circular shapes relate to the Mosque's dome-like structure. Note the placement of the words "greenery below," it's exactly where the trees appear in the target image. The drawing of clouds above implies a view of the sky, which is also accurate.

FEEDBACK by participant: Synchronicity

DOMES
HIGH TOWERS
TREES BELOW

Feedback descriptors *sent back* that do appear on the viewing transcript: "trees below" (as "greenery below")

Note the prominent drawing of the Mosque, which may be why the participant drew the large circle on their transcript. Not insignificantly, the phrase "trees below" is written *beneath* the drawing of the Mosque. In the transcript, the similar phrase "greenery below" appears *beneath* the large circles (which I assume represents the Mosque).

TRANSCRIPT by participant Star Gazer

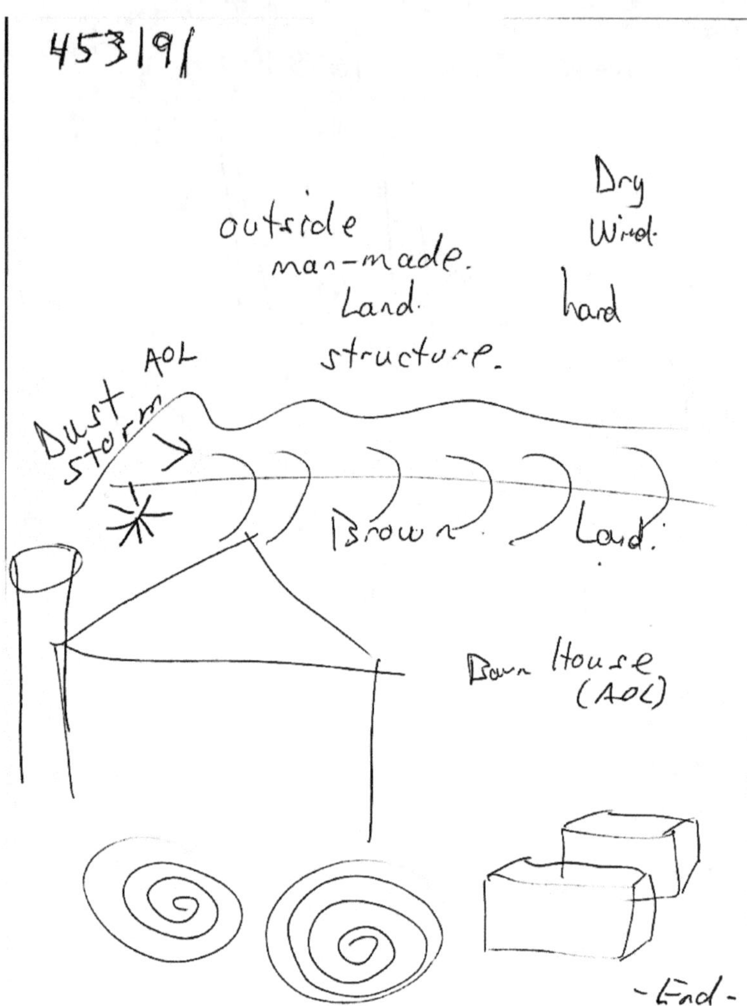

Accurate descriptors: “outside” “man-made” “structure” “dry” “hard” “brown” “land” “dust”

Accurate AOL: The participant also wrote “Brown House (AOL). In the color image of the target, significant parts of the Mosque appear brown. Also, note where they wrote “dust storm” with visual indicators. The color image of the target (accessible via Appendix 3) shows a low-lying layer of clouds closely resembling this drawing.

Graphic similarity: Note the spirals at the bottom, indicating multiple round shapes, which are seen in the target.

FEEDBACK by participant: Star Gazer

Feedback descriptors *sent back* that do appear on the viewing transcript: "dust"

Note how the participant drew the layer of clouds ("dust") here and compare to how this appeared in the viewing transcript.

Remote Viewing Coordinate: 522931 (color version in Appendix 3)

Dragon 2 Hover Test. Photo by Msaynevirta/SpaceX photos. Source: https://commons.wikimedia.org/wiki/File:Dragon_2_hover_test_(24159153709).jpg

TRANSCRIPT PAGE 1 by participant: Gentle Wolf

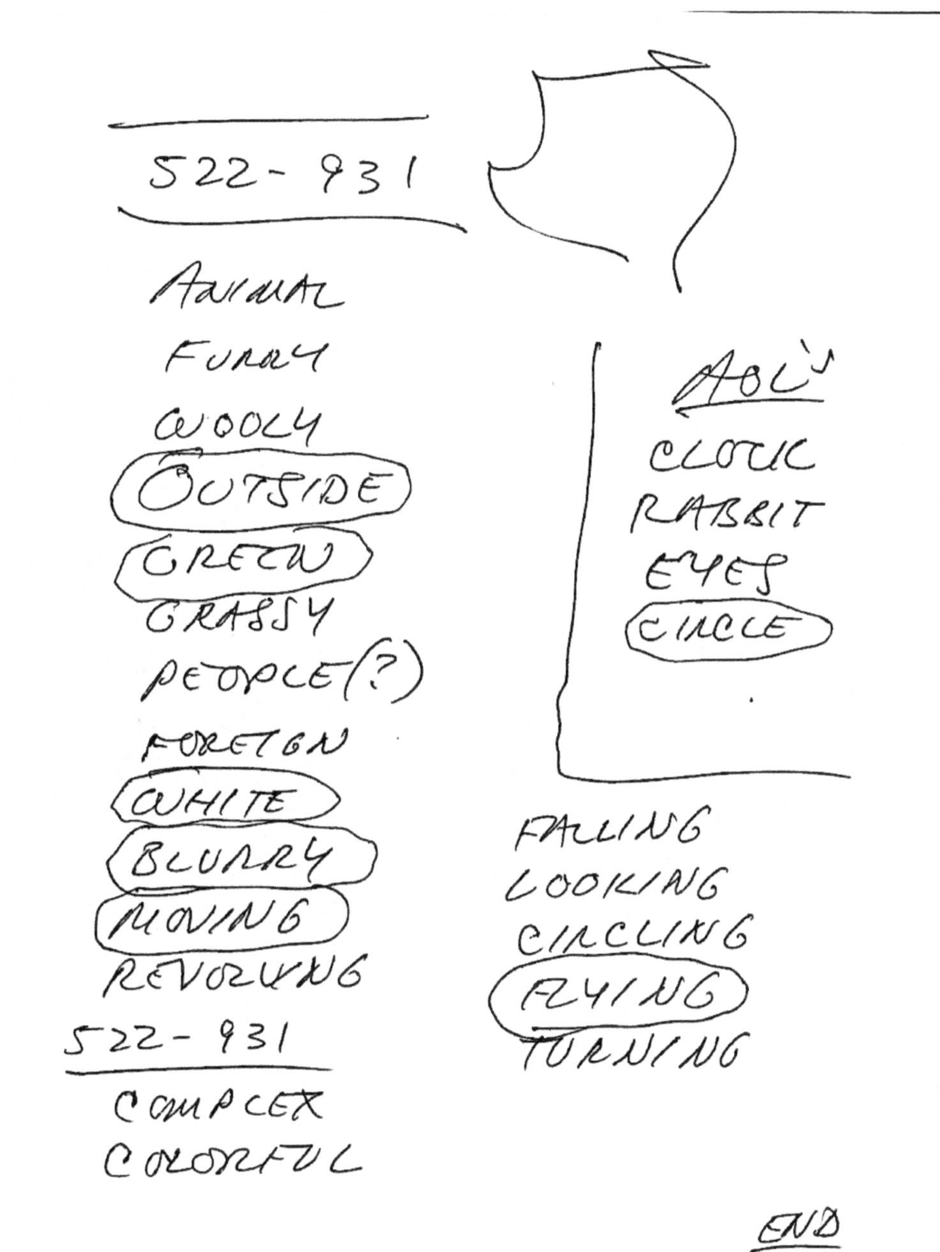

Accurate descriptors: "outside" "green" "white" "blurry" "moving" "flying"

TRANSCRIPT PAGE 2 by participant: Gentle Wolf

****NOTE** This is the second page of the transcript. The feedback is on the next page.**

Graphic similarity: A round object. Notice how the arrows convey a sense of movement.

FEEDBACK by participant: Gentle Wolf

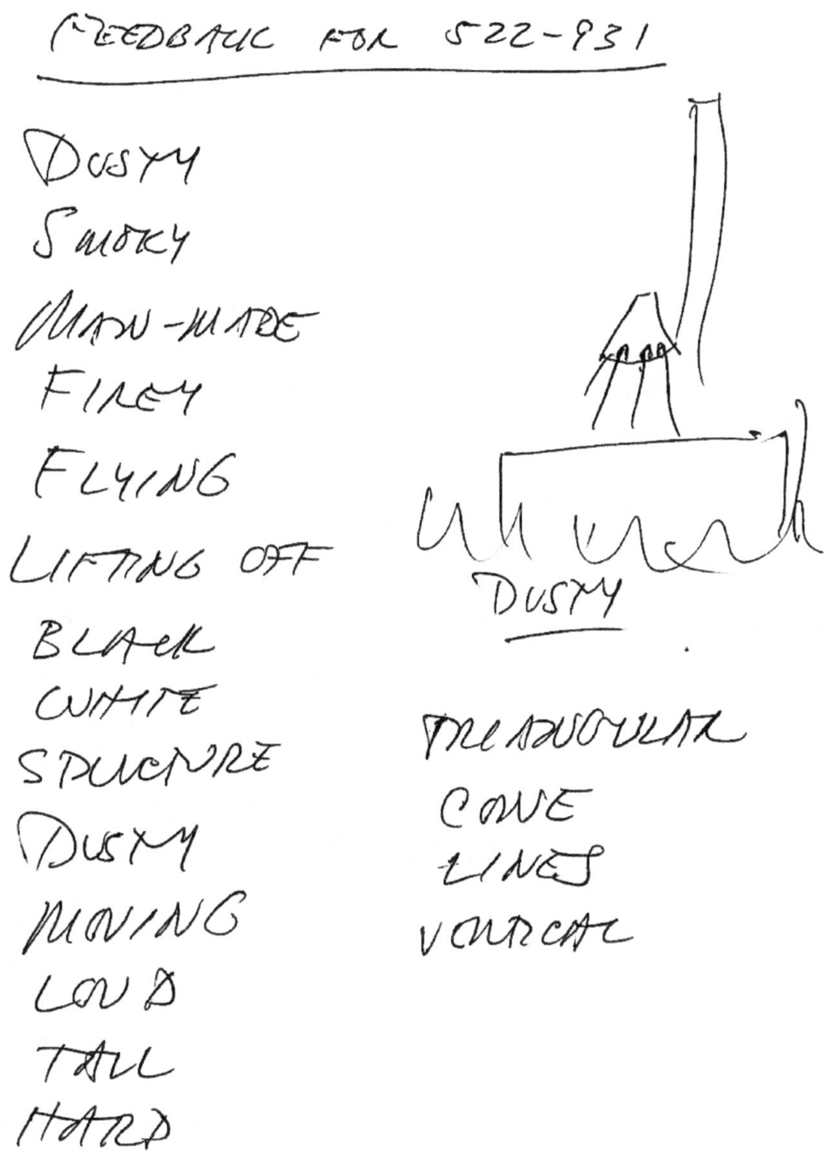

FEEDBACK FOR 522-931

DUSTY
SMOKY
MAN-MADE
FIREY
FLYING
LIFTING OFF
BLACK
WHITE
STRUCTURE
DUSTY
MOVING
LOUD
TALL
HARD

DUSTY

TRIANGULAR
CONE
LINES
VERTICAL

Feedback descriptors *sent back* that do appear on the viewing transcript: “white” “moving” “flying”

TRANSCRIPT by participant Atlantis

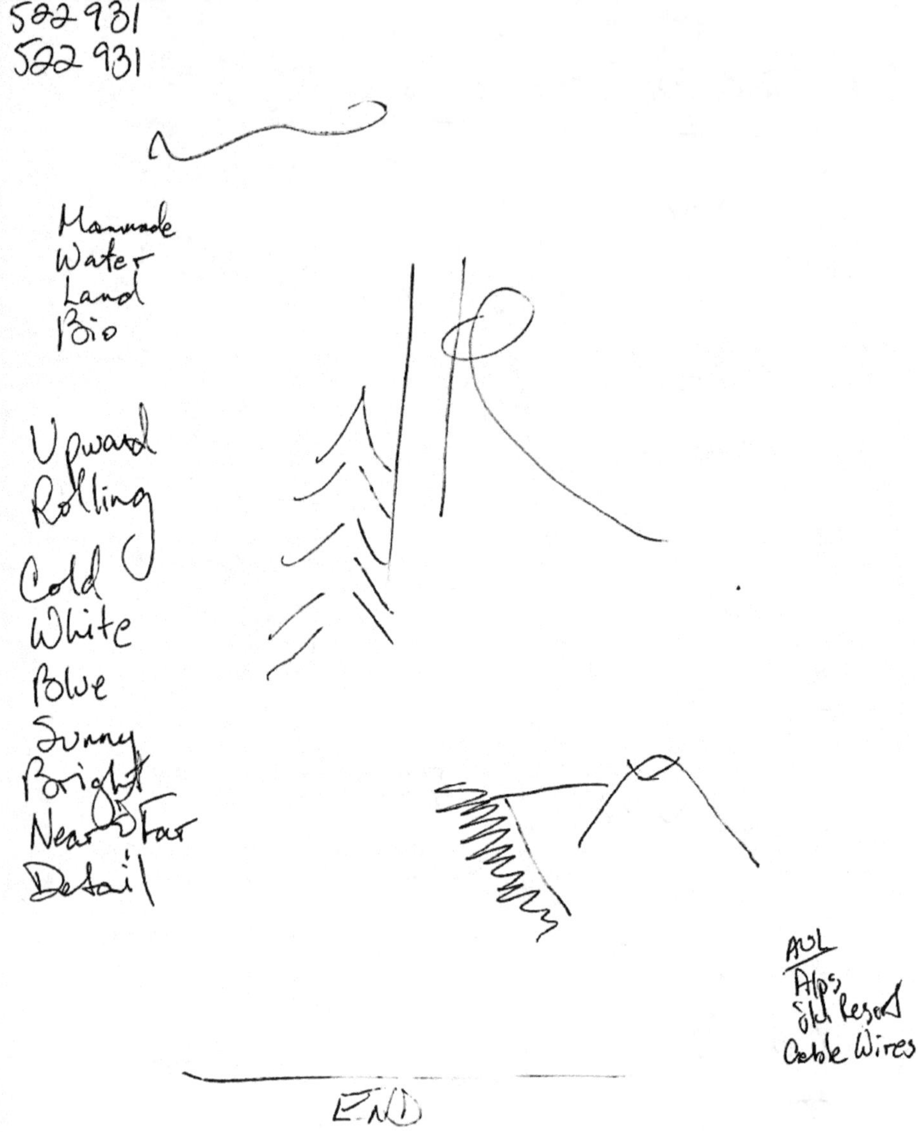

Accurate descriptors: “manmade” “land” “upward” “white” “bright”

Accurate AOL: “cable wires”

Graphic similarity: Strong similarity with the target and with the drawing sent back during the feedback session (next page)

FEEDBACK by participant: Atlantis

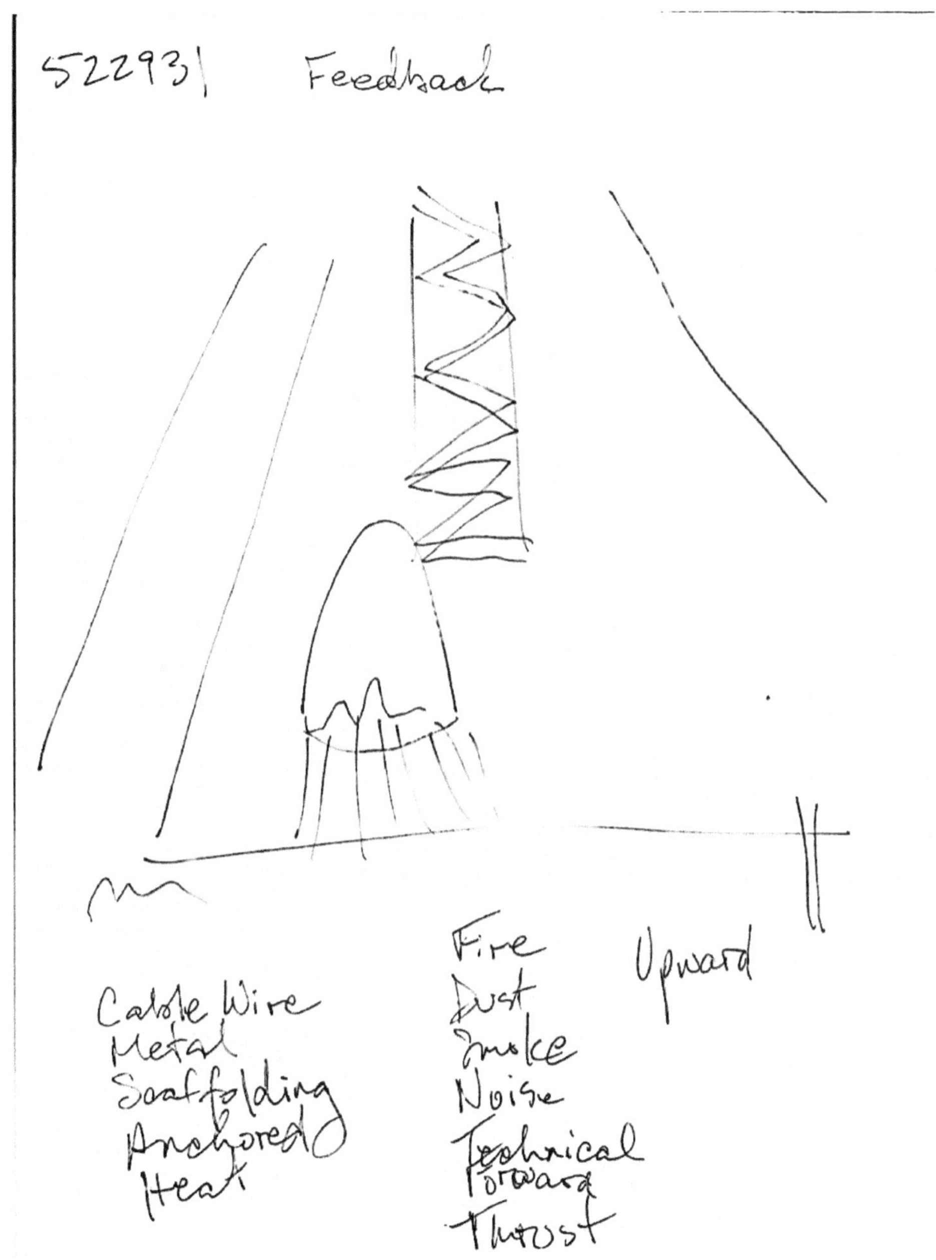

Feedback descriptors *sent back* that do appear on the viewing transcript: "upward" "cable wire" (appeared as AOL)

TRANSCRIPT by participant Lord of Water

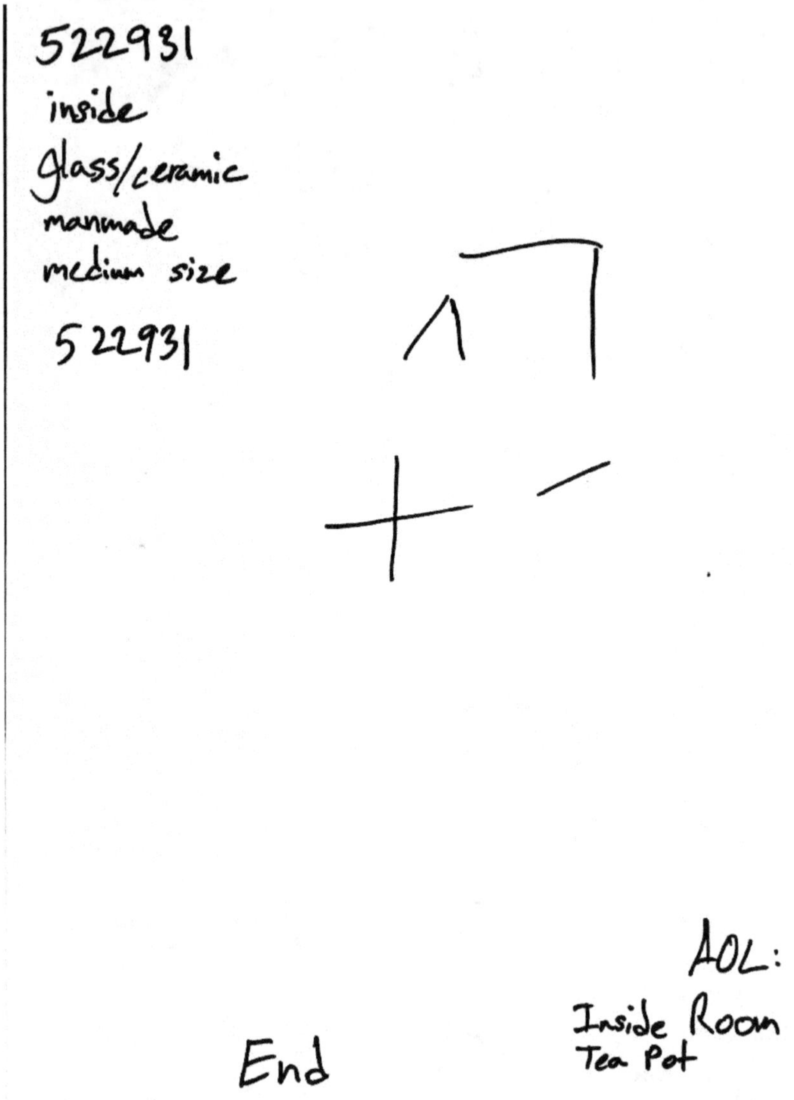

522931
inside
glass/ceramic
manmade
medium size
522931

AOL:
Inside Room
Tea Pot

End

Accurate descriptors: "manmade" "glass/ceramic" (Dragon 2 uses a specialized ceramic composite for its heat shield.)

Graphic similarity: This transcripts appears to be a proto-perception of the target and/or the feedback transcript. Note the similarity in the right-leaning triangle representing the capsule here with the right-leaning drawing of it in the feedback transcript (next page).

FEEDBACK by participant: Lord of Water

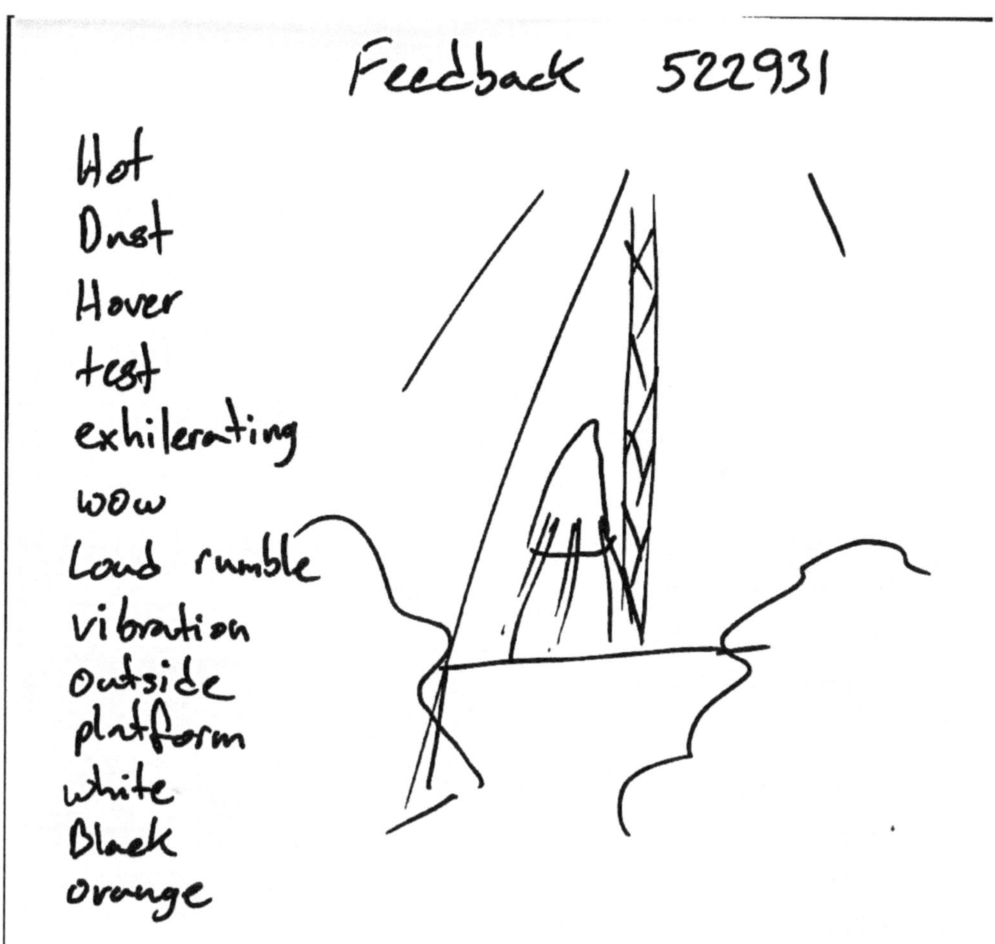

TRANSCRIPT by participant Power of Love

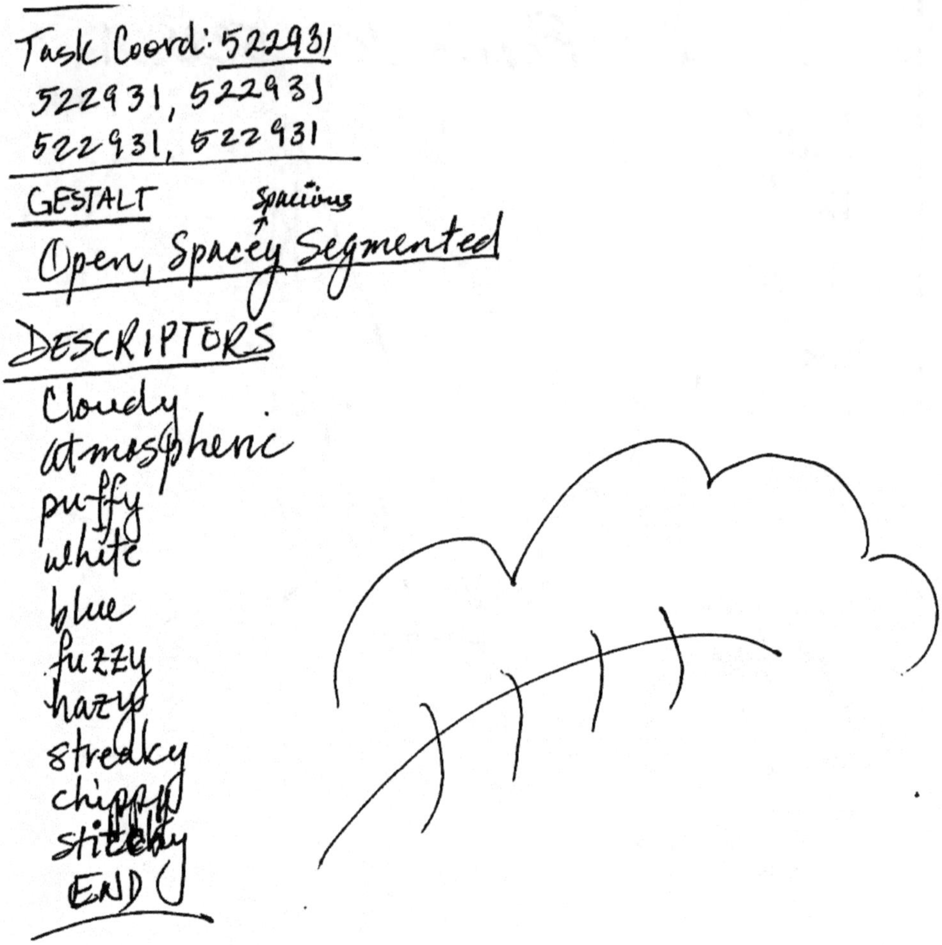

Task Coord: 522931
522931, 522931
522931, 522931

GESTALT
Open, Spacey (Spacious) Segmented

DESCRIPTORS
Cloudy
atmospheric
puffy
white
blue
fuzzy
hazy
streaky
chippy
stitchy
END

Accurate descriptors: "cloudy" "atmospheric" "puffy" "white" "blue" "fuzzy" "hazy" "streaky" "stitchy"(It's best to see the color image of the target for comparison. See the QR codes in Appendix 3 to easily find it online.)

Graphic similarity: The drawing captures the quality of billowing smoke and vapor.

FEEDBACK by participant: Power of Love

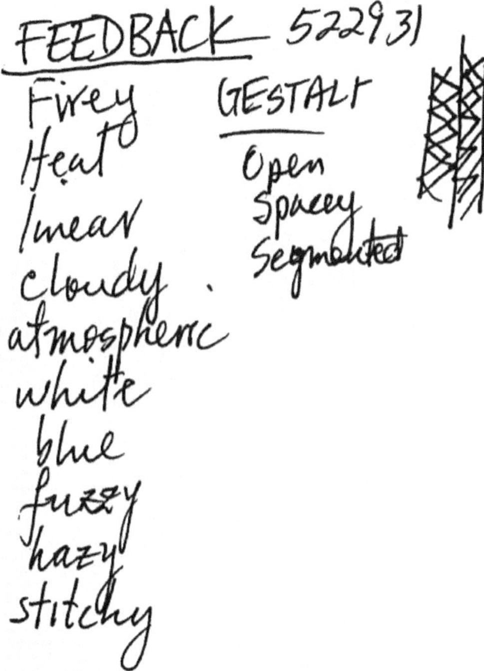

Feedback descriptors *sent back* that do appear on the viewing transcript: "cloudy" "atmospheric" "white" "blue" "fuzzy" "hazy" "stitchy"

This is a **great** example of the use of the feedback session to send information back in time to the viewing session.

TRANSCRIPT by participant Kindness Smiling

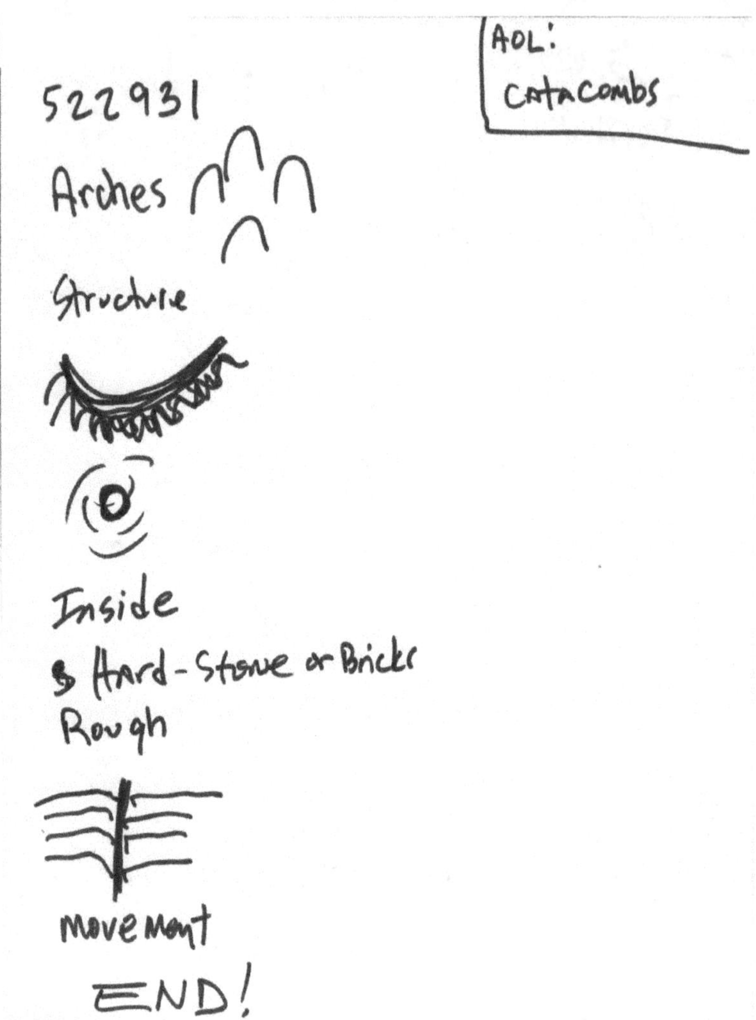

Accurate descriptors: "arches" "movement"

Graphic similarity: Note the sketch of arches near the top. What other similarities do you see with the target and with the feedback on the next page?

Note: Isn't it curious that the participant wrote "catacombs" (top right) as an AOL? "Catacombs" was the word Dalia used to test Lidu's telepathy during our Zoom call (page 27).

FEEDBACK by participant: Kindness Smiling

Feedback
522931

Firey
smokey
Energetic
lift off ↑

white

Noisey
Sound

TRANSCRIPT by participant Rain of Energy

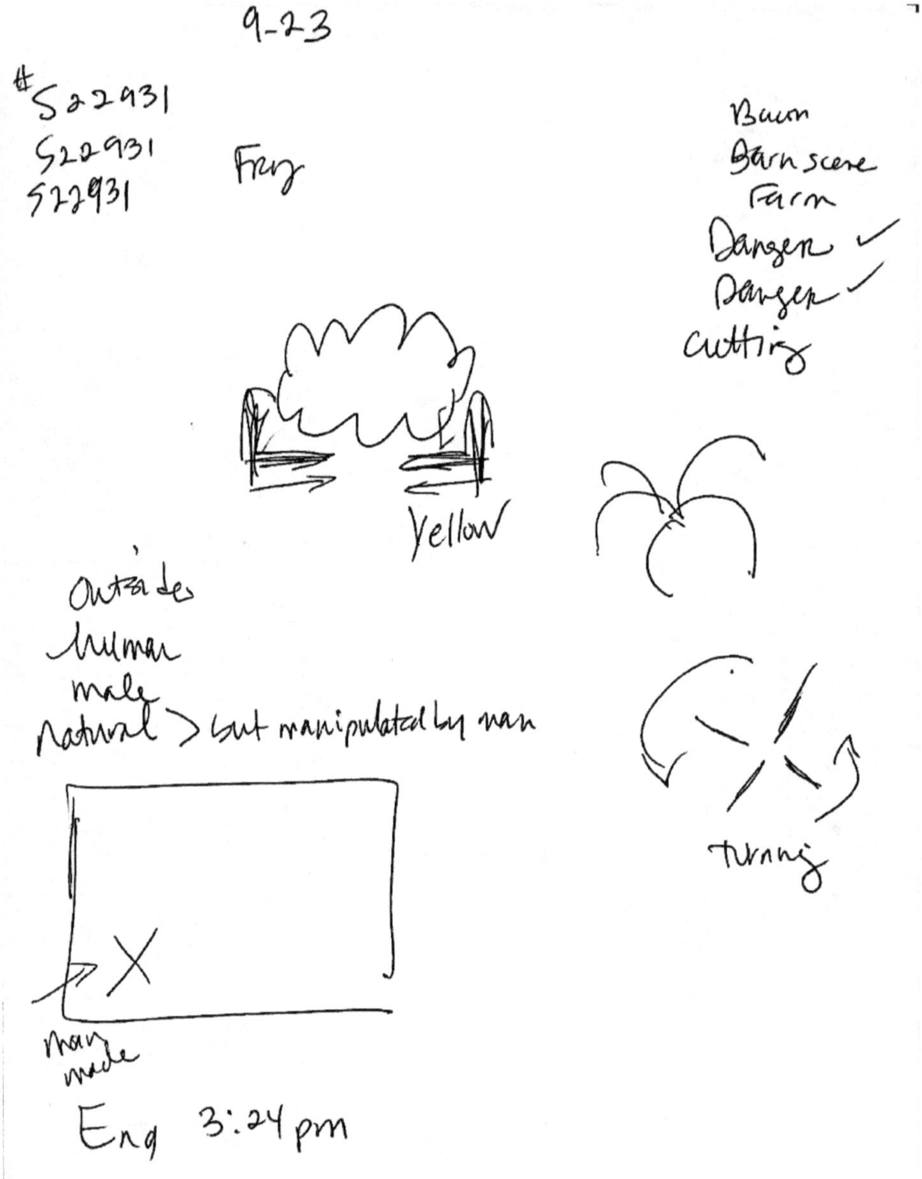

9-23

#522931
522931
522931

Frey

Baum
Barn scene
Farm
Danger ✓
Danger ✓
cutting

Yellow

Outside
human
male
Natural > but manipulated by man

X

man made

Turning

End 3:24 pm

Accurate descriptors: "danger" "outside" "manipulated by man"

Graphic similarity: Note where the participant noted the "X" with an arrow in their drawing. See how "SpaceX" appears on the left side of the platform in the target image on page 180 as well as on the feedback (next page).

FEEDBACK by participant: Rain of Energy

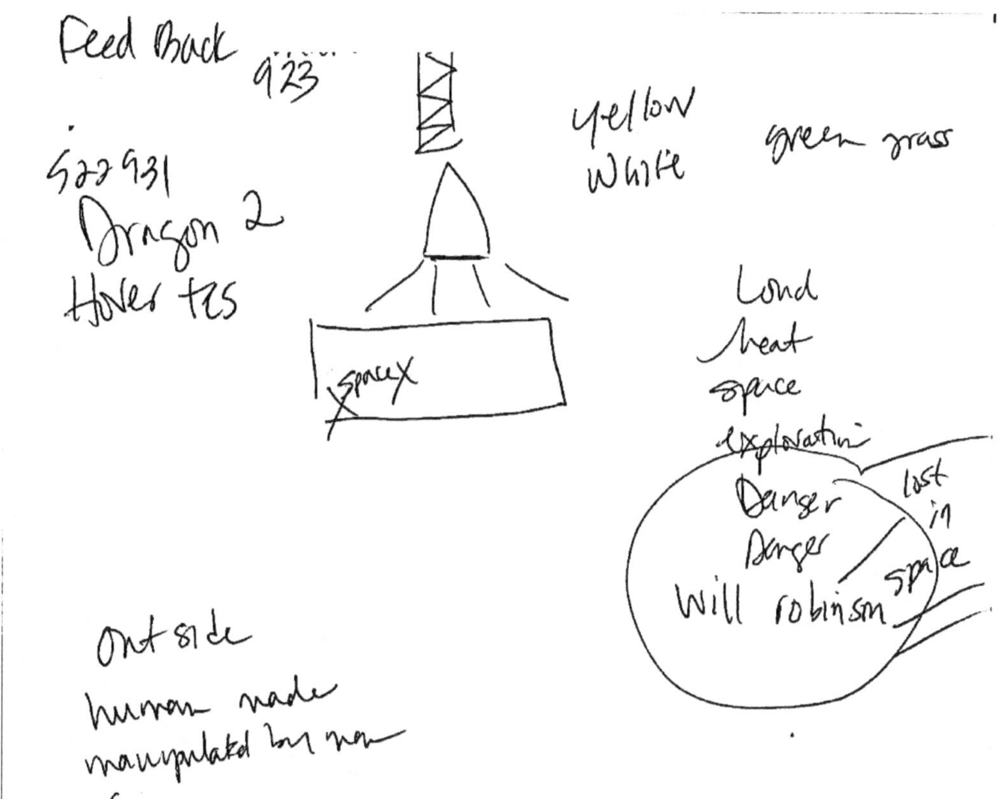

Feedback descriptors *sent back* that do appear on the viewing transcript: “danger” “manipulated by man”

TRANSCRIPT by participant Insight at Dawn

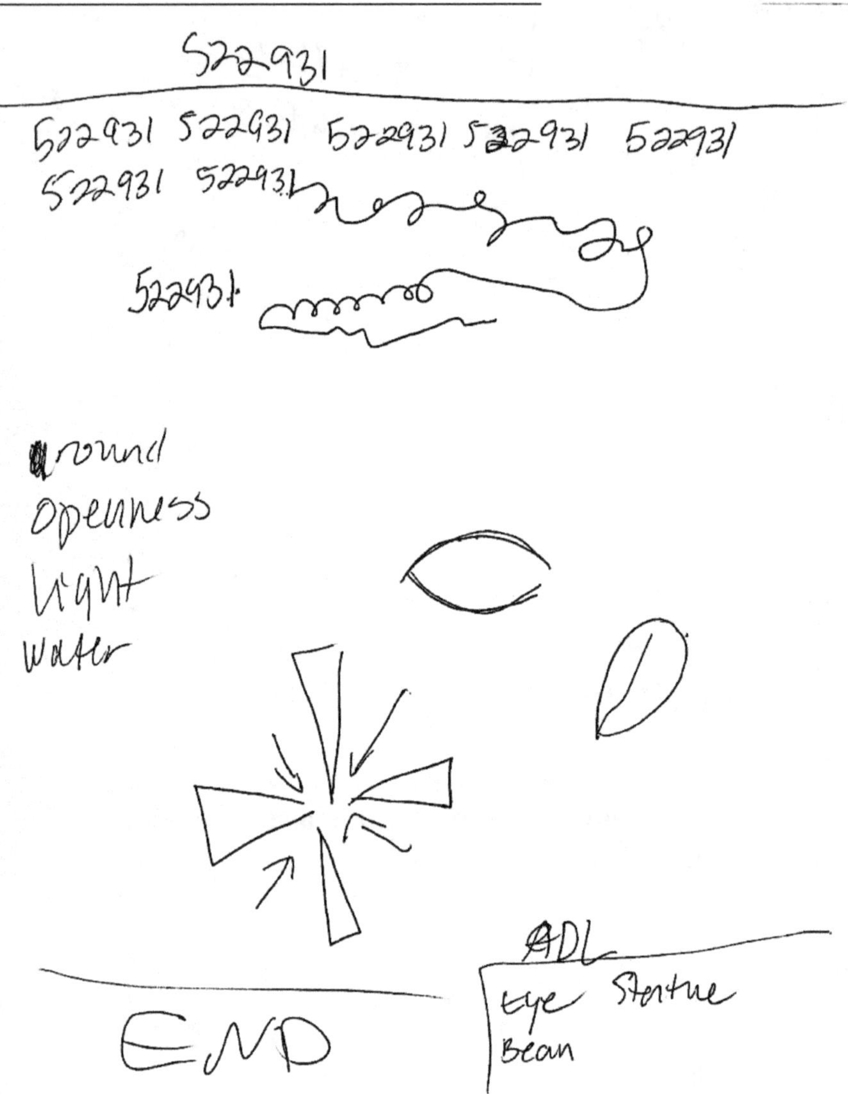

Accurate descriptors: "round" "light"

Graphic similarity: What do you think about the drawing above with the 4 arrows pointing in ward? How many rocket thrusters do you see on the capsule in the target image? Also, note the presence of arrows and triangles on the feedback transcript (next page).

FEEDBACK by participant: Insight at Dawn

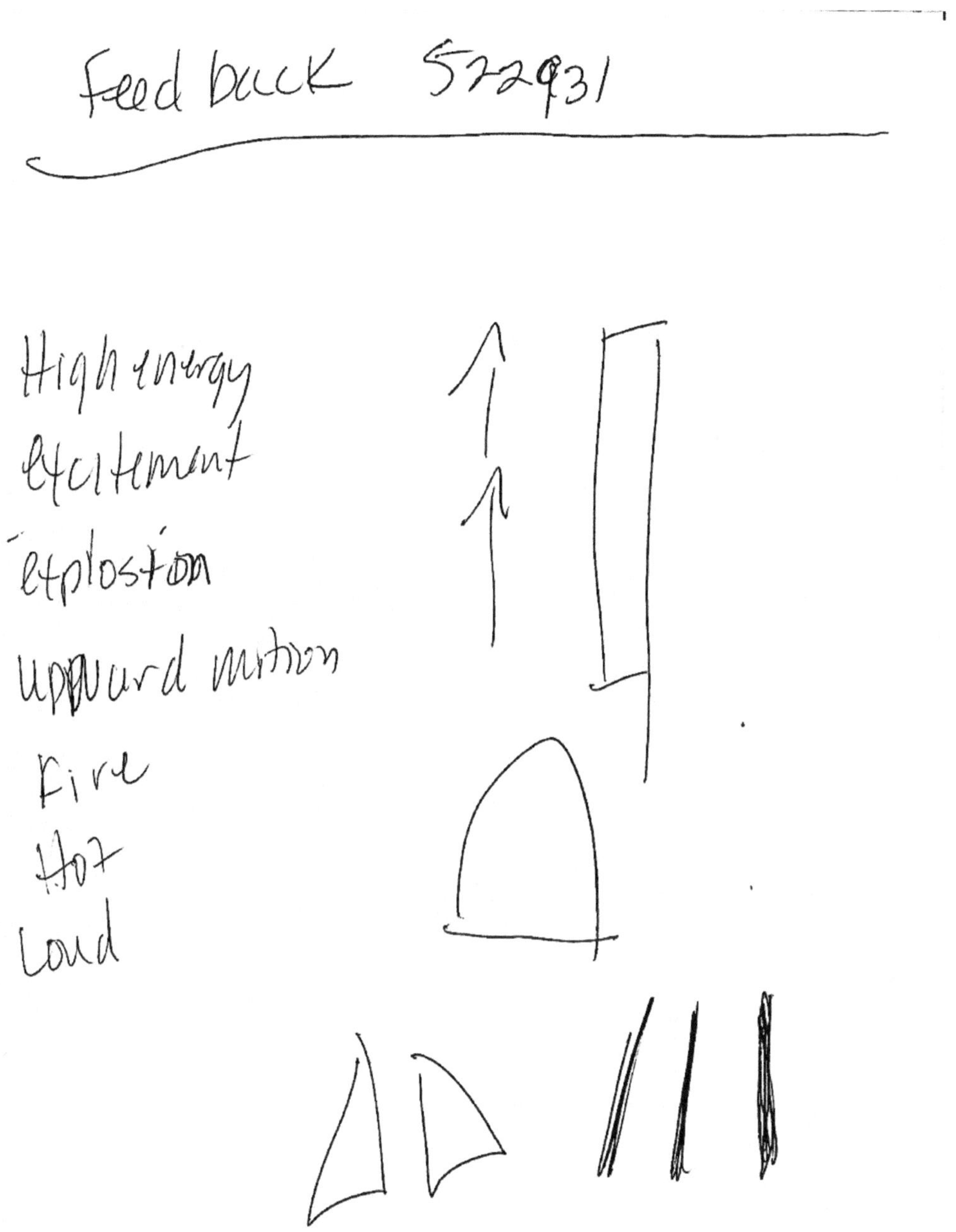

Feedback 522931

High energy
excitement
explosion
upward motion
Fire
Hot
Loud

TRANSCRIPT by participant Star Gazer

Accurate descriptors: “blue” “white” “tall/up (with **arrow**)”

Graphic similarity: notice the vertical lines atop a horizontal scene

FEEDBACK by participant: Star Gazer

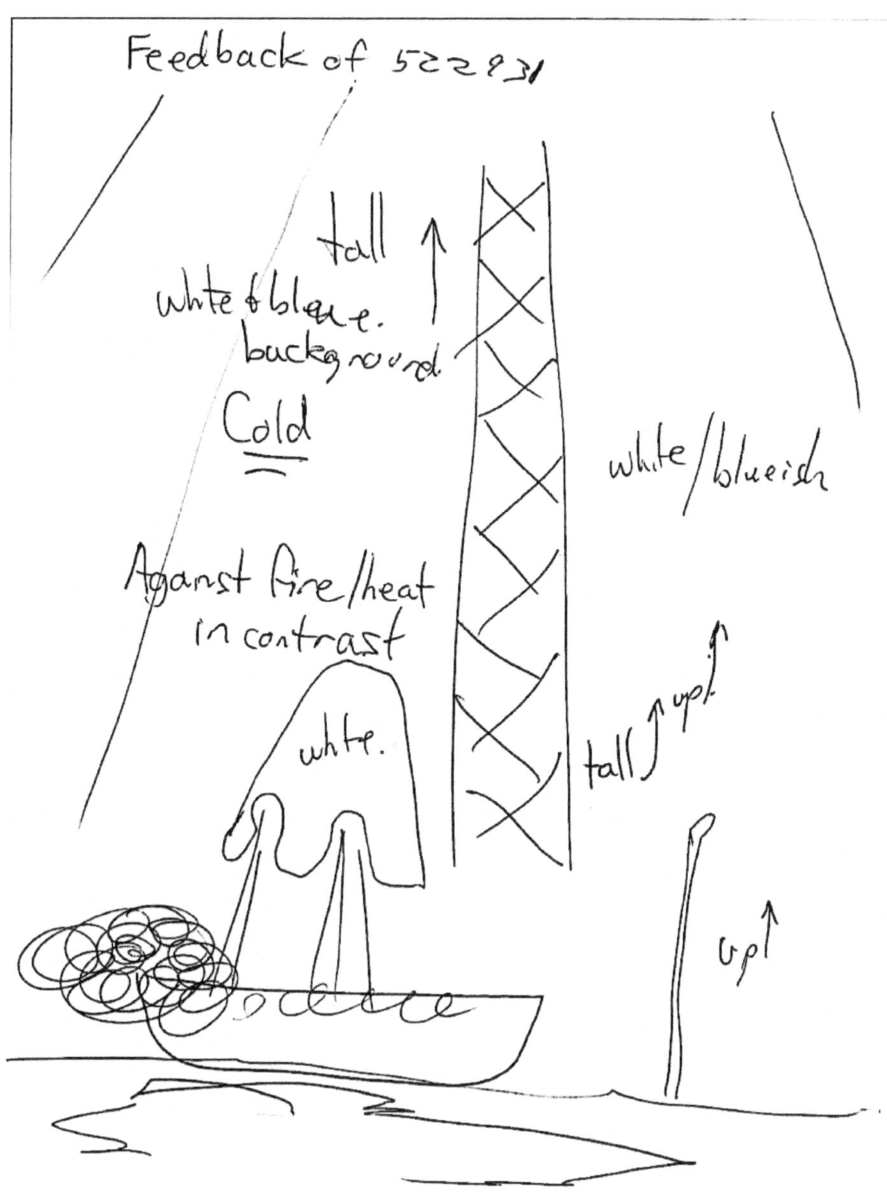

Feedback descriptors *sent back* that do appear on the viewing transcript: "white" "blue" "tall" "up" Note the arrows next to "up" (lower right) and next to "tall" (upper left). Now, find the arrow on the previous page (next to "tall/up", lower left).

TRANSCRIPT by participant Joyful Explorer

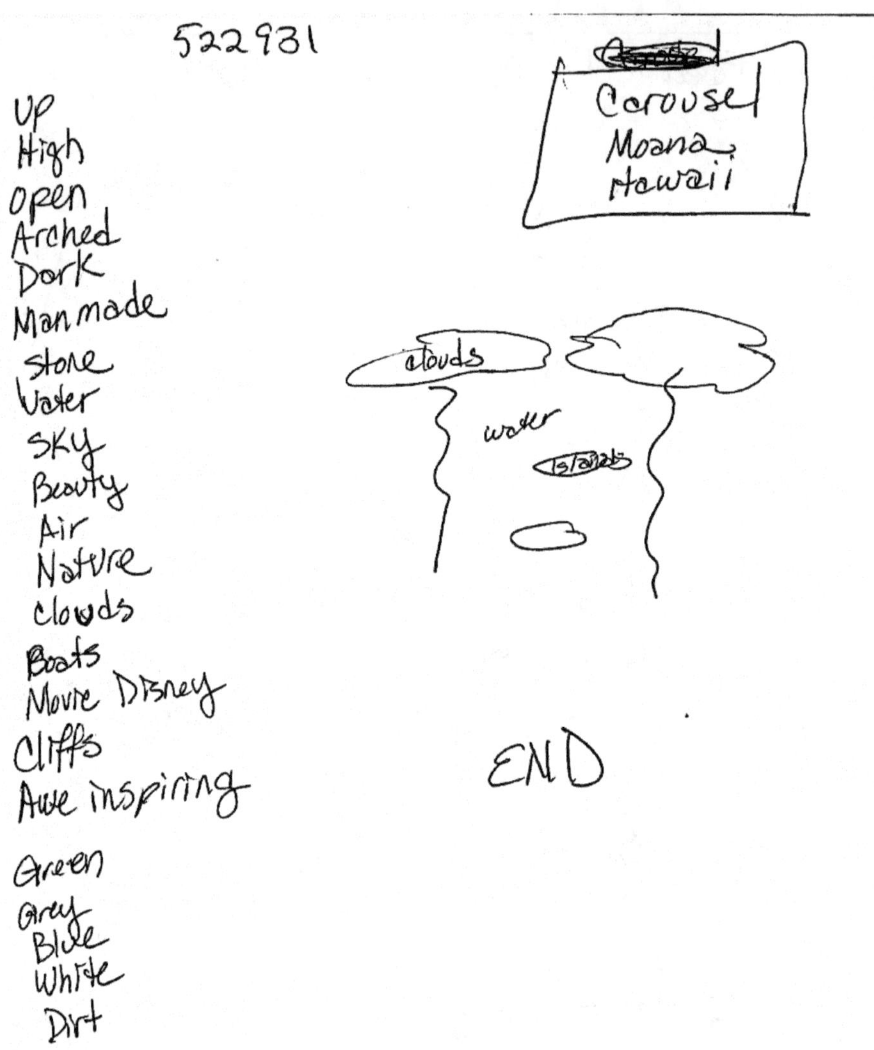

Accurate descriptors: “up” “high” “open” “manmade” “sky” “clouds” “green” “grey” “blue” “white” “dirt”

Accurate AOL: “carousel” – The target isn’t a carousel. But do an online image search for “carousel” and decide for yourself if you think they are somehow similar.

Graphic similarity: Compare the sketches labeled “clouds” above to the smoke in the target image and the feedback (next page).

FEEDBACK by participant: Joyful Explorer

Feedback descriptors *sent back* that do appear on the viewing transcript: "grey" "white" "dirt"

TRANSCRIPT by participant Mountain Seer

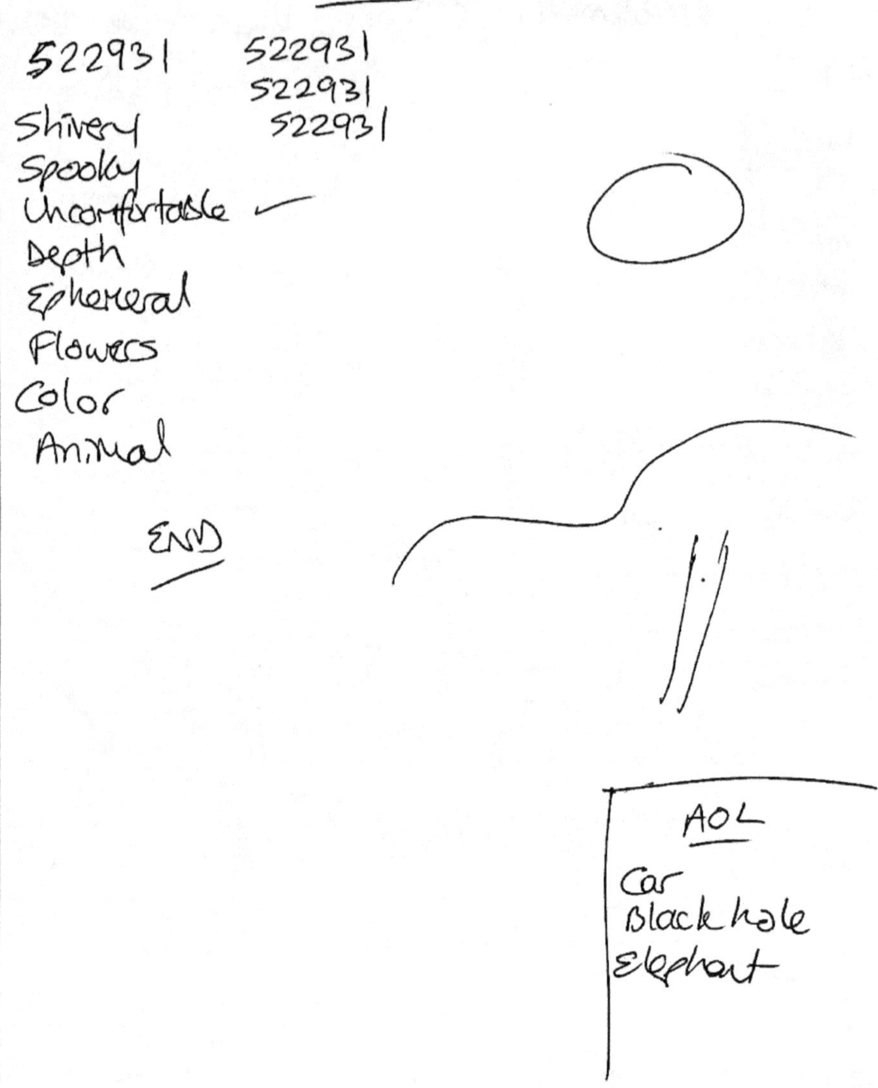

Graphic similarity: The sketches here capture the essential shapes, a circle for the capsule and two vertical lines for the scaffolding. Compare them to the images sent back during the feedback session (next page).

Accurate AOL: “car” – It’s a space capsule, not a car, but they are both vehicles.

FEEDBACK by participant: Mountain Seer

feedback : S22931

Speed
Space
Heat
Pollution
Noise
Groundshake
Force
Exploration
Metal
smoke

TRANSCRIPT by participant Snow Lion

522331
522331
522331

522331

BROWN
DRY
BEIGE
NATURAL
BLUE
AIRY
WHITE
METALLIC
SMOOTH
AOL: CUTLERY
GREY
MANMADE
ORANGE
SPONGY
SOFT
BROWN
AOL: ICE CREAM
GREEN
TRANSLUCID
SEMI-TRANSPARENT
WOBBLY
JELLY LIKE
POWDERY
SANDY
WHITE

Accurate descriptors: "brown" "blue" "airy" "white" "metallic" "smooth" "grey" "manmade" "orange" "green" "semi-transparent" "wobbly" "powdery" "white"

Graphic similarity: The drawing on the left is a strong match for the target image (the bottom half of the capsule) as well as the drawing in the feedback (next page).

FEEDBACK by participant: Snow Lion

FEEDBACK FOR 522831

BROWN
DRY
BEIGE
NATURAL
BLUE
AIRY
WHITE
METALLIC
SMOOTH
GREY
MAN MADE
ORANGE
BROWN
GREEN
TRANSLUCID
SEMITRANSPARENT
WOBBLY
POWDERY
SANDY
WHITE
METALLIC
STRINGY
DANGLING
TECHNOLOGICAL
HOT
HOVERING
VERTICAL

Feedback descriptors *sent back* that do appear on the viewing transcript: "brown" "blue" "airy" "white" "metallic" "smooth" "grey" "manmade" "orange" "green" "semi-transparent" "wobbly" "powdery" "white"

This is a **great** example of the use of the feedback session to send information back in time to the viewing session.

TRANSCRIPT by participant Forest Tantrika

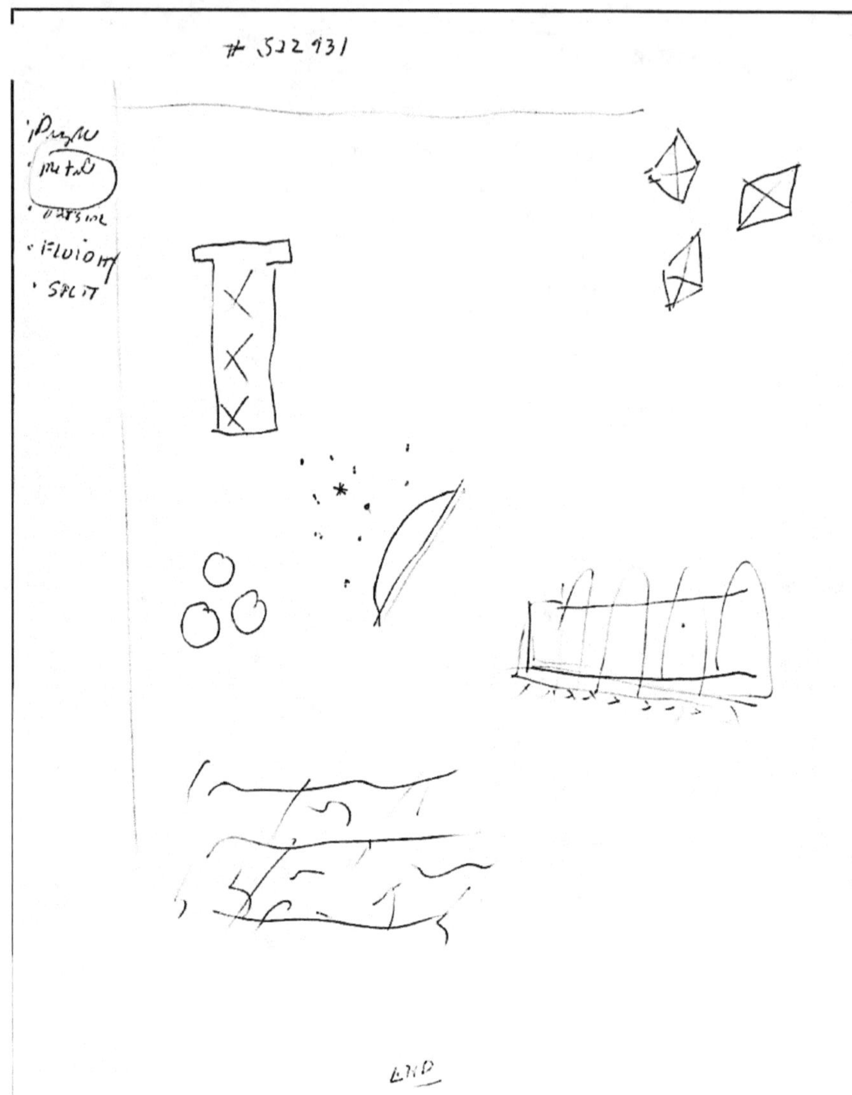

Accurate descriptors: "metal" "outside"

Graphic similarity: Notice how the object in the middle with stars to its left conveys the idea of a UFO (or UAP). To its right, notice the dome-like shapes. Other shapes here resemble the scaffolding. Also, compare the horizontal lines at the bottom with those in the feedback transcript (next page).

FEEDBACK by participant: Forest Tantrika

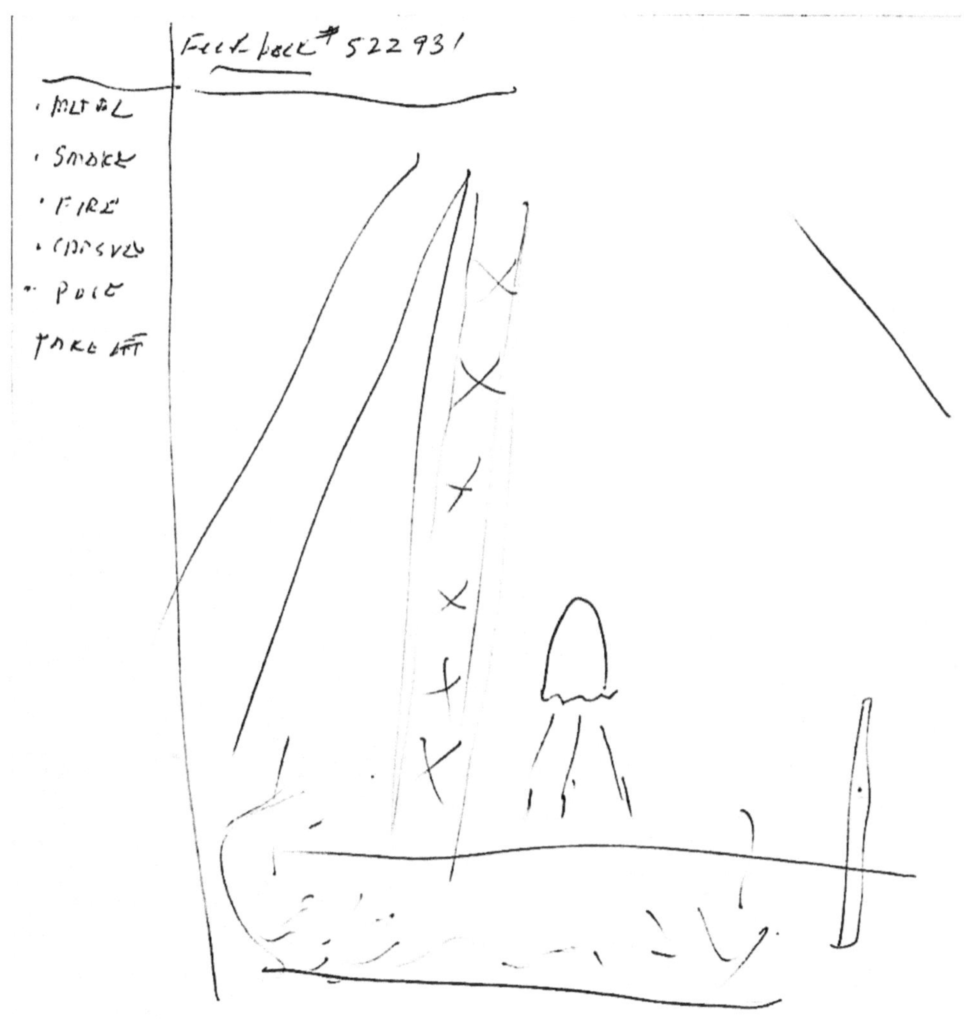

Feedback descriptors *sent back* that do appear on the viewing transcript: “metal”

TRANSCRIPT by participant Cosmic Dancer

Accurate descriptors: “waves” “fear” “motion”

Accurate AOL: “storm” “wind”

Graphic similarity: The wavy lines convey the effect of the rockets heating the surrounding air. Obviously, the rocket-like shape on the right is a strongly accurate association.

FEEDBACK by participant: Cosmic Dancer

Feedback descriptors *sent back* that do appear on the viewing transcript: “motion”

Remote Viewing Coordinate: 553904 (color version in Appendix 3)

NOTE: The feedback for this target was in the form of a **360-degree video** I recorded several years ago. The fun thing about this type of feedback is that when watching it on a smartphone, you can "look around" by moving the phone. On a laptop, use the cursor to click and drag on the video screen to change the angle of perception. To watch the video yourself, use the **QR code in Appendix 3** to find it easily. Or enter this URL: https://www.youtube.com/watch?v=arJC47W6aKo. My book, *Signal and Noise,* includes a link to its site hosting many remote viewing targets with 360-degree video feedback for training purposes. **I also provide the link and QR code here in Appendix 4.**

TRANSCRIPT PAGE 1 by participant: Snow Lion

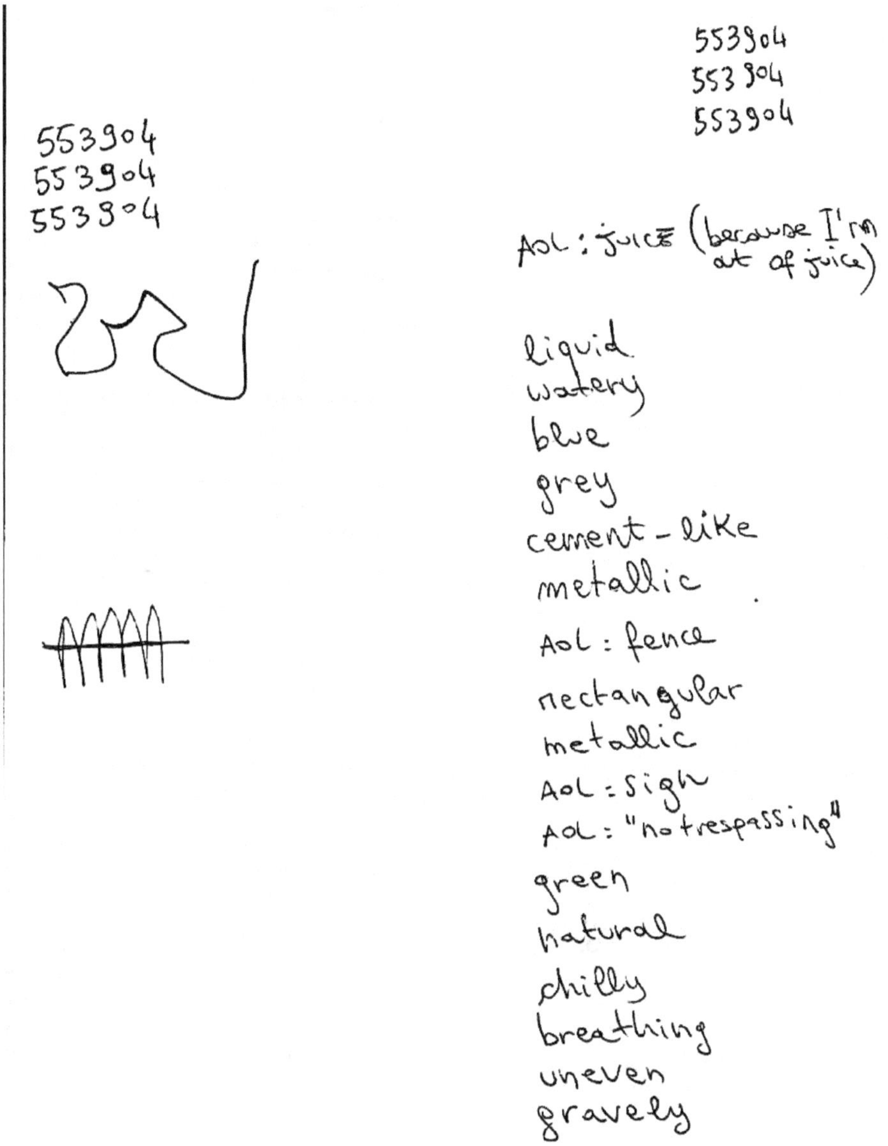

553904
553904
553904

553904
553904
553904

AOL: juice (because I'm out of juice)

liquid
watery
blue
grey
cement-like
metallic

AOL: fence
rectangular
metallic
AOL: sign
AOL: "no trespassing"
green
natural
chilly
breathing
uneven
gravely

Accurate descriptors: "grey" "cement-like" "metallic" "rectangular" "gravely"

Graphic similarity: Note the similarity of the sketch on the left (resembling a fence) with the two sketches in the feedback (page 211). They seem to be *combined* into one image here.

TRANSCRIPT PAGE 2 by participant: Snow Lion

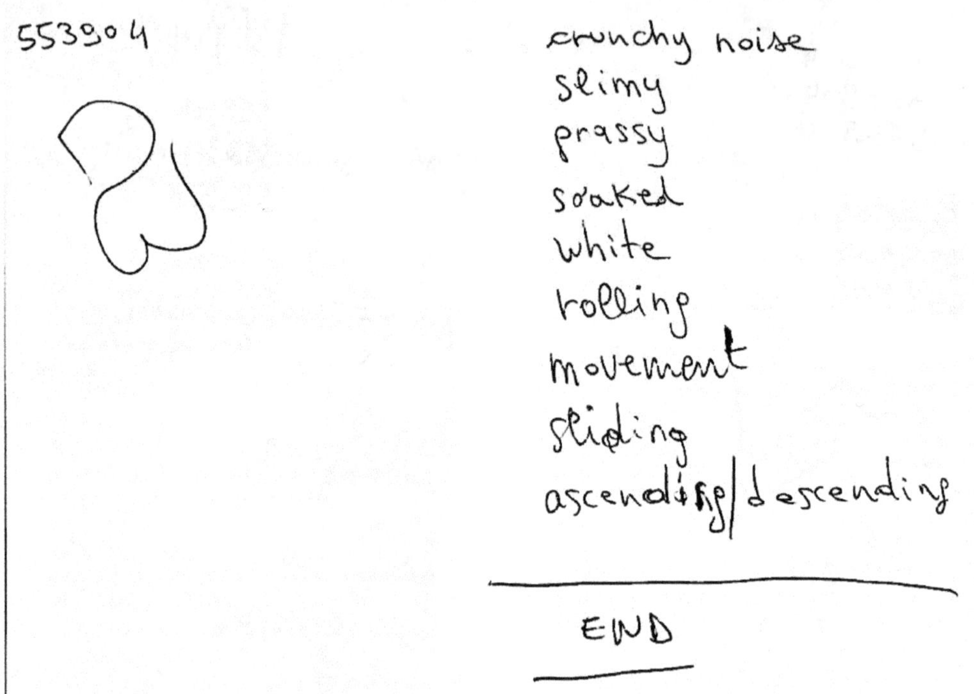

****NOTE** This is the second page of the transcript. The feedback is on the next page.**

Accurate descriptors: "rolling" "movement" "sliding" "ascending/descending"

FEEDBACK by participant: Snow Lion

The encircled sketch above is from the first page of the viewer's transcript. It appears to be a combination of the two feedback sketches on the left.

Feedback descriptors *sent back* that do appear on the viewing transcript: "grey" "cement-like" "metallic" "rectangular" "gravely" "rolling" "movement" (as "moving forward") "sliding" "ascending/descending"

This is a **great** example of the use of the feedback session to send information back in time to the viewing session.

TRANSCRIPT by participant Forest Tantrika

Graphic similarity: Compare the sketches here to those from the feedback (next page).

FEEDBACK by participant: Forest Tantrika

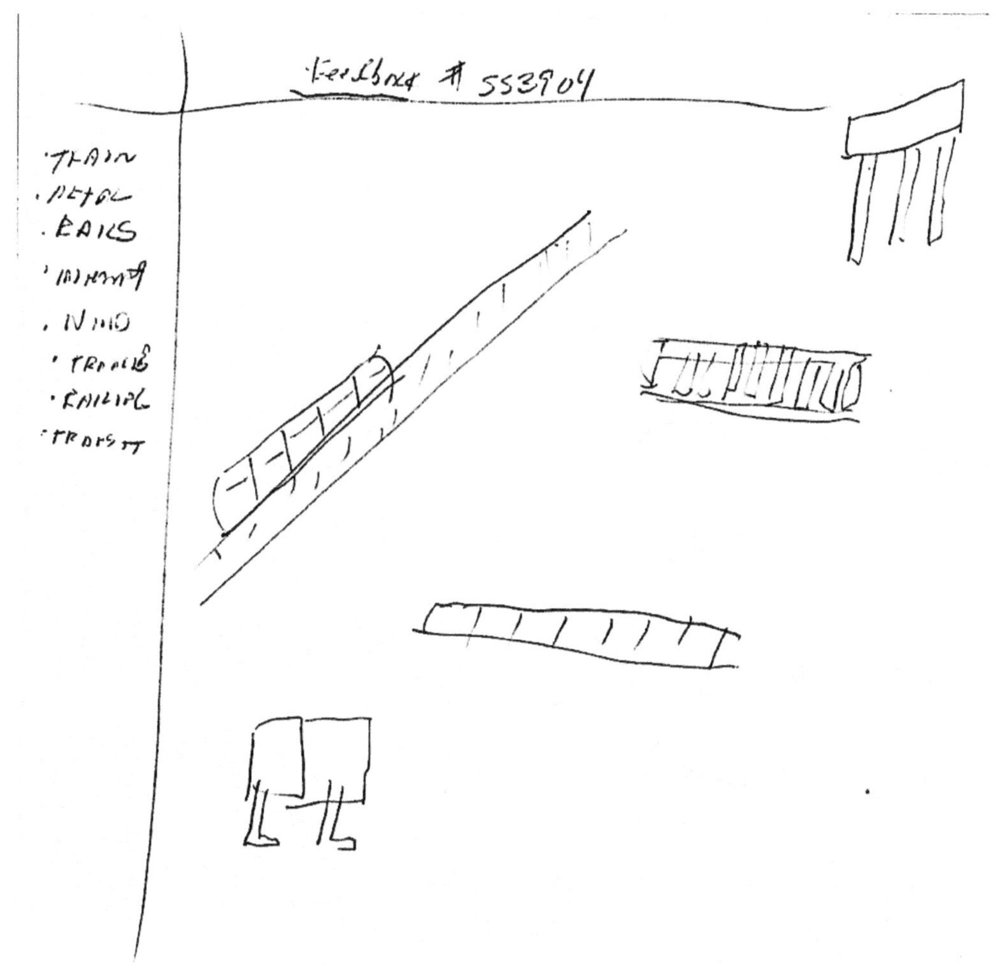

TRANSCRIPT by participant Time Traveler

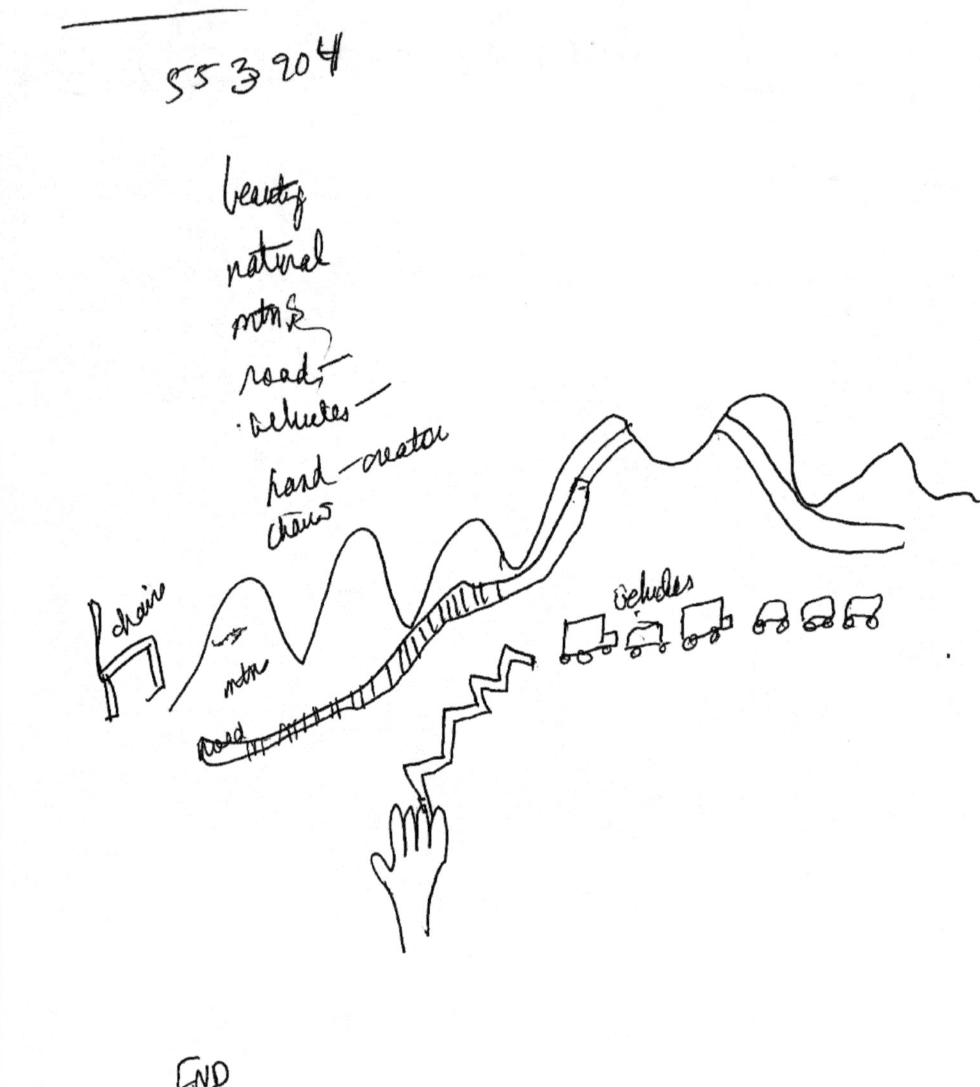

Accurate descriptors: “chair” “vehicles” “road”

Graphic similarity: Note the chair on the left and compare with the chairs in the feedback (next page).

FEEDBACK by participant: Time Traveler

Feedback 553904

vehicles lined up

road - tracks

seats - chairs

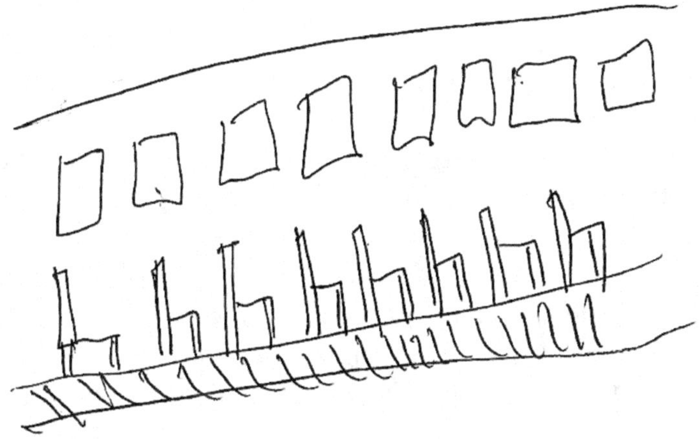

Feedback descriptors *sent back* that do appear on the viewing transcript: "vehicles" "chair" "road"

DAY 2 – PSYCHOKINESIS WITH RANDOM EVENT GENERATORS: THE OWLS

After completing the remote viewing segment, the group took a break and then reconvened to participate in another spoon-bending session. Then, we engaged in exercises using special random event generators (REGs) that I had procured several years ago from John Valentino and Herb Mertz[49] through their association with a company named Psyleron[50]. Its website featured a product called The Psyleron Mind Lamp™.

Their device was designed to change colors according to the REG's output. In a physicalist's version of the universe, the shifting colors should remain completely random. But research and experimentation have shown that *paying attention* to the REG (or the lamp) changes the output from random to non-random. This is very much a mind-over-matter phenomenon.

The lamp can reflect the state-change by slowing or stopping the constant shift from one color to another, and for some, changing to an intended color and remaining that color for a significant period.

I was only able to acquire the REG-light system, but not the frosted glass container. So, for the intensive, I went to Ikea, visited their lamp department, and purchased three children's lamps in the shape of owls. You can see one in color on the back cover of this book. The plastic was frosted in such a way that it worked well with the REG-light system I inserted inside.

---

[49] I highly recommend Mertz' book *The Selection Effect: How Consciousness Shapes Reality.* (2020). Penn Wolcott Press. In my opinion, it is one of the most sophisticated, detailed books on psychokinesis and should be required reading for every consciousness researcher.

[50] https://www.psyleron.com/lamp.html

Participants formed three groups of eight and went to their separate areas to work with their owl. This was not only an excellent opportunity for teamwork and creativity, but for bonding.

The groups were encouraged to experiment and try different ways to mentally affect their owls. They could try the brute force approach of applying a strong mental focus. They could also try developing a feeling of group cohesion and see if that would affect their owl's REG and cause it to stop changing from one color to another. They could chant, sing songs, hold hands, etc.

Afterward, Wendy Gallant told me how her group successfully caused their owl to move to a specific color. Someone in the group suggested, "Why don't we ask Spirit to help?" And so, they did. They asked, "Spirit, please turn the owl yellow." It did. The group responded by thanking Spirit. Then, they asked Spirit for another color, and the owl changed to that color.

Wendy told me they did this successfully *five times in a row*. This was a significant result and obviously leads to many more questions which are beyond the scope of this book.

Let the final point be that once communication with Spirit (as a second participant) was initiated, what began as psychokinesis ended as *telepathy*.

DAYS 2 and 3 – OUTBOUNDER REMOTE VIEWING

Outbounder remote viewing differs from the type of remote viewing shown earlier in the book because of the feedback method.

In some outbounder experiments, the viewer tunes into the experience another person (the outbounder) is having in the present, during the viewing, or will have in the future. In this case, feedback can take the form of interviewing the person who had the experience or looking at photos or video of the person having the experience and their environment.

At the intensive, the outbounders were the viewers themselves. Their feedback was to go to the target site and have their experience there, then to mentally *send* information about their experience back in time to themselves during their initial remote viewing session.

Carrying pen and paper would have been unwieldy, so the next few pages only show their initial remote viewing transcripts. There were no paper feedback transcripts. Going to the site *was* the feedback. As you'll see, this didn't hinder several of the participants.

The viewing session was done on the evening of Day 2, and the following morning, the viewers were shuttled to the target site, the Estes Park Aerial Tram.[51] They boarded the tram, exited at the top of the mountain, and enjoyed the beautiful views and hiking trails before returning.

Afterward, some of them walked into the town of Estes Park, whose streets are filled with shops and antique wooden architecture. Many of the transcripts (not included here) accurately depicted these scenes of the town instead of the aerial tram. This was a lesson for me as the tasker to select more specific and isolated outbounder experiences in the future.

---

[51] https://EstesTram.com

Outbounders experiencing their feedback.

Outbounders experiencing their feedback.

TRANSCRIPT by participant Cosmic Dancer

Accurate descriptors: "viewpoint" "top of the hill" "hills" "hilltops"

Accurate AOL: "fenicula" (third word on the left) – An online image search using the term "fenicula" returned results matching that term and the variation "funicular," which is a railway that goes up a mountain. The online images bear a strong thematic and visual resemblance to the target. Most image results for "funicular" returned *red* rail cars, another strong association.

Graphic similarity: The similarity to the target is extraordinary.

TRANSCRIPT by participant Lord of Water

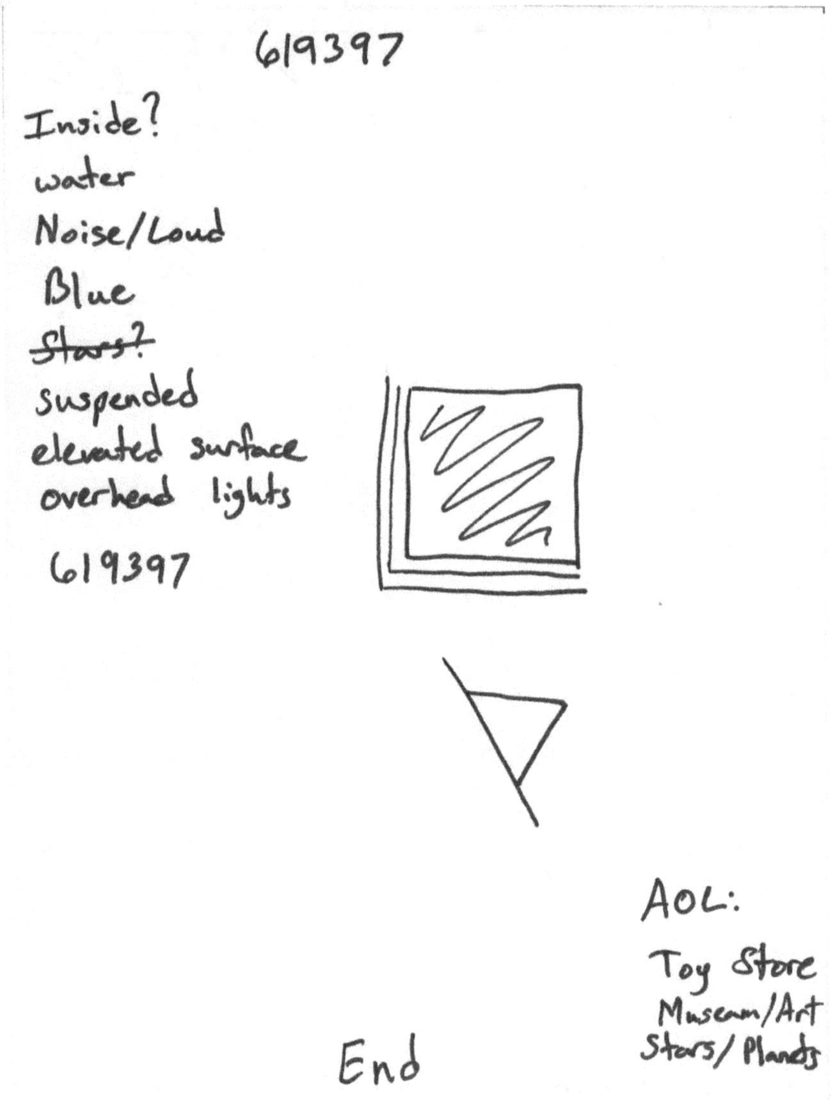

619397

Inside?
water
Noise/Loud
Blue
~~Stars?~~
suspended
elevated surface
overhead lights

619397

AOL:
Toy Store
Museum/Art
Stars/Planets

End

Accurate descriptors: "suspended" "elevated surface"

Graphic similarity: The triangle on a plane seems abstract but is evocative of an object traversing an incline. Without the presence of the accurate descriptors, my statement could be said to be the result of confirmation bias. Yet the descriptors together with the graphic similarity makes me confident this transcript shows evidence for psychic perception.

TRANSCRIPT by participant Light of Wisdom

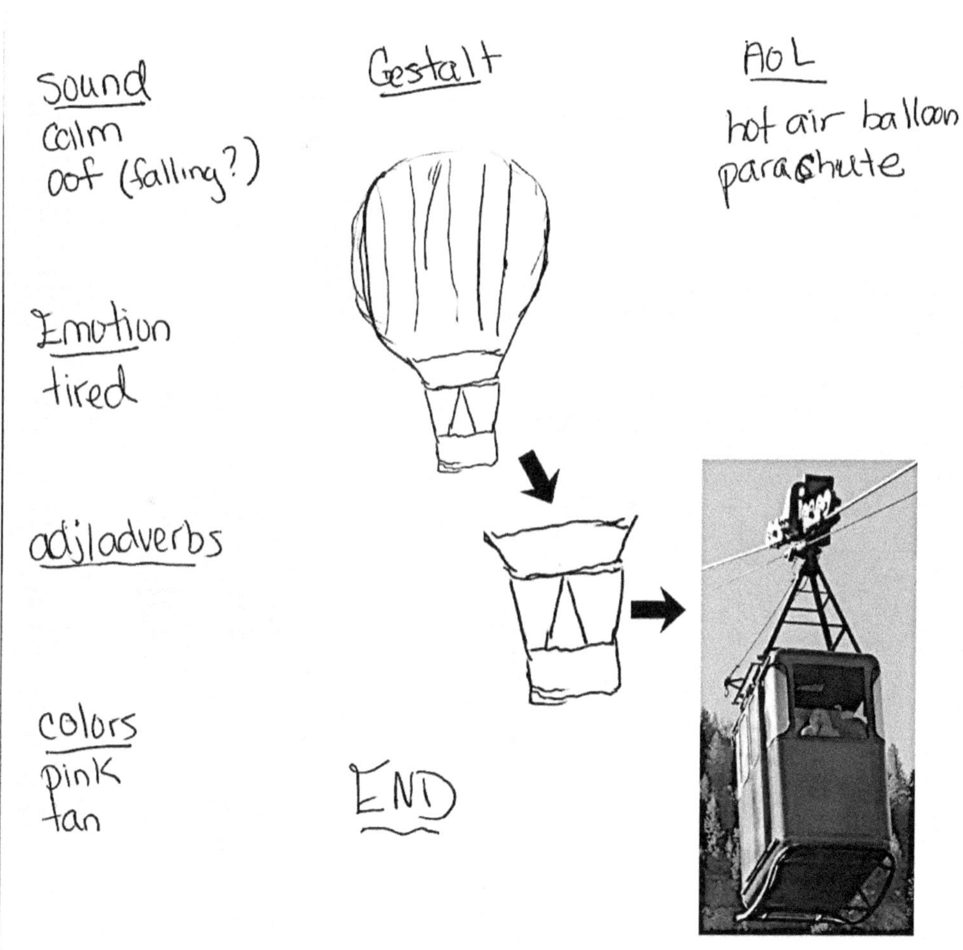

Observed attribute: Analytical Overlay - "hot air balloon"

Observed attribute: Thematic similarity

Graphic Similarity: The triangle inside the balloon basket resembles the triangular frame connecting the suspended tram to its cable. The triangle's appearance in the balloon sketch is unusual because balloon baskets/gondolas don't have that kind of structure.

TRANSCRIPT by participant Forest Tantrika

Graphic similarity: (A) resembles the tram, (B) resembles the triangular frame on top of it.

Observed attribute: Contamination by another telepath – Is it possible (C) is related to the hot air balloon drawn by the remote viewer whose transcript appears on the previous page? And what of (B), the triangle which also appears on the other transcript?

DREAM TRANSCRIPT by participant Synchronicity

On the night of doing the remote viewing session, the participant with code name Synchronicity had a dream that included aspects of the target site which she would see the next day. These aspects were inside the gift-shop section of the aerial tram's building. The VW bus in the painting below was red. This is an example of dream-precognition.

"In my dream, I was riding with my husband in a long boat that was shaped like a **red** VW bus. When the canal would turn into a street, the wheels automatically came out and it turned into a car my husband could drive this vehicle so smoothly. I was very proud of him."

* Remember that the actual tram was red. See the color photo on the back cover of this book.

DAY 3 – TEAM TELEPATHY EVENTS

We were halfway through the intensive at this point and had spent the morning off-site at the remote viewing outbounder feedback location, the aerial tram. After lunch, it was time to engage in four different team-style telepathy exercises: identifying colors, identifying colored shapes, locating small objects, and identifying the Gestalt[52] of a complex image.

IDENTIFYING COLORED PAPER

Earlier in the week, participants had practiced their clairvoyance with colored paper. The difference now was that, as a member of a team, the designated receiver would sit blindfolded up front while someone held the colored paper behind or above their head. Their teammates, as senders, would focus on the color and attempt to psychically assist their receiver in correctly identifying it.

There were four teams of six participants. So, with four receivers up front, I indicated to each assistant which color to hold up for their teammate. This ensured all four receivers were working with the same color at the same time.

Each round was limited to three minutes, and when time was up, each receiver stated aloud which color they thought it was. Each correct receiver's team received a point.

[52] See page 149 in a previous chapter about remote viewing for the definition of *Gestalt*.

IDENTIFYING COLORED SHAPES

The colored shapes exercise followed the same format, with an assistant holding a colored shape glued onto a black, cardstock sheet. Like the color exercise, each correct receiver's team received a point.

IDENTIFYING SMALL OBJECTS

This exercise resembled the format from Day 2 (page 139). As you'll see in the photos on the next pages, the use of a folder as their workspace was replaced with four sheets of white paper.

To set up the round, a member from *another* team was responsible for setting the four physical objects onto the workspace as quietly as possible so the blindfolded receiver had no way of knowing where each object was placed.

Receivers were permitted to make six attempts to locate their four objects and pull them off their workspace. But the first person to find and remove all their objects would be the winner. If nobody succeeded at removing them all, the winner would be whoever had removed the most objects after six attempts.

Limiting their attempts to six prevented receivers from reaching out many times rapidly and randomly finding objects like chickens pecking at grain. That would not be telepathy, obviously. They had to work mindfully, slowly, and deliberately, trusting the subtle impressions arising in their mind's eye.

Once all four receivers' workspaces were set, I would say, "Begin." Since their teammates, as senders, could see where the objects were located, their task was to telepathically transmit that information to them.

IDENTIFYING A COMPLEX IMAGE

For the exercise of identifying a complex image's Gestalt, the target image was projected on the back wall, behind the blindfolded receivers. The instructions were for each receiver to state their perceived Gestalt aloud at the end of the round, like the other two exercises. They needed to limit it to a single word or phrase.

Judging their performance was difficult because it was subjective. And if two or more receivers were accurate but used different descriptors, that made it more difficult. It was up to me to decide whose description best matched the target, and not everyone agreed with me. Luckily, this was all in fun, so the debates never got serious.

I didn't record their descriptions. But I do remember one winning participant's description of her target. Behind her on the wall was the image of a raging nighttime forest fire. The orange glow from the massive flames radiated out against the dark sky. She uttered a single word to win the round, "Warm." You can see the color version of the photo on the back cover of this book.

Just as when we'd done similar exercises a couple of days before with clairvoyance, Wendy Gallant and Bob Leander[53] won their rounds in two seconds flat because of their enhanced clairvoyant abilities to perceive their surroundings as if they weren't wearing blindfolds at all. It was inspiring to see.

To make the afternoon's exercises more fun, I created a scoreboard by making a simple racetrack out of a couple of tables marked with tape. Each team was assigned a plastic horse, and each had its team name taped on its side.

As you'll see in the photos on the following pages, two of the team names were "Gestalt" and "Thunder and Lightning." Each time a team received a point, their horse progressed to the next mark made with masking tape on the racecourse.

In the end, we all won because of the wonderful blend of entertainment and insight we shared that afternoon.

[53] Find their websites in Appendix 5. Bob Leander's is found by clicking the link for Mind Possible Authorized Teachers.

Below assistants hold colored-paper above and behind the receiver's heads. Their teammates are to telepathically assist their receiver.

Below assistants hold colored-shapes on black card-stock behind the receiver's heads.

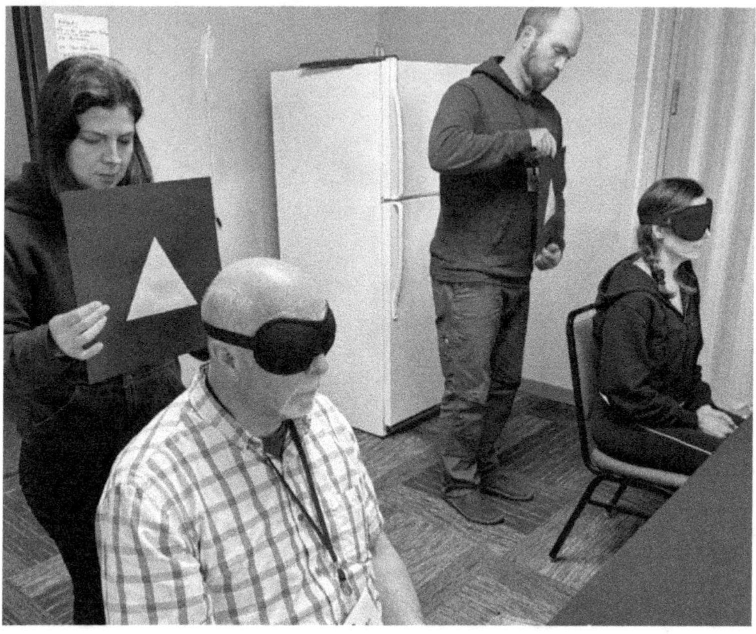

A participant using telepathy and clairvoyance to find his physical objects.

Below: Wendy Gallant, renowned teacher of Seeing Beyond Eyes, succeeded immediately because of her ability to perceive as if she wasn't wearing a blindfold at all. Learn more about Wendy in Appendix 5.

Below: Horses with team names on their sides progress up and down the racetrack when their team earns a point.

Below: Teammates focus on the target image projected behind the receivers, attempting to send them information about the target with telepathy.

Top: A receiver attempting to receive information about the target sent telepathically by his teammates. No, this is not a real photo of a UFO.

Below: This receiver gave an impressive single-word description, her *Gestalt* for the target image of a raging wildfire was "Warm." See the color version on the back cover.

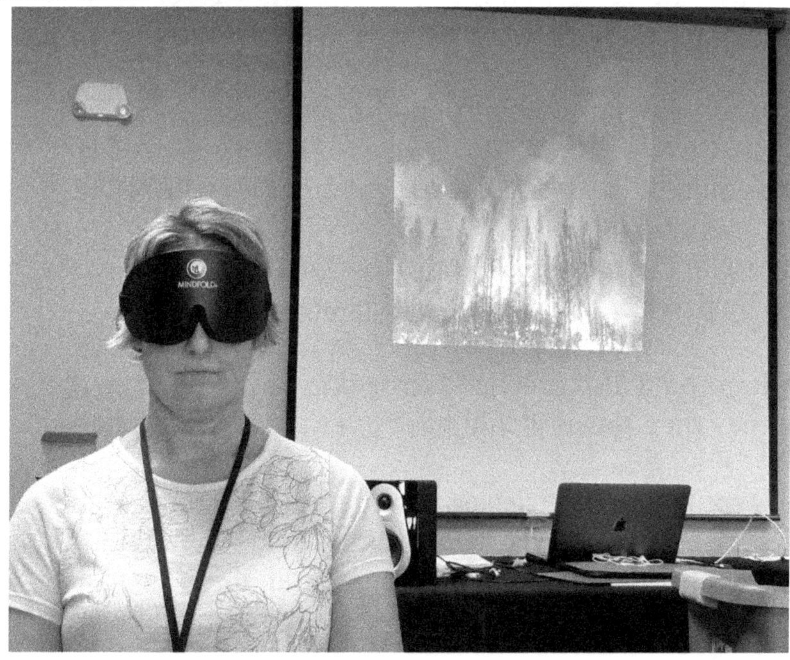

Day 3 - WHAT'S IN THE BOX? #1

"What's in the box?" is an exercise I created for exploring telepathy and clairvoyance with large groups. It was also designed for exercising dream-precognition. I explained to the group that the following day, half the group (senders) would participate in "an experience" together, and the other half of the group (receivers) would try their clairvoyance and telepathy from their bedrooms to see if they could pick up on what the senders were experiencing.

Everyone could practice the lucid dreaming technique I'd presented at the start of the program and try to dream about the next day's event. They were to write any dream recollections down for me to collect the next morning. The box would be opened that evening.

When it was time to have "the experience" contained in the box, the receivers were sent to their bedrooms. They were told the experience would begin in about 20 minutes, so they knew when to start applying their intention and attention.

The senders were given the opportunity to practice precognition by writing down any impressions they received about the experience they would have 20 minutes or so in the future.

To clarify, there were four psychic opportunities:

1. **Everyone** could practice *dream-precognition* the night before.

2. The **senders** in the room could practice *clairvoyance* before the box was opened by psychically perceiving its contents.

3. The **senders** could also practice *precognition* by perceiving the experience they themselves would have *after* the box was opened.

4. **Receivers** could practice *telepathy* from their bedrooms at the same time the experience was being had by the senders. They could choose one of the senders to focus on, or choose several, if not the whole group. At the designated start time (when the box would be opened),

the receiver's intention would be, "What is [participant] experiencing right now?" Or, "What is the whole group of senders experiencing right now?"

I chose a large cardboard wardrobe box to contain all aspects of the experience. I needed it to conceal the contents without giving any clues.

It was just large enough to fit all the parts that would be necessary to create the scene: a small circus tent (folded up), a dozen red clown noses, a couple of clown wigs, and three dozen colorful juggling scarves. I cut a flap into one side of the box and hung a foam mannequin head from a bar at the top with a wig and clown nose affixed to it.

When it was time to start the experience, I opened the flap to reveal the clown head suspended inside. My intention was to produce a little bit of shock and awe in the participants' minds, in the hopes of making an impression at the psychic level. I knew that at the same time the participants in the room, as senders, were having this experience, the others, as receivers, were lying in their beds using telepathy to pick up on what was happening in the room and writing down their impressions.

After the dramatic reveal, I emptied the box. Everyone put on a clown nose and grabbed a few of the scarves. I turned on the projector and played a YouTube video which included the kind of music you could expect to hear at the circus with circus-themed imagery in the background.

Several participants put together the children's circus tent while the others formed a circle around it and began dancing in sort of a conga line.

As they danced and laughed in the circle, they threw their colorful scarves up and backward into the air so the person behind them would catch the scarf and pass it on. Some participants practiced their juggling skills with the scarves, and one displayed gymnastic skills with cartwheels and doing the splits.

I've included four transcripts that include significant results. The subheading of each indicates the participant's method of perception. Given this was the first time anyone had done this type of exercise, I was grateful for their wholehearted participation.

DAY 3 - WHAT’S IN THE BOX? #1

Top photo: Preparing to reveal the contents of the box.

Middle photo: The surprise of the clown head suspended inside.

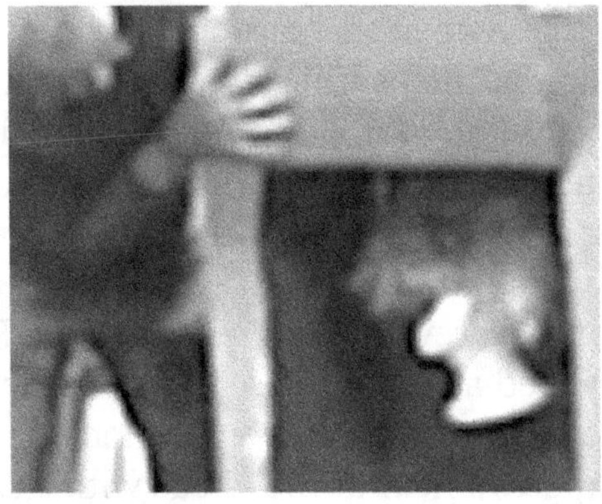

Bottom photo: Emptying the box.

While the senders' experience progressed (below), the receivers practiced telepathy from their bedrooms while lying in bed and writing down their impressions.

TRANSCRIPT by participant Cosmic Dancer

Dream Precognition (done the night before the box was opened)

LUCID DREAMING

"TEAM EXPERIENCE"

MORNING NOTES

box is empty or almost empty

the size is misleading -> It is a decoy

the "experience" is human connection like dancing together

probably just chatting or sharing thoughts

maybe while standing in a circle

AOL

my mind finds this "unsuccessful attempt"

my mind was obsessed with the idea, that the "experience" is a game or activity.

I could not find any evidence for this oversight while dreaming

Accurate descriptors:

"Box is empty or almost empty." – This was true, it was mostly empty.

"The size is misleading -> it is a decoy."

"The 'experience' is human connection like line dancing together…maybe while standing in a circle."

"My mind was obsessed with the idea that the 'experience' is a game or activity."

TRANSCRIPT by participant Lord of Water

Telepathy (done from another room *during* the event)

Items being tossed/passed
multi-colored
laughter
game
video
physical activity
music
boardgame(s)
warmth

AOL:
Twister
musical chairs

Accurate descriptors: "Items being tossed/passed" "multi-colored" "laughter" "game" "video" "physical activity" "music" "warmth"

TRANSCRIPT by participant Insight at Dawn

Precognition & Clairvoyance (done in the room *before* the box was opened)

Group of people repeling off the side of a roof. Like a house roof.

- 2 dragons flying over head
Very colorful.

Accurate AOL: "2 dragons flying overhead" "very colorful" – Participants were tossing the colorful juggling scarves up into the air and backward while dancing in a circle for the people behind them to catch.

Also, note the sentence, "Group of people repeling [rappelling] off the side of a roof. Like a house roof." Look again at the photos on page 237 and see that a participant is holding the "house" by its roof.

TRANSCRIPT by participant Snow Lion

Telepathy (done from another room *during* the event)

Date / /

BOX #2

PINK
SOFT
FUN
MOVEMENT
JUMPING
BLUE
WHITE
ORANGE
GOING AROUND
PLASTIC
RED
MAKING NOISE
AWE
LIGHT-EMANATING
ROUND
"ding ding ding"

Date / /

TUNING IN FROM
S BEDROOM

- MAKING NOISE
- TOUCHING FLOOR CARPET
- BEING SLOWED DOWN BY PERSON IN FRONT OR WAITING YOUR TURN
- TREPIDATION
- CLAPPING HANDS OR MOVING HANDS IN THE AIR
- ROUND
- AOL = BALLOONS
BALLOONS
POPPING
- ENERGY BUILDUP
- WORKING TOGETHER TO ACCOMPLISH SOMETHING
- TRYING TO BE COHESIVE
- HESITATION

Accurate descriptors: "fun" "movement" "blue" "white" "orange" "going around" "red" "making noise" "round" "touching floor carpet" "being slowed down by person in front or waiting your turn" "trepidation" "clapping hands or moving hands in the air" "round" "energy buildup" "working together to accomplish something" "trying to be cohesive" "hesitation"

DAY 4 - HEART RATE TELEPATHY (DMILS)

Have you ever been out in public and felt a sudden urge to turn around, only to find someone staring at you? Or have you ever stared at someone just beyond their line of sight, until they suddenly turned to catch you? In either case, it would seem that one person's focused attention had affected the other.

What if one person's attention on another could physically affect them? Isn't that the premise of prayer? And of long-distance (or hands-off) energy healing, such as Reiki? Or group intention-setting, such as described in Lynne McTaggart's book *The Power of Eight*?[54]

To me, this phenomenon is associated with telepathy but goes one step further. Instead of only transmitting information to another's mind, a sender uses their intention to affect another's *physical body* through that receiver's mind. And research on this has been going on for nearly half a century.

In his 2003 systematic literature review titled ***Direct Mental Interactions with Living Systems*** *(DMILS) – Assessing Healing in the Physiological Lab*, Stefan Schmidt of the Institute for Environmental Medicine and Hospital Epidemiology (IUK) writes that DMILS experiments, which began in the late 1970s, were to "investigate whether there is an interaction between two spatially separated persons," and that "This interaction is operationalized as covariation

---

[54] McTaggart, L. (2018). The Power of Eight: Harnessing the Miraculous Energies of a Small Group to Heal Others, Your Life, and the World. Atria Books.

between the intentions of one person and the physiological reactions of the other person." [55]

Schmidt's paper referenced twenty-two studies on DMILS done between 1978 and 1999. He writes that nine of the twenty-two (37.5%) "yielded significant results according to their hypotheses."

I'd known about DMILS for a long time, but until I began planning for the 2025 intensive had never thought about doing my own experiment. Since the focus was to be telepathy, though, I knew this might be the best opportunity I'd ever get to do it, and to provide the participants with such a unique experience.

The design for our experiment was partly inspired by periodic bouts of insomnia I'd been having recently. The cause was no mystery.

Over the past few years, my interest in playing music has increased significantly. This interest was born out of several months of microdosing psilocybin. It was as if the musical part of my brain, which had been largely shut down all my life, suddenly awakened, and it was ravenous for music, especially anything involving overtones.

Suddenly, I could hear them from unexpected sources. For example, my ears could pick up overtones emanating from the kitchen faucet as water streamed out of it. I heard beautiful overtones from the wind buffeting my car's frame when driving eighty miles per hour from Colorado to Nebraska.

This led me to learn to play instruments like the didgeridoo, the jaw harp, and the Slovakian shepherd's flute called a Fujara. I taught myself to sing in overtones in the Western style, as well as similarly to the Tuvan throat singing style *khoomei*.

Still today, hearing and singing in overtones satisfies my brain like nothing else in my daily experience can. It grants me a unique type of fulfillment difficult to put into words. Because of how my

---

[55] Schmidt, Stefan. (2003). *Direct mental interactions with living systems (DMILS).* DOI 10.1016/B978-0-443-07237-6.50008-5.
https://www.researchgate.net/publication/279719074_Direct_mental_interactions_with_living_systems_DMILS

brain changed through microdosing psilocybin, playing this type of music *makes me very happy*.

And when I play my instruments or listen to others' recordings of overtone-based music at night, which is usually the only time of day I have to myself, that special joy I feel inside keeps me awake after going to bed.

In planning our DMILS experiment, I wondered, "What if a sender telepathically sent happy thoughts to a receiver? Could the sender physiologically affect the receiver?" In the spirit of making it an objectively measurable experience, I knew affecting someone's heart rate would be the easiest way to go.

I had a feeling it would be worthwhile to be as specific and personal as possible when deciding what kind of happy thoughts should be sent.

So, seven weeks before the intensive, I sent a video message to all the participants asking them to send me a brief narrative: "In three or four sentences, describe an activity that you currently do or have done at some point in your past. Maybe even when you were in school. Something that really got you excited. Ideally, this could be a physical activity, like a sport or a hobby. Or maybe theater. Something that, when you're doing it, gets your blood pumping and really excites you…This should be something that makes you feel exhilarated and positive and happy."

Aside from the specific activity, I asked them to also describe what they were wearing at the time, who else was present, and the overall environment.

I was also transparent with the participants by telling them I was asking for this information so far in advance of the intensive in the hopes they would forget I even asked them for it. I did not tell them exactly why I needed the information other than that it would be part of our time together.

Responses came in soon after. One person wrote about swimming with dolphins. Other experiences included a *very* romantic first date, watching the clouds part to reveal Machu Picchu at the end of a four-day hike, and performing a pole-dancing showcase for the first time. Reading everyone's experiences, which I came to refer to as *stimulus-narratives*, I was confident the experiment would be worth the effort. And it would take a lot of effort.

We did the experiment over two days so that everyone could experience the role of receiver. Each day, everyone was put into groups of four. A group was comprised of a receiver, a monitor, and two senders.

The **receiver's job** was to lie down during the experiment. They wore a small heart rate and oxygen tracker on their finger. Each tracker had a unique digital signature linking it to its designated phone app. This prevented the signal from one device from being sent to the wrong monitor's phone.

The **monitor's job** was to sit close by and track the receiver's heart rate using a phone app wirelessly linked to the heart rate monitor. I gave each monitor a tracking sheet they could use to periodically record the receiver's heart rate. Their special instruction was to be watchful of significant changes, up or down, and record them on the form.

The **two senders' job** was to sit in the hallway outside the room and send one of two telepathic commands to their team's receiver. The command sent depended on my instructions given at precise times during the experiment.

One of the two commands they sent was "Sleep." While telepathically sending the command, the senders were instructed to imagine the receiver entering a very relaxed state and sleeping deeply.[56]

The other command they sent wasn't a command at all but rather a visualization of the receiver's *stimulus-narrative*. I'd pasted each receiver's stimulus-narrative onto a Word document and found online photos closely depicting the scene.

---

[56] While creating this exercise, and indeed the whole intensive, I was inspired by the book *Experiments in Mental Suggestion* by L.L. Vasiliev.

Then I printed out two copies of each receiver's stimulus-narrative to give each pair of senders. I waited until the specific time to hand them the narratives so they would be undistracted by them beforehand.

Each round of the experiment lasted twenty minutes after the receivers were fully settled. Before the round began, I randomly determined which five-minute period would be the *stimulation* period. The three other five-minute periods would be the *sleep-command* periods. Only I knew how each period was designated, and I never told the senders and receivers how long each round would last.

At the start of each round, each group's pair of senders in the hallway were instructed to remain silent until further instructions were given.

Inside the main room, six receivers wearing pulse trackers lay on the floor with their monitors sitting nearby, tracking sheets and apps in hand.

I spent several minutes giving a hypnotic induction to bring the receivers into a relaxed state. No doubt they were excited and curious about the experiment, and the novelty of lying on the floor while being closely observed would be a factor.

When I believed they were well-settled, I exited the room to spend the rest of the round with the senders.

During the **sleep periods**, the senders were instructed to send their sleep commands to their team's receiver. It was not surprising to observe some senders becoming drowsy and nodding off themselves during these periods.

When it was time for the **stimulation period**, I handed each sender their copy of their receiver's stimulus-narrative. I asked them to read it, focus on the photos, and imagine the scene in as much detail as possible. All the while, they were to mentally *send the scene,* imbued with color, motion, sound, emotion, and the rest, to their receiver. But how to send it? By imagining the receiver living the scene out *right now*.

All of this was done as silently as possible to prevent hallway sounds from disturbing the receivers inside the room.

At the end of the round, I entered the room and gently announced it was over. Then I collected the monitor's tracking sheets for evaluation after the program. I regretted not being able to give them their results right away, but I was working alone and didn't have the time during the intensive.

When I finally had the time to review the tracking sheets, I was happy to see that six of them (25%) showed significant variations in heart rate correlated with the stimulus and sleep periods of each round. I've included them in the following pages. Each is labeled with the receiver's code name for confidentiality.

For each receiver, I've included:

- their stimulus-narrative with photos (the original photos have been replaced with similar royalty-free ones for this publication)
- their monitor's tracking sheet with hand-written notes
- a "normal" chart using the actual heart rate noted on the monitor's hand-written chart
- an "exaggerated" chart created by subtracting the lowest recorded heart rate on the chart to make the differences more visibly discernible

At the bottom of each chart, a bolded bracket helps you note which of the three five-minute periods was the stimulus period. I'll let you decide for yourself if the heart rate in each period correlates with the command being sent. It's subjective, but interesting enough to consider.

As you review each chart carefully, it will be important for you to remember that two different commands were sent. It's too easy to focus on whether the heart rate increased during the stimulus period and ignore the rest. Keep in mind that during the sleep periods, the senders were strongly influencing the receiver to become deeply relaxed. This means that a heart rate's **decrease** during sleep-command periods is *just as significant* as its increase during the stimulus period.

In case there's any doubt about the telepathic aspect of this exercise, I'll share an interesting anecdote. After the intensive, participant Desi told me that she'd felt compelled to disregard the instructions for the exercise and do something else instead. The results of trusting her gut were as remarkable as they were valuable.

I'll let her tell you about the experience in her own words below, which she sent me via audio recording. Her teammates' names are replaced by the letters X and Y for confidentiality, and her report is lightly edited for readability.

Desi's experience during the heart rate telepathy exercise:

When we were doing our partnered meditation, X and I were outside [as senders], and we were sending energy into Y. So, I relaxed and got myself into a meditative state and focused on Y.

I felt a really strong connection between her, me, and X. But when I went into sort of that meditative state, I felt this really strong, overwhelming sense that I needed to send her healing. It felt like it was coming from maybe her sons. That's what I was picking up on. And so, I just focused on sending loving, healing energy, sort of like sending her a lot of white light.

I knew I was supposed to be doing the exercise, but it was such a strong, overwhelming feeling that I just went with it. And then after a little while, I felt like I had done what I was supposed to do, and then I was able to focus on the exercise. And so, I did that.

But when we walked in the room, the very first thing she said to X and me was, "Which one of you was sending me healing?" And I was like, "Oh, that was me." So, she knew instantly that I had been sending healing and not doing the exercise.

It was really validating for me because I knew I wasn't doing what I was supposed to be doing, but I felt like I was doing what I was supposed to do from the point of view of what Y needed.

And it was just really awesome to have that be the first thing she said, like, nothing about the exercise, just, "Which one of you was sending the healing?" It was really nice to know that she had felt it, and I hugged her and everything. So anyway, that's the story.

* * * *

This was a spontaneous telepathic occurrence, but it also produced more *meaning* than the pre-planned exercise. Perhaps the Great Mystery had a hand in it?

Top: One of the oxygen and pulse trackers used by the receivers while lying down.

Bottom: A screen-capture of the app while recording the input from the tracker. The app's readout differs from the tracker because the photos were taken at different times. The monitors periodically hand-recorded the app's readout on their tracking sheets for me to convert into charts afterward.

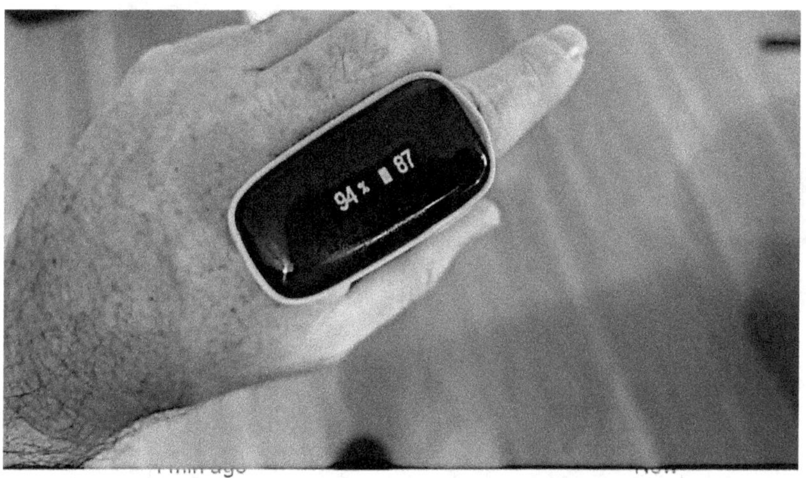

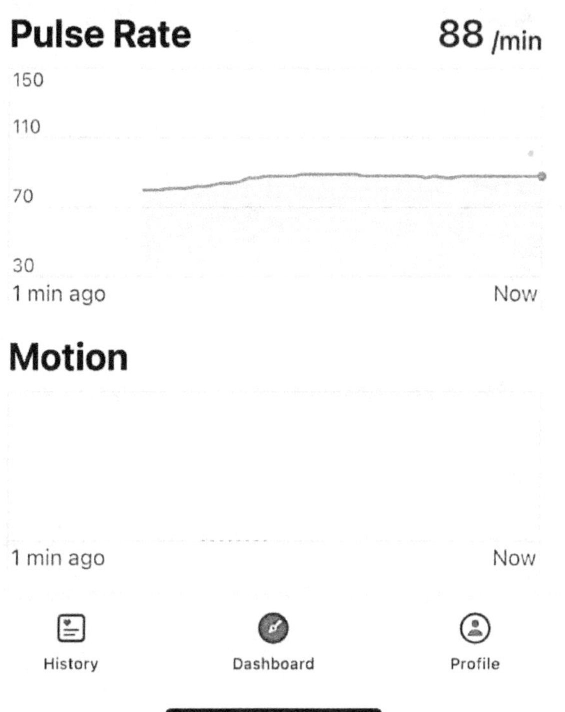

Below: Monitors sit by their receivers, who are lying down to prepare for the exercise. The senders are situated outside the room and will work in pairs to raise and lower their receiver's heart rate when signaled by the author.

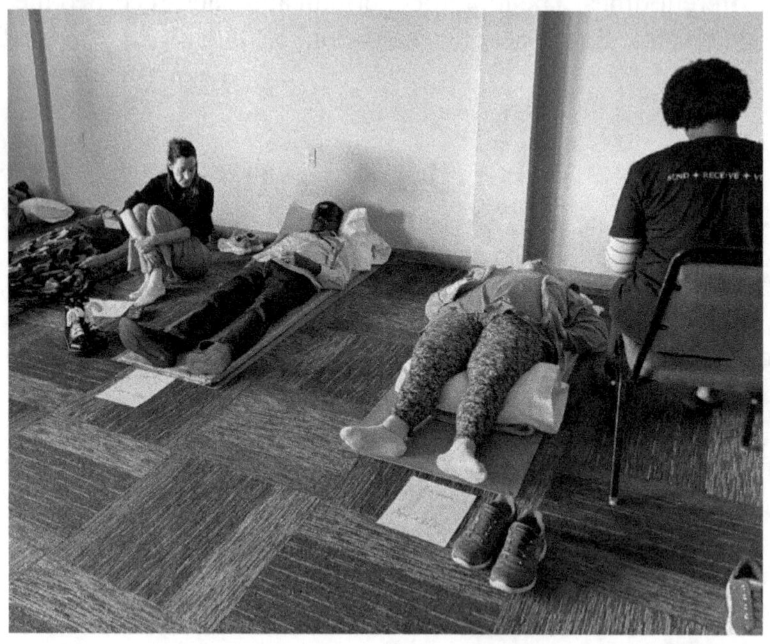

Stimulus-narrative for receiver *Power of Love*

Ages 11-17, Martial arts, wearing a Karate gi (uniform), at the dojo. Students were practicing hitting bags, performing katas, practicing self-defense moves with others, or engaging in kumite (simulated combat).

See footnote for photo credits.[57]

[57] Top photo by Jjskarate https://commons.wikimedia.org/wiki/File:JJS_Karate_Kids_on_Training.jpg.

Bottom photo by Jjskarate https://commons.wikimedia.org/wiki/File:JJS_Karate_Kids.jpg

Monitor's Chart for receiver *Power of Love*

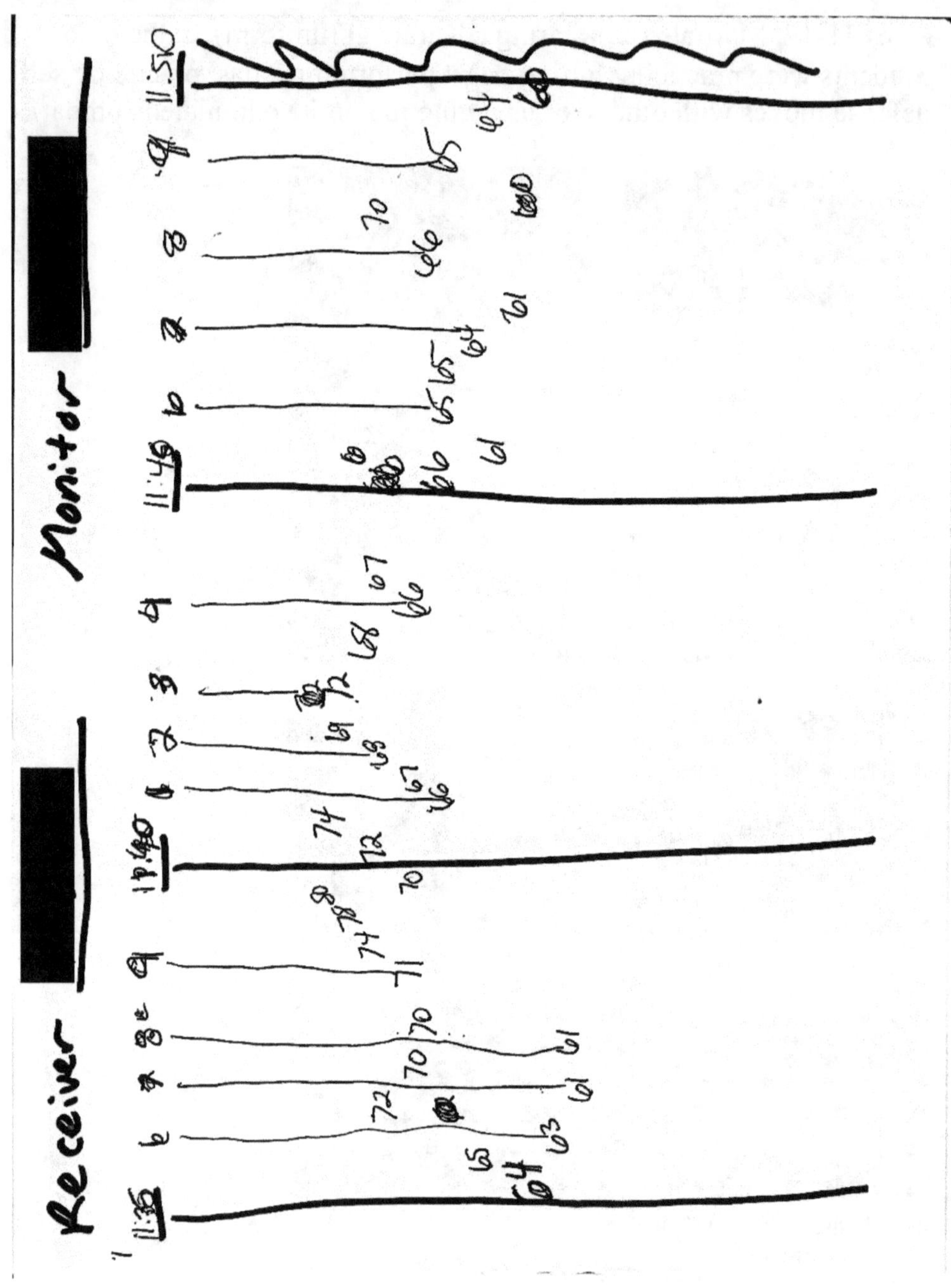

Normal chart for receiver Power of Love

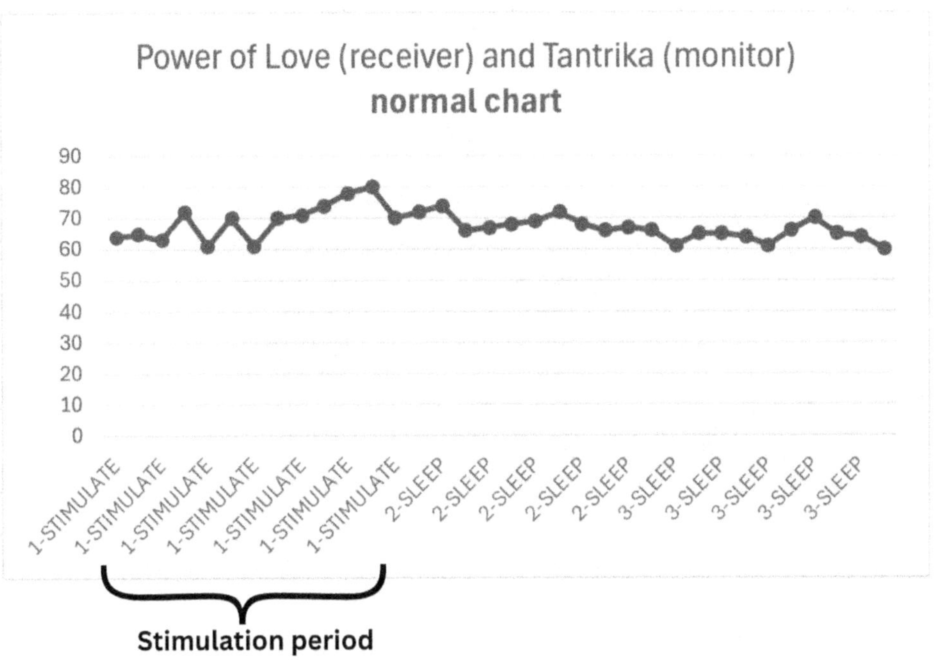

Exaggerated chart for receiver Power of Love

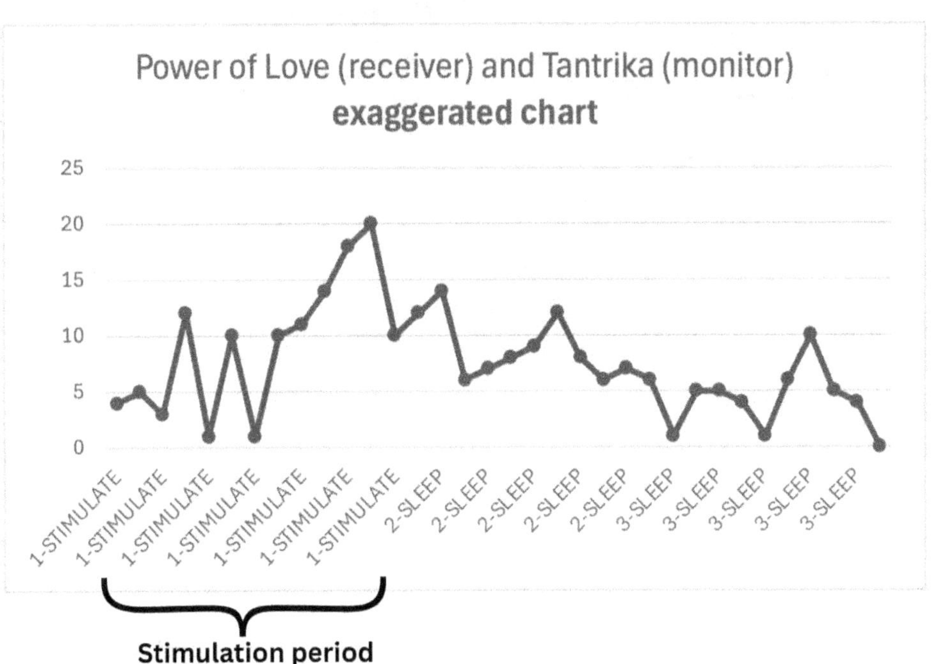

Stimulus-narrative for receiver *Force of Water*

Whitewater rafting the grand canyon, Wearing lifejackets, dry suits, helmets, shorts and sun shirts, fun costumes, Typical scene is tall red rock walls, warm sunshine, large whitewater rapids, multiple rafts, cooking meals on sandy beaches, laughter, campfires.

See footnote for photo credits.[58]

---

[58] Top photo by Costaricapro
https://commons.wikimedia.org/wiki/File:White_Water_Rafting_Costa_Rica.jpg

Bottom photo by https://www.flickr.com/photos/simplysahil5/
https://commons.wikimedia.org/wiki/File:A_camp_site_by_the_Ganga,_Rishikesh.jpg

Monitor's chart for receiver *Force of Water*

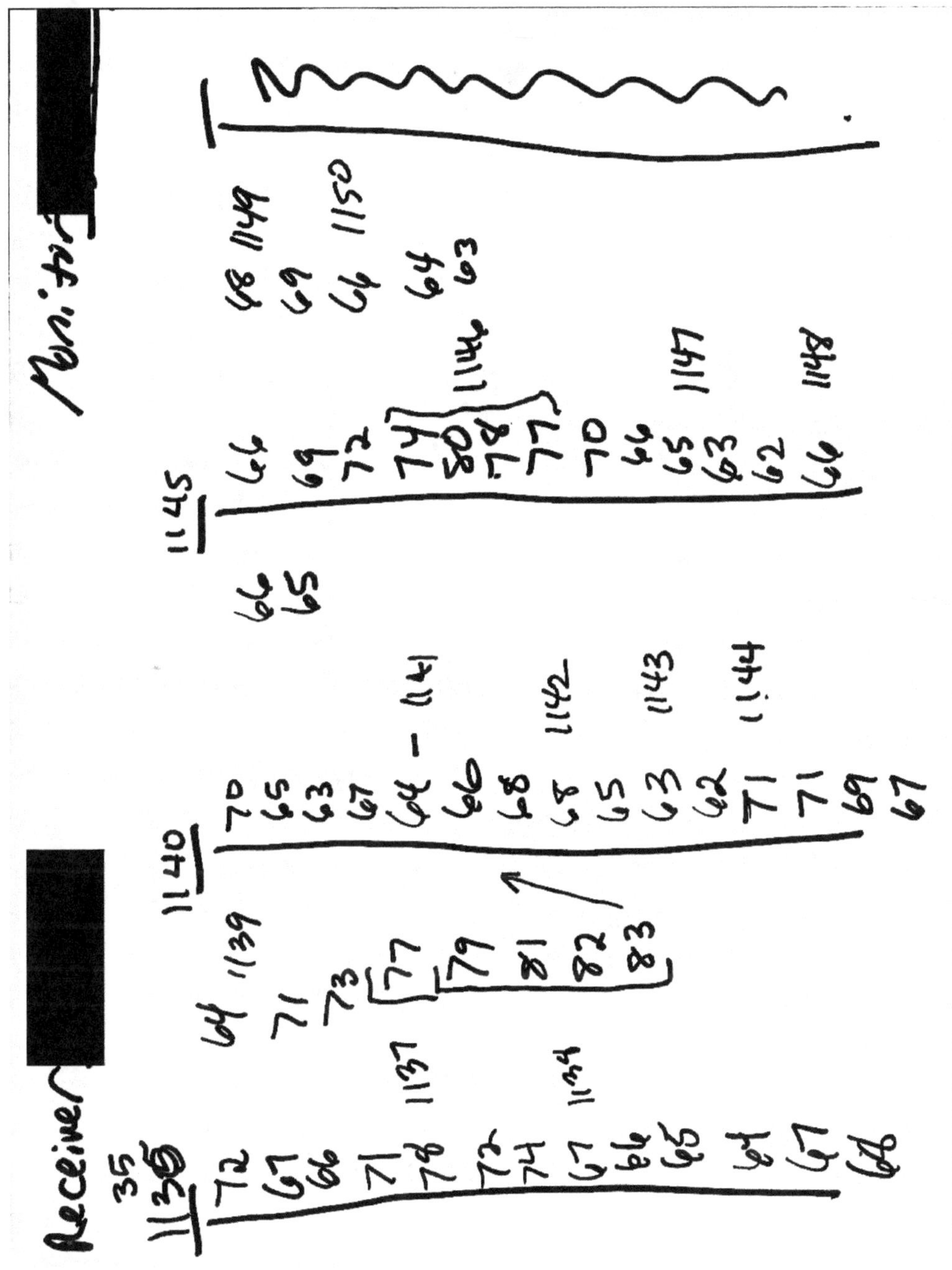

Normal chart for receiver Force of Water

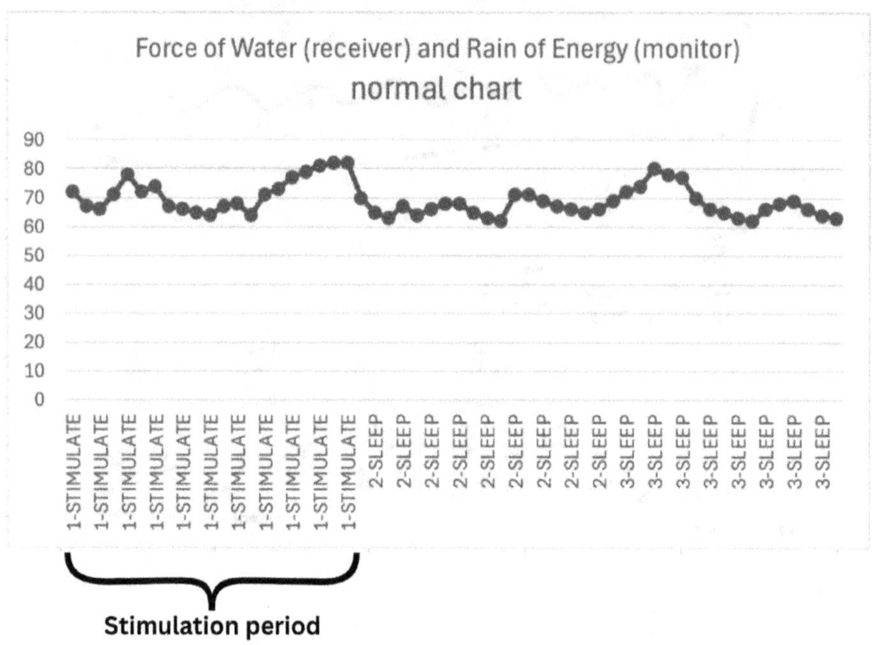

Exaggerated Chart for Receiver Force of Water

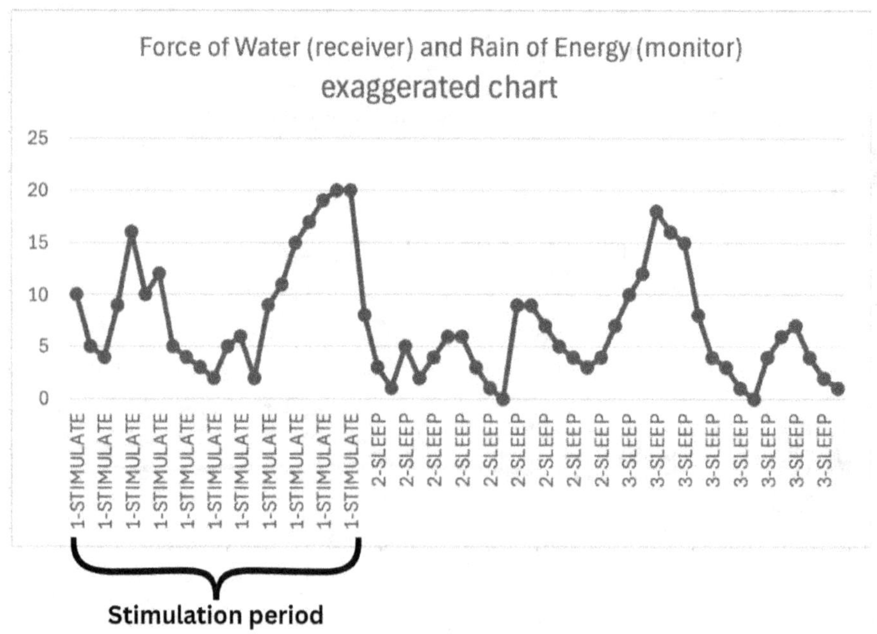

Stimulus-narrative for receiver *Synchronicity*

This activity took place in January of 2005. I was 38 years old. I took my athletes to a Gymnastics meet in Cancun, Mexico. We stayed for almost a week. At the meet, I had a white jacket and black pants. The gymnastics meet was held in a large ballroom. During the awards ceremony, my team won first place, and I was called up and a black and gold sombrero was placed on my head. My team stood behind me on the awards podium holding a large gold colored Mayan Calendar as the 1st place award.

See footnote for photo credits.[59]

[59] Top photo by David Jones
https://commons.wikimedia.org/wiki/File:Olympic_women%27s_individual_all-around_artistic_gymnastics_medal_ceremony_(2).jpg

Bottom photo by Martin Rulsch
https://commons.wikimedia.org/wiki/File:2018-10-13_Gymnastics_at_2018_Summer_Youth_Olympics_–_Girls%27_Artistic_Gymnastics_–_Apparatus_finals_–_Uneven_bars_(Martin_Rulsch)_187.jpg

Monitor's chart for receiver *Synchronicity*

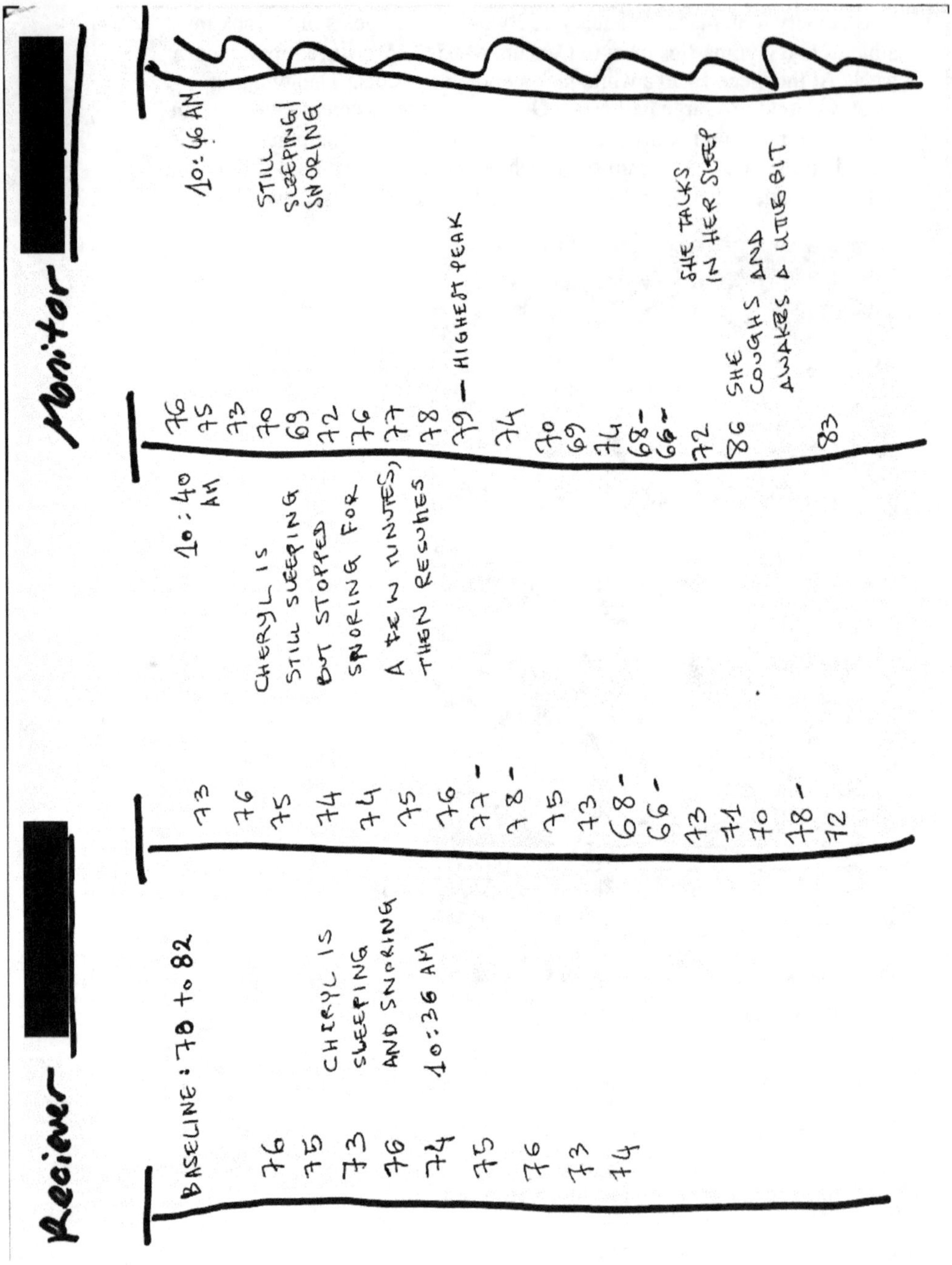

Reciever

BASELINE: 78 to 82

76
75
73
76
74
75
76
73
74

CHERYL IS SLEEPING AND SNORING
10:36 AM

73
76
75
74
74
75
76
77 -
78 -
75
73
68 -
66 -
73
71
70
78 -
72

10:40 AM

CHERYL IS STILL SLEEPING BUT STOPPED SNORING FOR A FEW MINUTES, THEN RESUMES

Monitor

76
75
73
70
69
72
76
77
78
79 — HIGHEST PEAK
74
70
69
74
68 -
66 -
72
86 SHE COUGHS AND AWAKES A LITTLE BIT
83

10:46 AM

STILL SLEEPING/ SNORING

SHE TALKS IN HER SLEEP

Normal chart for receiver Synchronicity

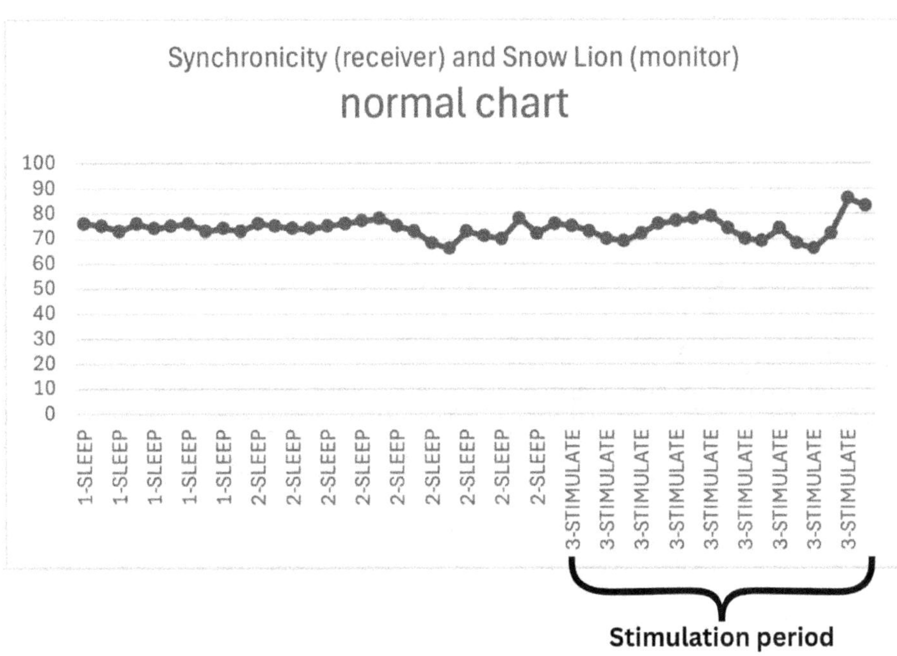

Exaggerated chart for receiver Synchronicity

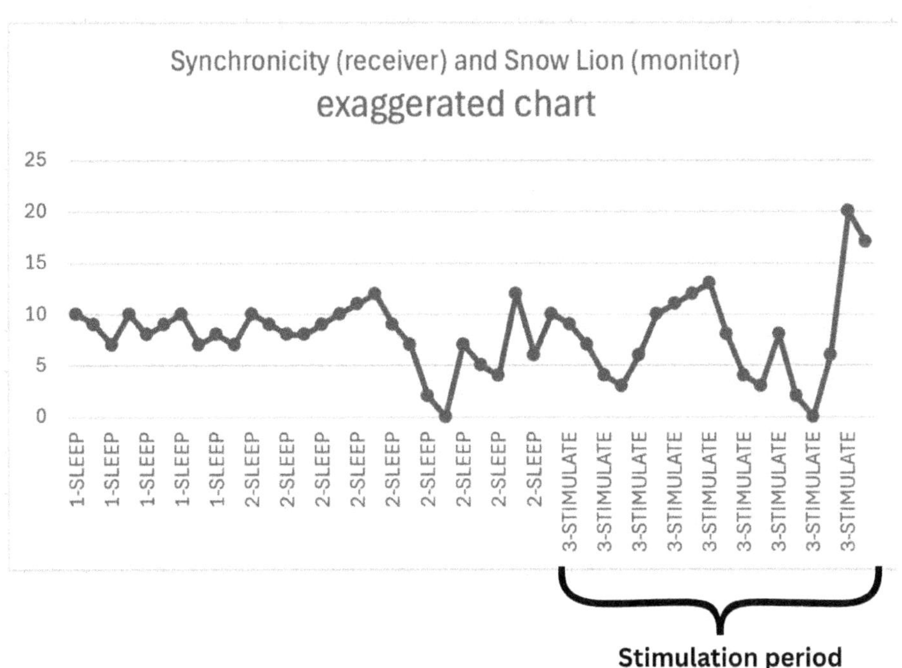

Stimulus-narrative for receiver *Across Dimensions*

Roller coasters and high intensity / adrenaline-oriented activities like bungee jumping. Probably wearing jeans & t-shirt.

See footnote for photo credits.[60]

---

[60] Top photo by Roger Tuttle
https://commons.wikimedia.org/wiki/File:Laughter_Rides_With_Fear_(25189031).jpeg

Middle photo by Thomas Wagner
https://commons.wikimedia.org/wiki/File:VR_Coaster_Train_at_Six_Flags_New_England.jpg

Right photo by Pilarmoret
https://commons.wikimedia.org/wiki/File:Dani_Bungee_Jump.jpg

Monitor's chart for receiver *Across Dimensions*

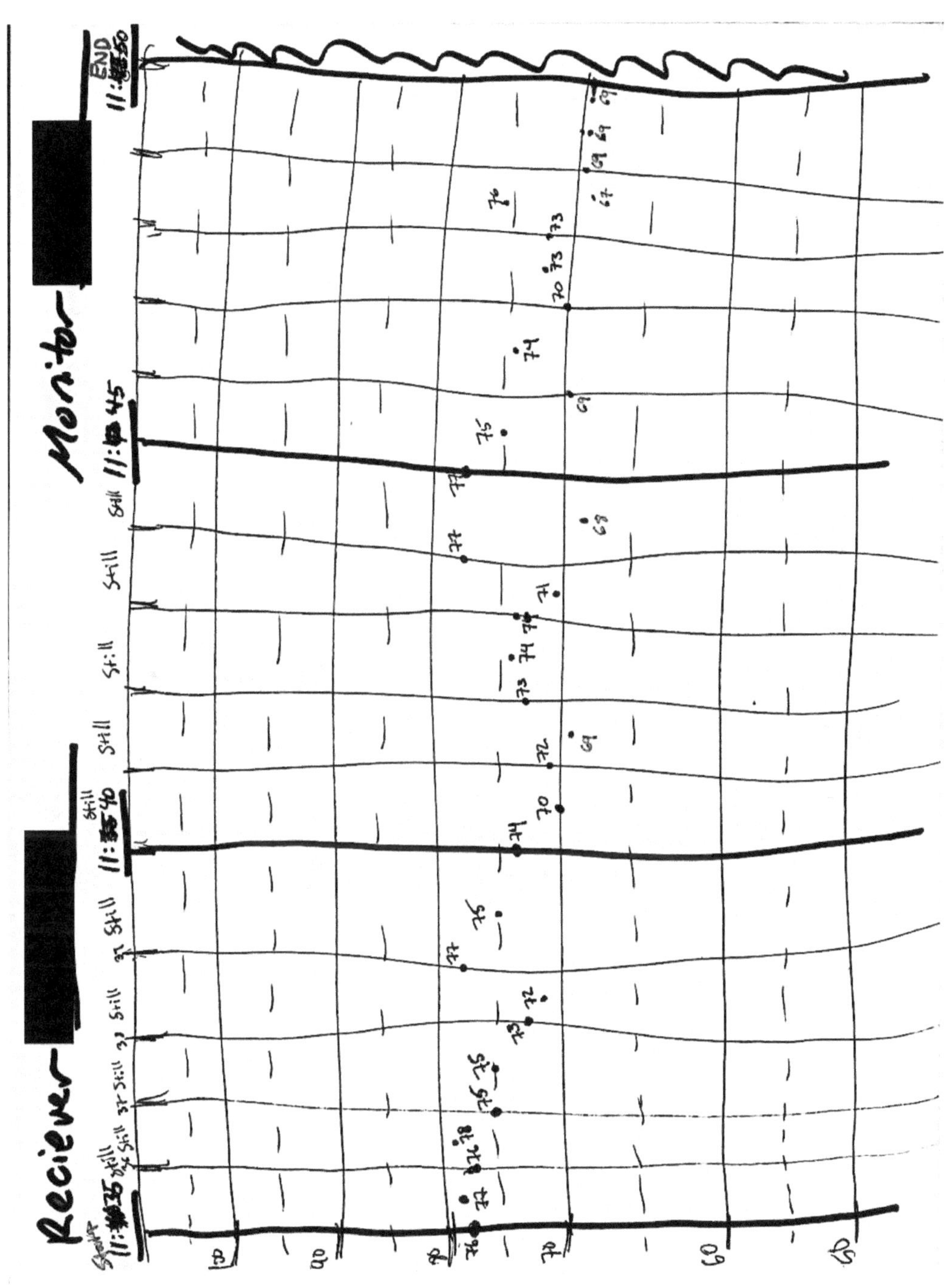

Normal chart for receiver Across Dimensions

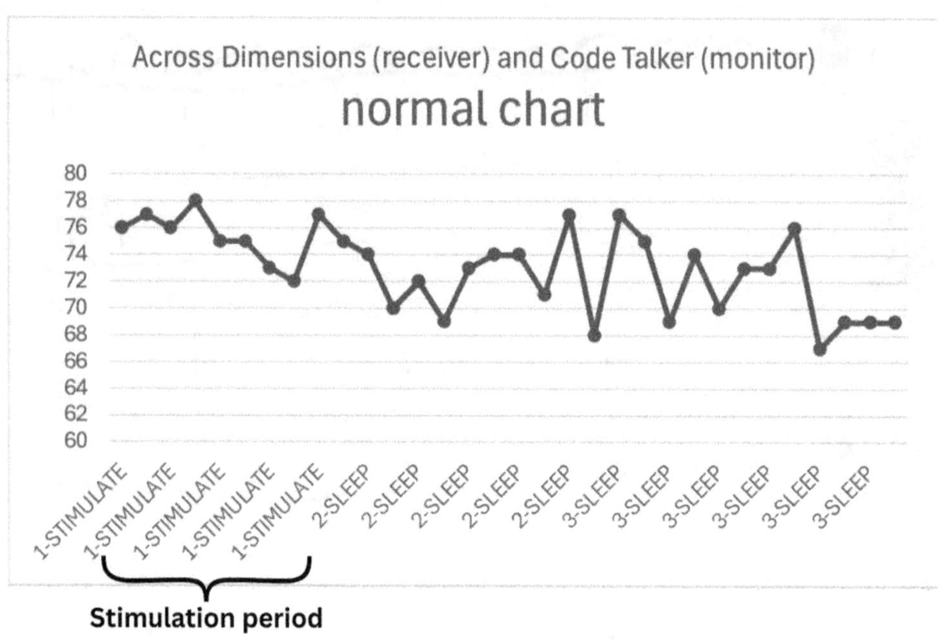

Exaggerated chart for receiver "Across Dimensions"

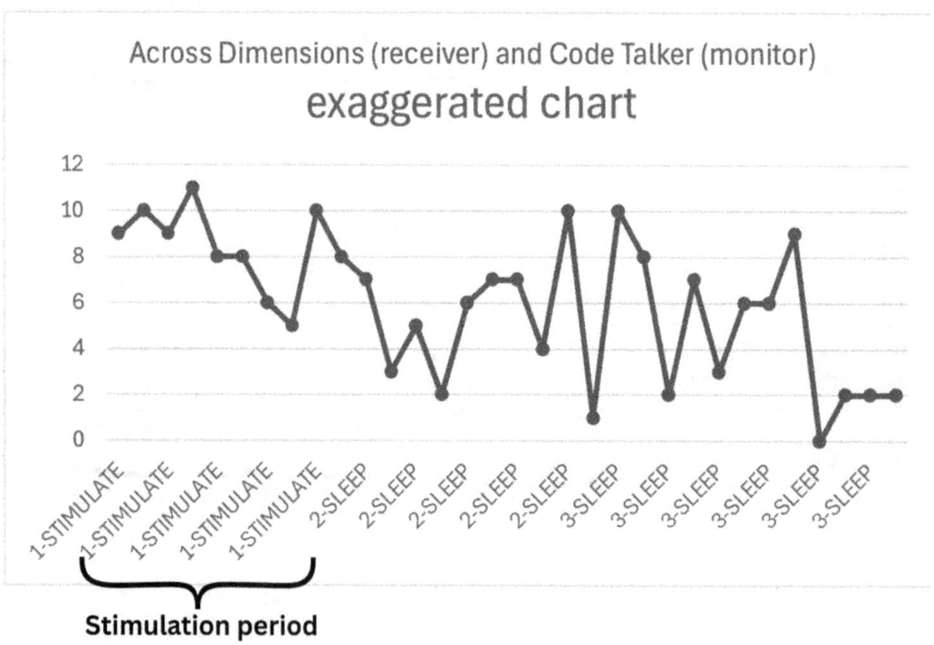

Stimulus-narrative for receiver *Diamond Eyes*

When I was about 12, my father was complaining about how bad our garden looked because there hadn't been rain for a while, and no rain in the forecast for at least a week. So, I decided I would do a rain dance to call forth rain. I recruited my brother and sister to join me in the back yard. We started dancing, whooping it up, going in circles, louder and more intense. After a while, my brother and sister quit on me and left me to dance alone. I continued, building the energy, whipping myself into a frenzy. I stayed out dancing and dancing, UNTIL IT STARTED TO RAIN!!! I was thrilled and felt so empowered!

See footnote for photo credit.[61]

[61] Photo by Niharikaarun https://commons.wikimedia.org/wiki/File:Kidintherain.jpg

Monitor's chart for receiver *Diamond Eyes*

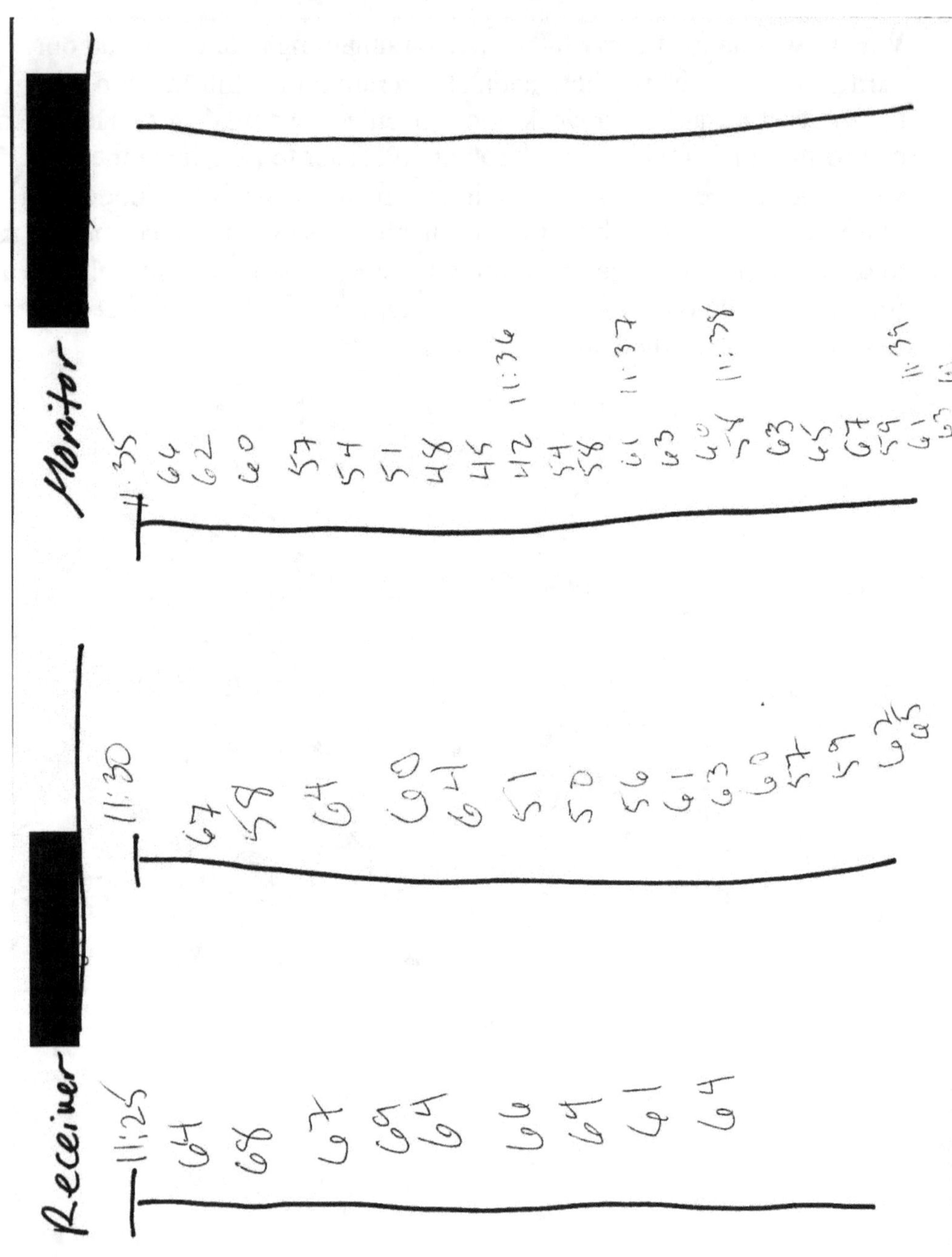

Normal chart for receiver Diamond Eyes

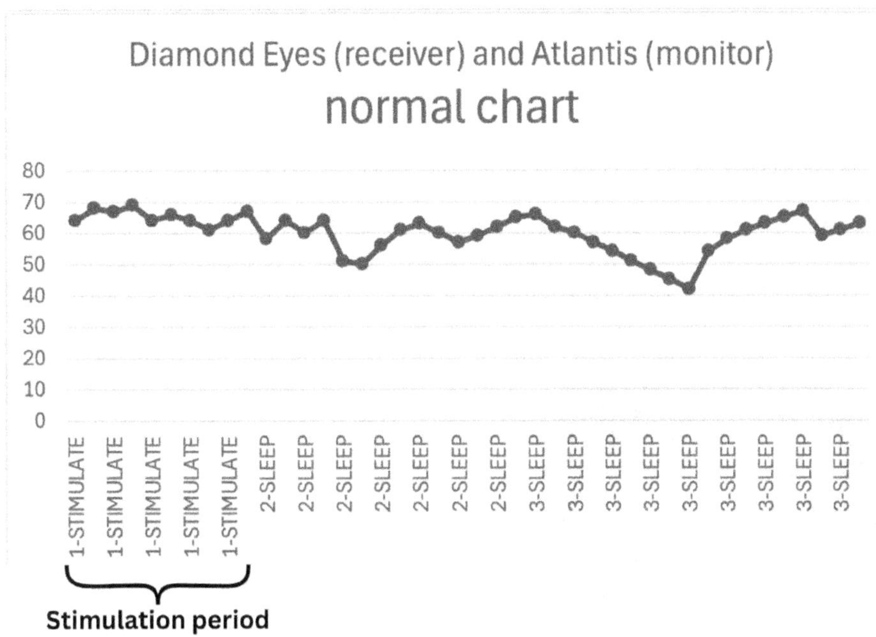

Exaggerated chart for receiver Diamond Eyes

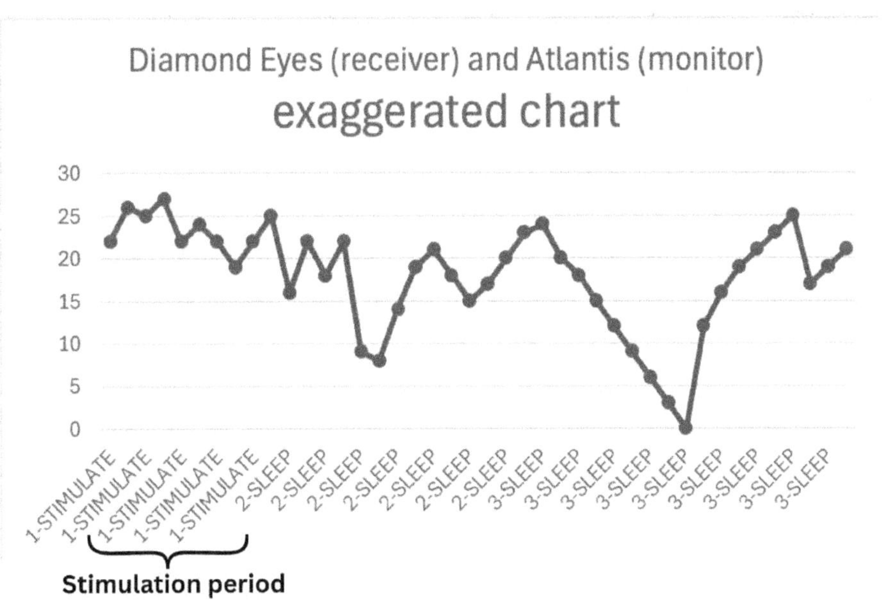

Stimulus-narrative for receiver *Joyful Explorer*

I do a couple of different styles of dance, including West Coast swing and Latin dance forms. I went to Bali for a 10-day dance experience in the fall of 2023. It was intense and amazing. Usually I wear feminine, flowy clothing like a dress or wide-bottom pants and a blouse. I love to couples dance because it allows me to let go and someone else to direct my body movements. I feel like I'm skating or flying and in a life that a lot of times feels like I need to be so in control, this allows me to feel free and trust someone else to care for me and move me.

See footnote for photo credit.[62]

[62] Photo by Sheba_Also 43,000 photos https://commons.wikimedia.org/wiki/File:Ready_to_Latin_Dance-2_(26120105111).jpg

Monitor's tracking chart for receiver *Joyful Explorer*

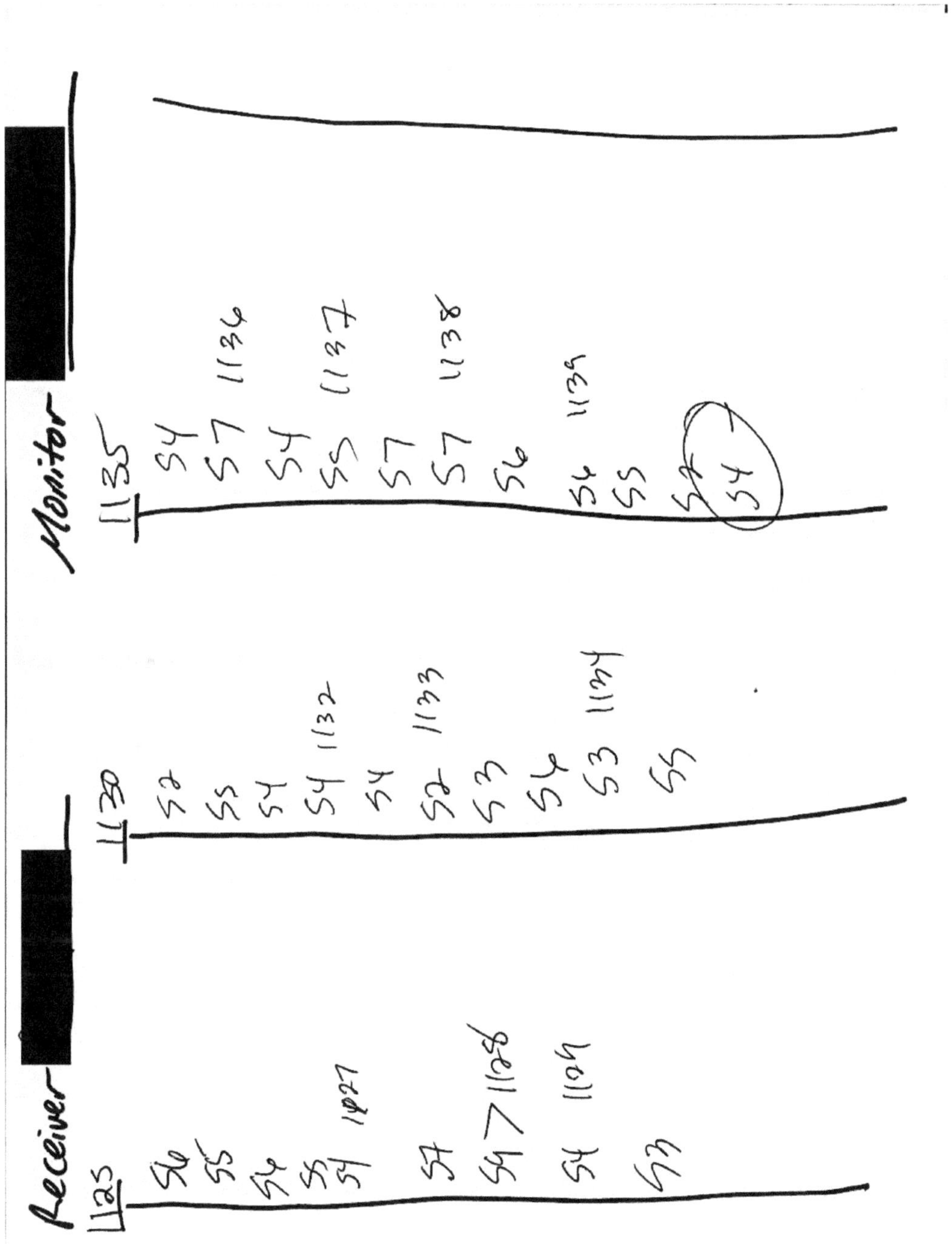

Normal chart for receiver Joyful Explorer

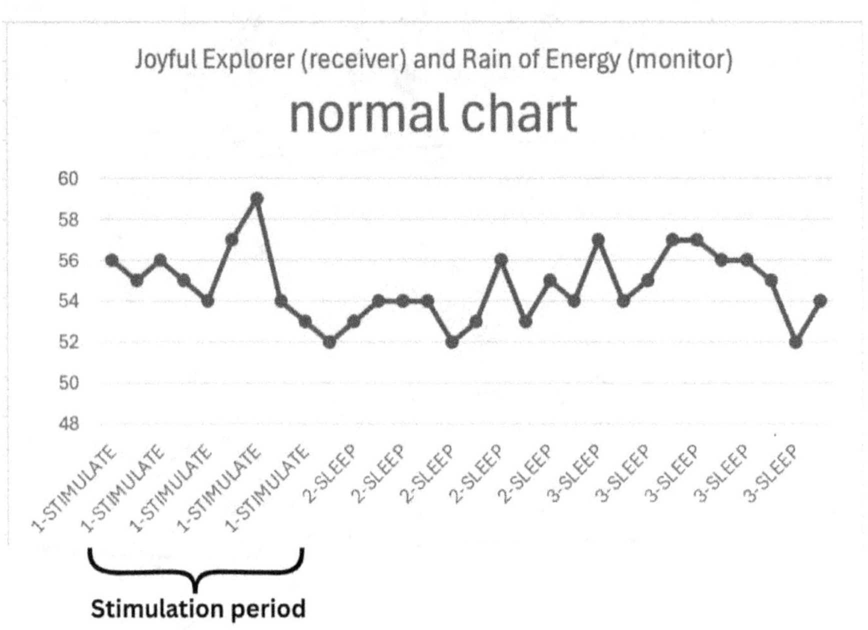

Exaggerated chart for receiver Joyful Explorer

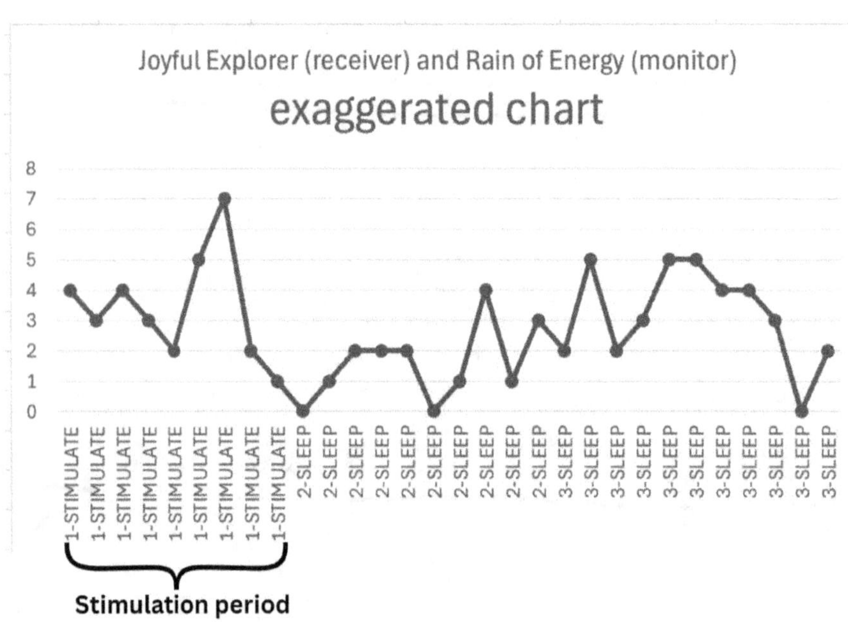

Day 4 - WHAT'S IN THE BOX? #2

This exercise was the same as What's in the Box? #1 from the night before (page 234). Last night's senders were today's receivers, and vice versa. As you'll read in the subtitle for each transcript, the first three transcripts were done by receivers using telepathy from their lodge rooms at the same time the experience was happening downstairs in the meeting room.

The last three transcripts shown here were done by senders who were given time to use *precognition,* seeing into the future, to perceive the experience they were about to have themselves.

I needed to alter the box to contain this evening's experience. I had purchased a large black and white piñata which resembled a zebra. It was too broad and long to fit in the same box I used last time. I decapitated the zebra so the rest could fit inside the box. Along with the decapitated head and body, I included rope and several bubble-wands in the box. I needed to top the box with a second box to conceal everything inside.

The only components to the experience that didn't fit inside the box were the two long, wooden poles with screw eyes in their ends for tying the rope to. I'd kept them hidden all week behind a refrigerator in the corner of the room.

While we set up the piñata scene, including reattaching the zebra's head, I played festive music through the speakers. Participants attached the rope to the poles, suspended the piñata, and took turns beating the hidden lollipops out of it with a stick. Others added to the festive mood by making soap bubbles with their bubble wands.

I recorded the experience on video and played it for the receivers the next morning for their feedback session, after collecting their transcripts. Scenes from the video and participants' transcripts are on the following pages.

Below, the double-box used to store the components for this evening's experience: rope, bubble wands, and a piñata stuffed with lollipops.

* * * * * * * * * * *

Remember, the experience inside the box could've been *anything*.

Above, scenes from the second “What’s in the Box?” experience.

TRANSCRIPT by participant Code Talker

Telepathy/Clairvoyance (done from another room *during* the event)

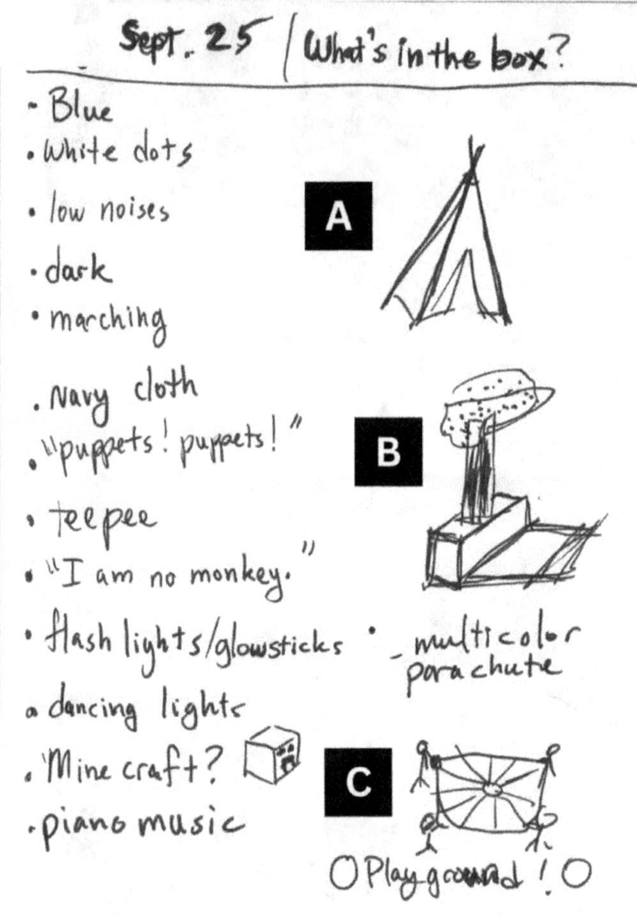

(A) Note that a teepee is a structure supported by poles. The piñata was held aloft by a rope supported by poles.

(B) An object raised up with dots on it, creating a patterned appearance like the zebra piñata.

(C) The playground scene shows people surrounding a central object, like the piñata event. If the scene is interpreted to be people pulling on the edges of a parachute to hold it aloft (which some people have experienced in school settings), the association with the piñata event is even stronger.

TRANSCRIPT by participant Kindness Smiling

Telepathy/Clairvoyance (done from another room *during* the event)

Thursday Night

Colored lights / Music
Movement

Swords Crossing
Sorcery

High Fives End,

The association of swords with the piñata event is strong, given that people took turns striking the piñata with a stick. Participants also grasped the two poles to which the rope was tied. Others were given bubble-wands for blowing soap bubbles.

TRANSCRIPT by participant Insight at Dawn

Telepathy/Clairvoyance (done from another room *during* the event)

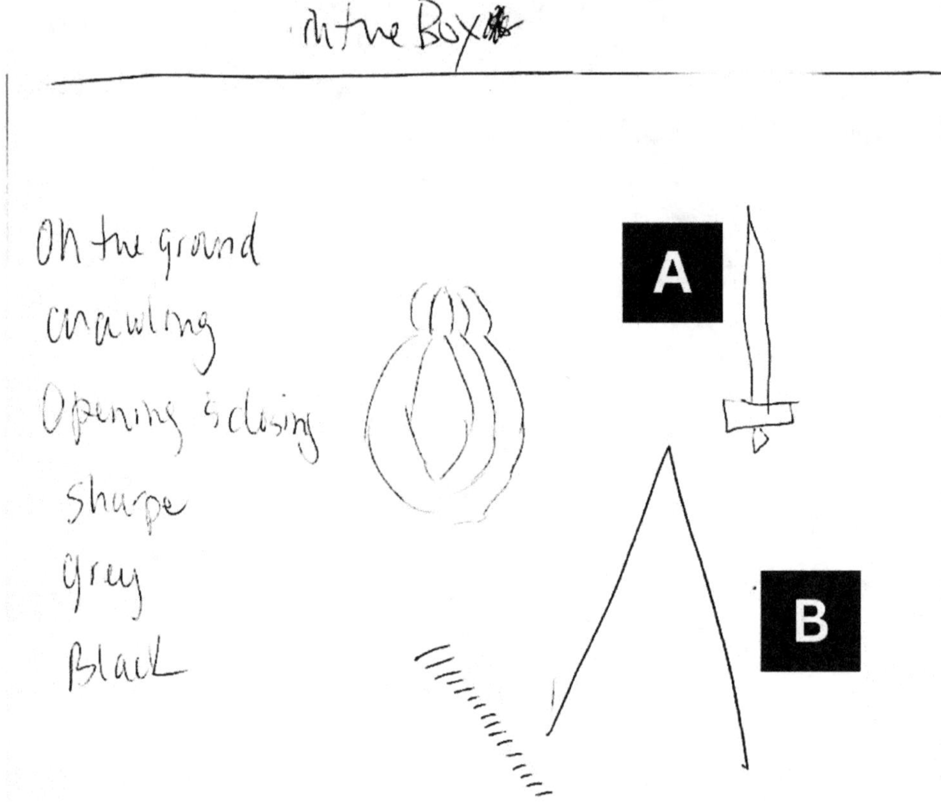

As with the transcript on the previous page, the association of a sword (A) with the piñata event is strong. Or is this the **observed attribute** of contamination by another telepath?

Note the similarity of shape (B) with the teepee in the transcript on page 272 and the "swords crossing" on page 273. This might represent the tension of the rope on the two long poles. It could also be the **observed attribute** of psychic soup.

TRANSCRIPT by participant Joyful Explorer

Telepathy/Clairvoyance (done from another room *during* the event)

What's in the box

Fun
Game
Balls
sticks
Mallets
Tent
Camping
Rolling around on the ground
Patting the back

Ping pong
Raquet
Balls
Ferris Wheel

Accurate descriptors: “fun” “game” “sticks”

Other associative descriptors: “mallets” and “raquet” [racket], as *things one strikes with or swings*. The word “tent” is associative here similarly to “teepee” on page 272, as *things held up by poles*.

TRANSCRIPT by participant Atlantis

Precognition (done in the same room before the box was opened)

What is in the box
In room impression
Musical
Singing
Playing
Twisted
Dice
Mini golf
Corn hole
Hopscotch

Long sticks
Pool Cues
Golf Clubs

Laying Down Hockey sticks

END 8:53

Accurate descriptors: "long sticks"

Other associative descriptors: "mini golf"
"pool cues" "golf clubs" "hockey sticks" – all imply holding a stick.

TRANSCRIPT by participant Sojourner

Precognition (done in the same room before the box was opened)

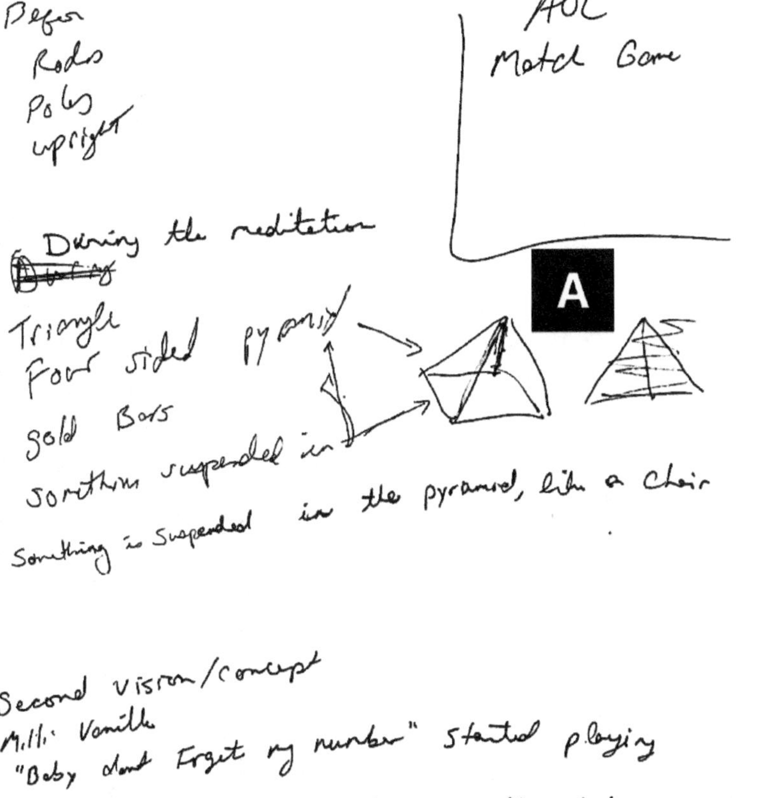

Accurate descriptors: "something suspended in the pyramid"

(A) bears similarity to "camping" and "tent" on the left side of page 275, the triangle on page 274, and the teepee on page 272. Could this be another instance of psychic soup[63]?

[63] Psychic soup is discussed as one of the Observed Attributes of Telepathy on page 79.

TRANSCRIPT by participant Synchronicity

Precognition (done in the room *before* the box was opened)

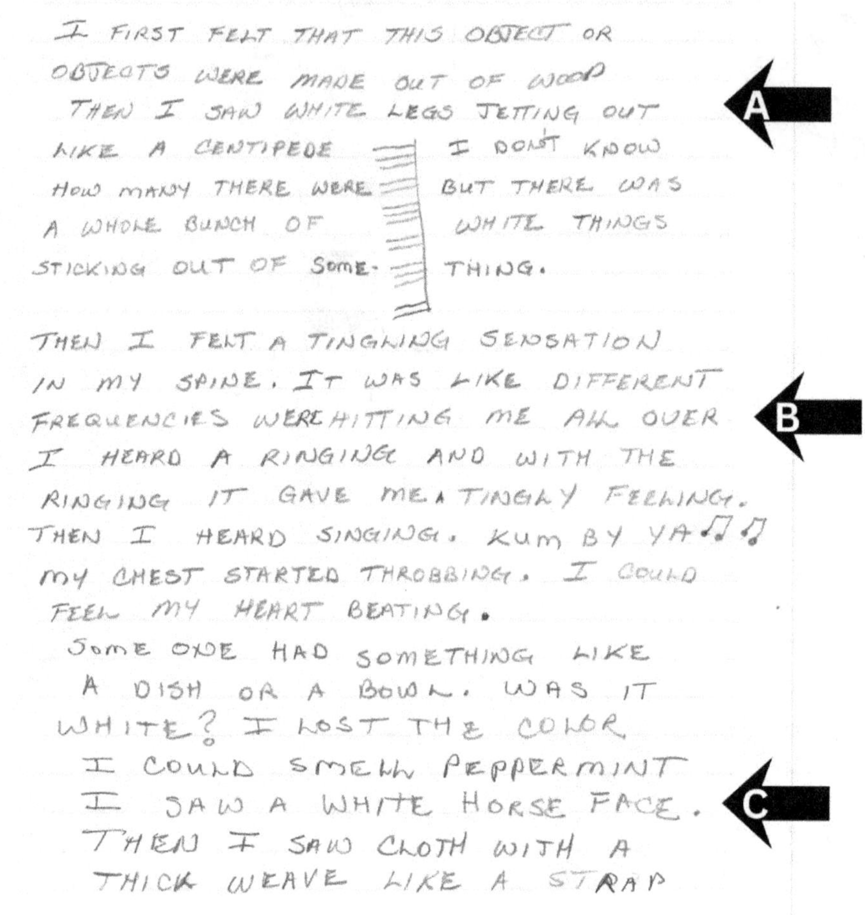
I FIRST FELT THAT THIS OBJECT OR
OBJECTS WERE MADE OUT OF WOOD
THEN I SAW WHITE LEGS JETTING OUT
LIKE A CENTIPEDE I DON'T KNOW
HOW MANY THERE WERE BUT THERE WAS
A WHOLE BUNCH OF WHITE THINGS
STICKING OUT OF SOME- THING.

THEN I FELT A TINGLING SENSATION
IN MY SPINE. IT WAS LIKE DIFFERENT
FREQUENCIES WERE HITTING ME ALL OVER
I HEARD A RINGING AND WITH THE
RINGING IT GAVE ME A TINGLY FEELING.
THEN I HEARD SINGING. KUM BY YA ♫♫
MY CHEST STARTED THROBBING. I COULD
FEEL MY HEART BEATING.
SOME ONE HAD SOMETHING LIKE
A DISH OR A BOWL. WAS IT
WHITE? I LOST THE COLOR
I COULD SMELL PEPPERMINT
I SAW A WHITE HORSE FACE.
THEN I SAW CLOTH WITH A
THICK WEAVE LIKE A STRAP

(A) "Then I saw white legs jetting out" – To hide the piñata in the box, the author had to remove the zebra's head to prevent the legs from "jetting out" of the box. He reattached the head before suspending the piñata by the rope.

(B) "Frequencies were *hitting me all over*"

(C) "I saw a white horse face."

DAY 5 - Team Telepathy with Blinking Shapes

I got the idea of this exercise by reading *Handbook of PSI Discoveries*[64] by Sheila Ostrander and Lynn Schroeder, the same duo who wrote *Psychic Discoveries Behind the Iron Curtain*[65]. *Psychic Discoveries* inspired me greatly when I first began exploring psychic phenomena years ago. I was happy to find a copy of *Handbook* while planning the intensive because it kept my wheels turning at night while I planned the events.

Handbook was published the same year I was born, and I wonder if half a century from now this book will find itself in the hands of a young or even a not-so-young consciousness researcher or teacher. I'll be long gone by then, but if you happen to be that future person reading these words sometime after the year 2075, please know that you were in my thoughts back in 2026. I wish you well on your path and in your efforts to help humanity understand itself. Keep the flame alight.

In *Handbook*, Ostrander and Schoeder report achieving significant results in a telepathy experiment using a *teleflasher*, which the authors write, "is basically a light box with a flashing light inside." The book describes several ways to build a teleflasher. Essentially, it uses a blinking light to make the target appear, then disappear, then appear...target on, target off, target on, target off....to help the sender

[64] Ostrander, S. & Schroeder, L. (1974). *Handbook of PSI Discoveries*. Berkley Publishing Corporation.

[65] Ostrander, S. & Schroeder, L. (1970). *Psychic Discoveries Behind the Iron Curtain*. Prentice Hall.

focus their mind or as they write, "Concentrate and saturate yourself with the target image."

Something about the rhythmically interrupted perception of the target either helped the sender to send, or the receiver to receive, or both.

Instead of using a version of the teleflasher described in *Handbook*, I created a video on my laptop to mimic the blinking appearance for each target and projected the video on the main wall for the senders to see. The target was set to appear for a second, then disappear for a second, then reappear for a second, etc.

The senders' task was to watch the target blinking on and off while holding the intention to send the information to their team's receiver, who sat with their back to the target.

Since the participants were divided into four teams, four receivers sat up front facing their teammates (see the next few photos).

The receivers were given a limited amount of time (it may have been three or four minutes, I can't remember) to decide what that target was. When time was up, each receiver stated their conclusion to the group, with points going to whichever team's receiver was correct.

After that round, another receiver from each team would replace the previous one, and the process was repeated with another shape. Since I randomly chose the shapes, there was always a chance the same shape would be projected twice in a row, if not more. It was not unusual for more than one receiver to correctly determine the shape.

To do this at home, it can be as simple as having a volunteer stand behind the receivers, holding a paper version of the target shape for the senders to see. The senders can simply blink their eyes in one-second periods to reproduce the effect.

Below, receivers with blinking target (circle) projected behind them.

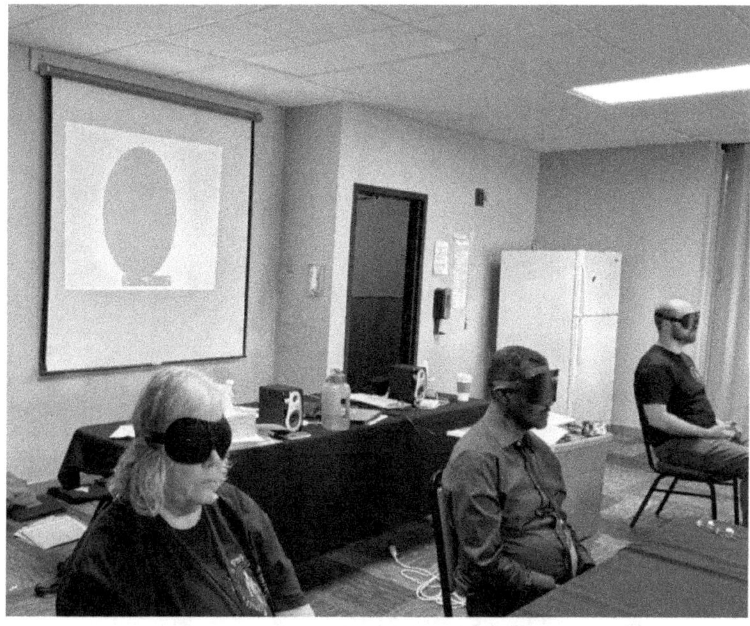

Below, a sender intensifies her perception by drawing the outline of the square in the air, hoping to assist her teammate to perceive the shape projected from her mind.

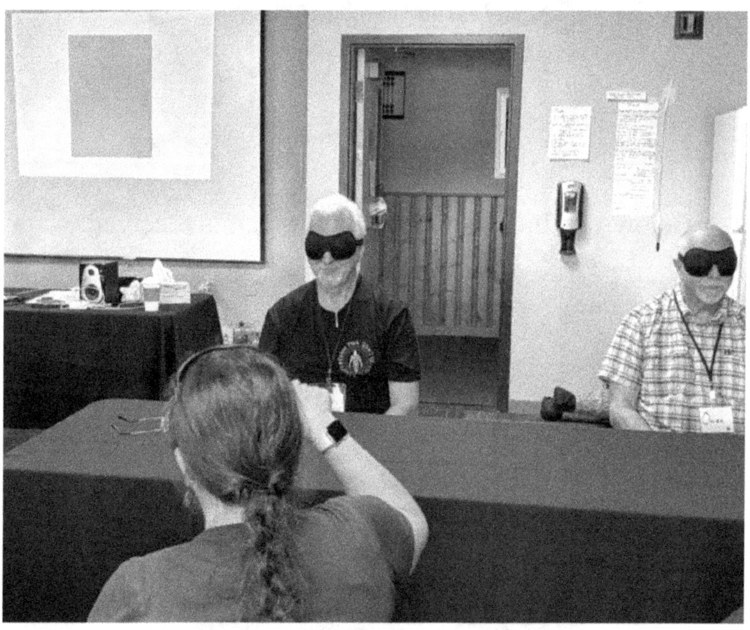

Below, receivers work the triangle target.

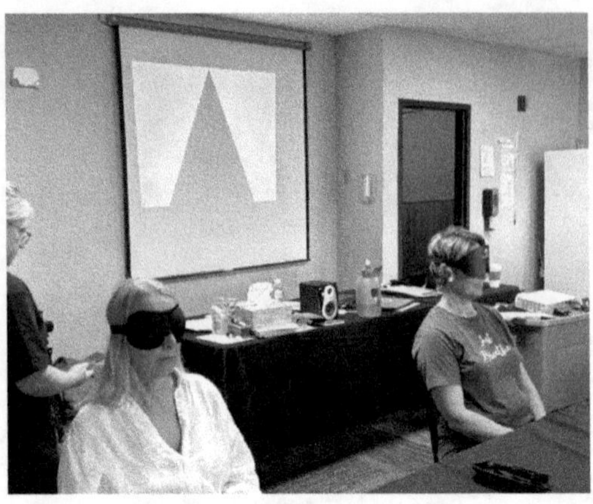

Below, senders silently intensify their efforts by making the shape of the target (circle) with their hands.

Below, sending "square" to their team's receiver.

DAY 5 - Team Telepathy with Color-Matching Abacus Test

Those who've read my other book *Dewdrops of Infinity*[66] will be familiar with the Matching Abacus Test (MAT). There, I credited Andrija Puharich and his book *The Sacred Mushroom*[67] for the idea. In it, he described experiments which in a psychic was seated at a table with two rows containing the same cards on it. The psychic's task was to rearrange the top row of cards to match the order of cards in the bottom row while blindfolded.

During my experiments for *Dewdrops of Infinity*, participants had to match two rows containing six cards each. Instead of playing cards, though, they used Tarot cards. I thought the complex and intense meaning of each card would give the participants' minds more associations to connect with in the psychic space. In those experiments, they performed simple clairvoyance since they were working alone.

They shuffled the cards while blindfolded, then used their sensitivity to rearrange the rows. Once complete, they would remove their mask and record their scores as part of the study. Their results are included in *Dewdrops*.

But for the 2025 intensive, this would be an exercise in telepathy as well as clairvoyance. For speed and simplicity, I decided

---

[66] McNamara, S. (2023). *Dewdrops of Infinity: Psychedelics, Psychic Abilities, UFOs, and The Puharich Project COLOR EDITION.* Mind Possible.

[67] Puharich, A. (1974). *The Sacred Mushroom: Key to the Door of Eternity*. Doubleday and Company, Inc.

to use two rows of three papers, each a different color. The colors were red, yellow, and blue. You can see a color photo of the setup on the back cover of this book.

Each receiver was seated at their table at the front. Once they were all blindfolded, their rows of colored paper were ordered in the same way as the other receivers' rows to avoid the idea of unfair advantage. I don't really think it mattered whether their initial rows looked the same because the receivers still needed to accurately determine the paper color while blindfolded. So, starting positions shouldn't have made a difference.

The receivers were given three or four minutes (again, I don't remember exactly) to perceive their papers via clairvoyance as well as telepathy, since their teammates were in full view of their table. As the receivers hovered their hands over the papers, picking them up and rearranging them, their teammates attempted to encourage and discourage their decisions with telepathy.

When time was up, the receivers removed their blindfolds to see if they successfully matched their top row to their bottom one.

This is one of the easiest psychic games to set up at home and can be done by taking turns with a partner or done with several people in teams using a timer, as was done during the intensive.

Below, senders attempt to influence their receiver-teammates in rearranging their colored papers correctly.

Below, the receiver has matched her left-most papers of her top and bottom rows. *One minute left, keep going!*

Below, the receiver on the left had a complete match of both rows.

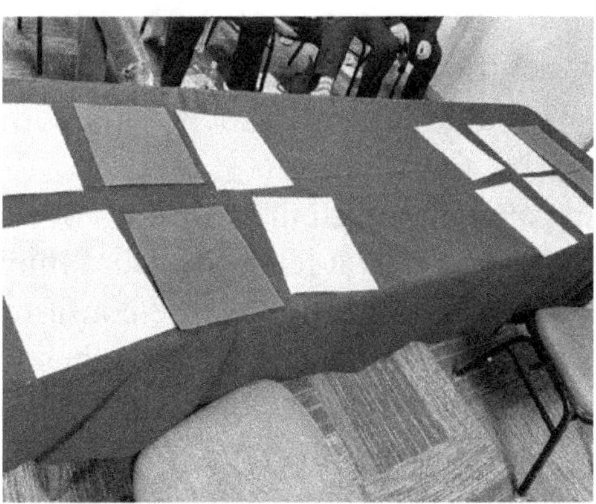

DAY 5 – TEAM TELEPATHY WITH LINE DRAWINGS

We finish our exploration of the participants' psychic development by reviewing their results of an exercise like the one they began the intensive with: line drawings. The targets were different from those used several days before. The procedure also differed since this was a team-style exercise.

Like the other team-style events, each of the four teams designated one receiver per round. Each receiver stood facing their own whiteboard. They were not permitted to turn their heads and look around since the target image was being projected on the wall behind them. And of course, they were not to look at another receiver's whiteboard.

They were to receive impressions about the target from their teammates, who could clearly see the target in front of them. If they wanted to, the senders (their teammates) could draw the target on their own paper and trace over the lines as I did for them on the first day. Or they could simply concentrate on the image and use intention to send it to their team's receiver.

Each round lasted four minutes. At the end of each round, Desi, who generously volunteered to help me, and I judged the whiteboard transcripts. The team of the receiver whose transcript was most associated with the target received a point for that round. In several rounds, it was difficult to choose a single winner because different transcripts revealed strong associations with the target but used different associative features.

Whether participants improved their abilities over the week may be difficult to determine based on only a few tests. But I think they did. And it's clear to me that their transcripts for this exercise confirmed their use of telepathy. You should form your own opinion, though, so please review them carefully. Enjoy them as if they were a fine dessert served at the end of a delicious feast.

Teammates (to the left) draw the target they're shown on the projector screen on their own paper to help them *send* the target to the receivers (to the right) who use whiteboards against the wall as their transcripts.

Close-up of the receivers working the target as teammates look on silently.

The author and Desi were the judges. Here, they compare the target image on the projector screen to the whiteboard transcripts.

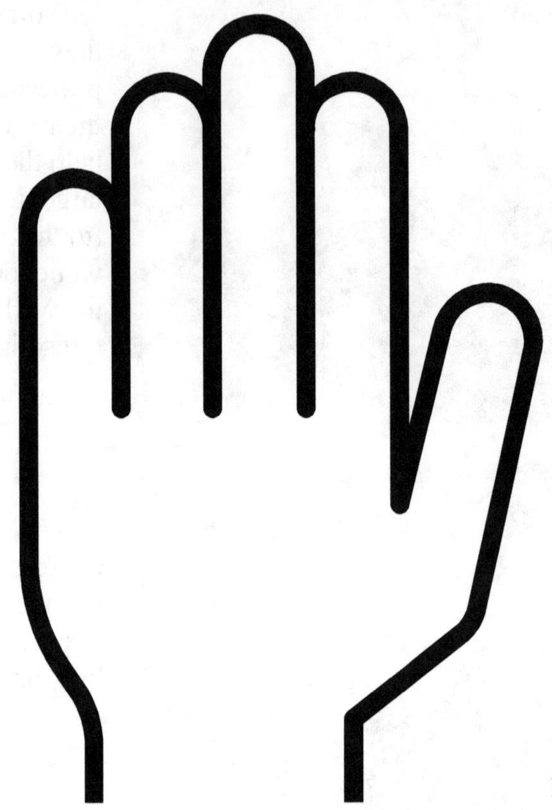

Target: Hand

Associative features:

- rounded top, or bumps
- multiple things coming out of a central thing
- upward directionality indicated by vertical lines

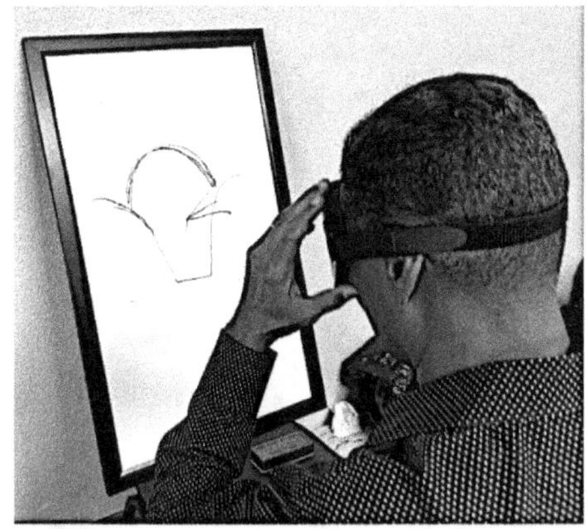

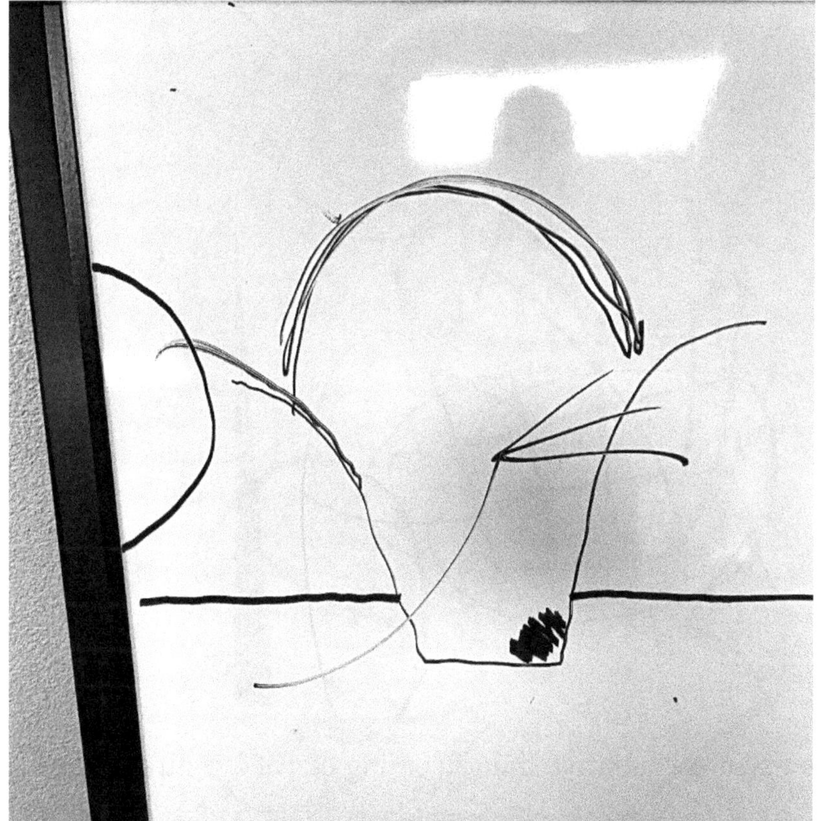

Associative feature: "rounded top, or bumps"

Try this - Hold your hand up with the back of the hand facing you about 10 inches (25.4 cm) away, fingers touching each other. Focus on the tops of the middle three fingers, including the fingernails. Now, look at the transcript again. Do you see the similarity?

Associative feature: "multiple things coming out of a central thing"

Associative feature: "upward directionality indicated by vertical lines"

Could the mind have associated the circle with the "roundedness" of the fingertips or of a hand's palm?

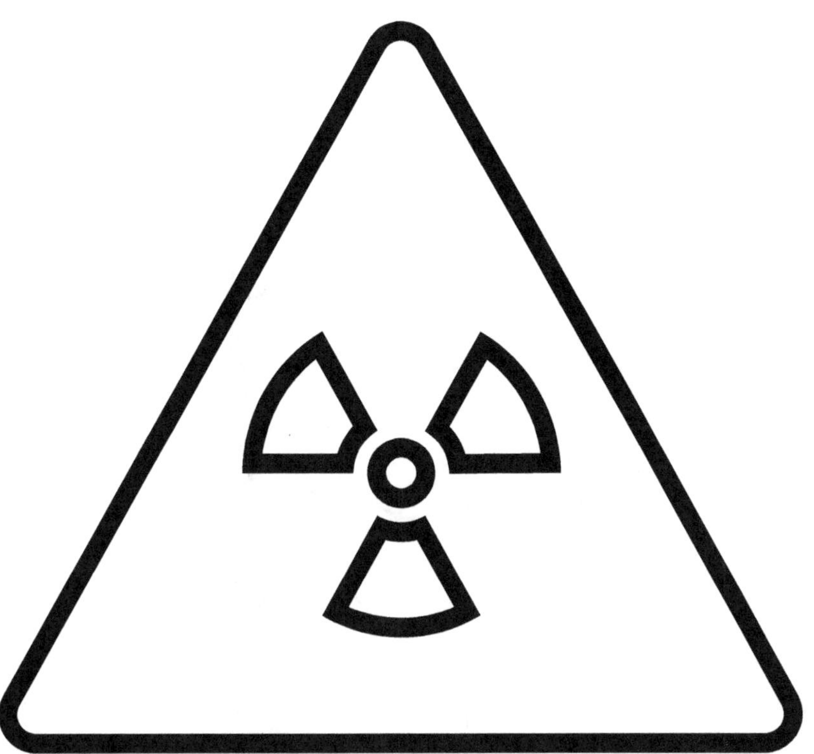

Target: Radiation symbol

Associative Features:

- main shape is triangular
- triangle contains shapes inside it
- the most central shape is a circle
- 3 shapes surround the circle
- the interior shapes seem like they could be moving toward contact, but they do not make contact

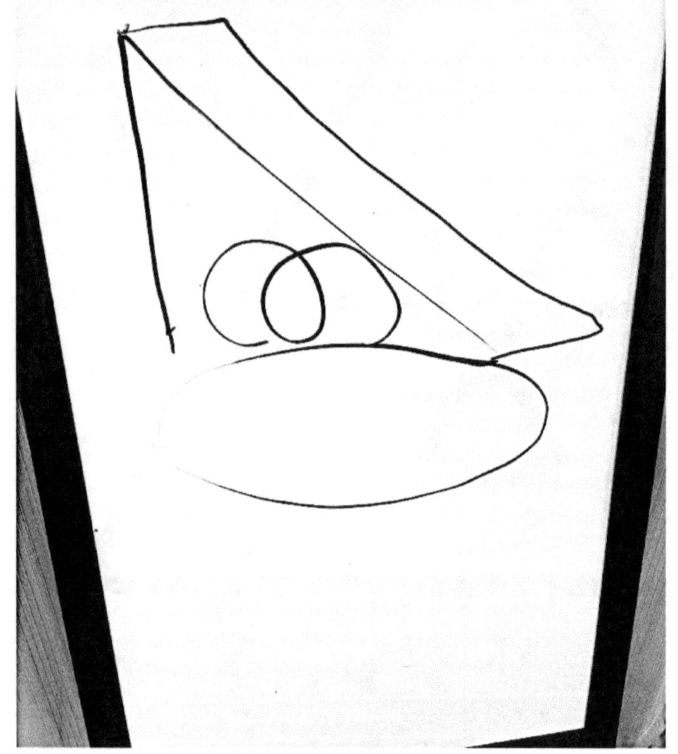

Associative feature: "main shape is triangular"

Associative feature: "triangle contains shapes inside it"

Associative feature: the most central shape is a circle"

How many circles/ovals/curved shapes do you see in the transcript and the target?

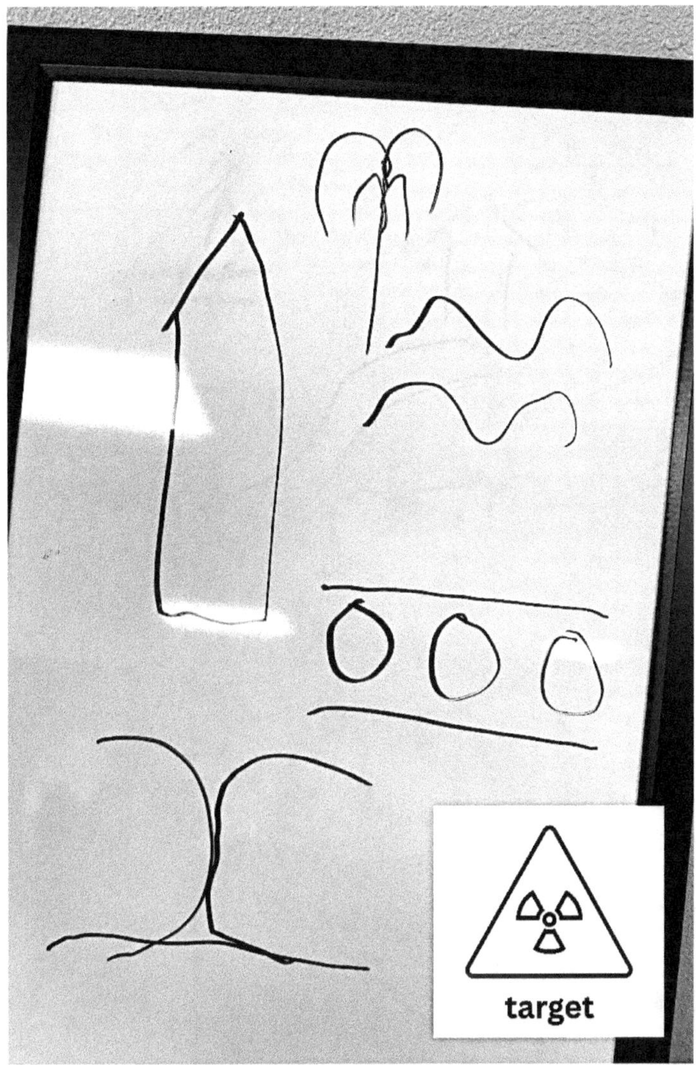

Associative feature: "3 shapes surround the circle" – Here we see three circles inside parallel lines. Did the mind combine the count of 3 with the concept of "circle" to produce this interpretation?

Associative feature: "the interior shapes seem like they could be moving toward contact, but they do not make contact" – The shapes at the very bottom convey this feeling of *almost touching*.

Do you see a triangular top in the shape to the upper-left?

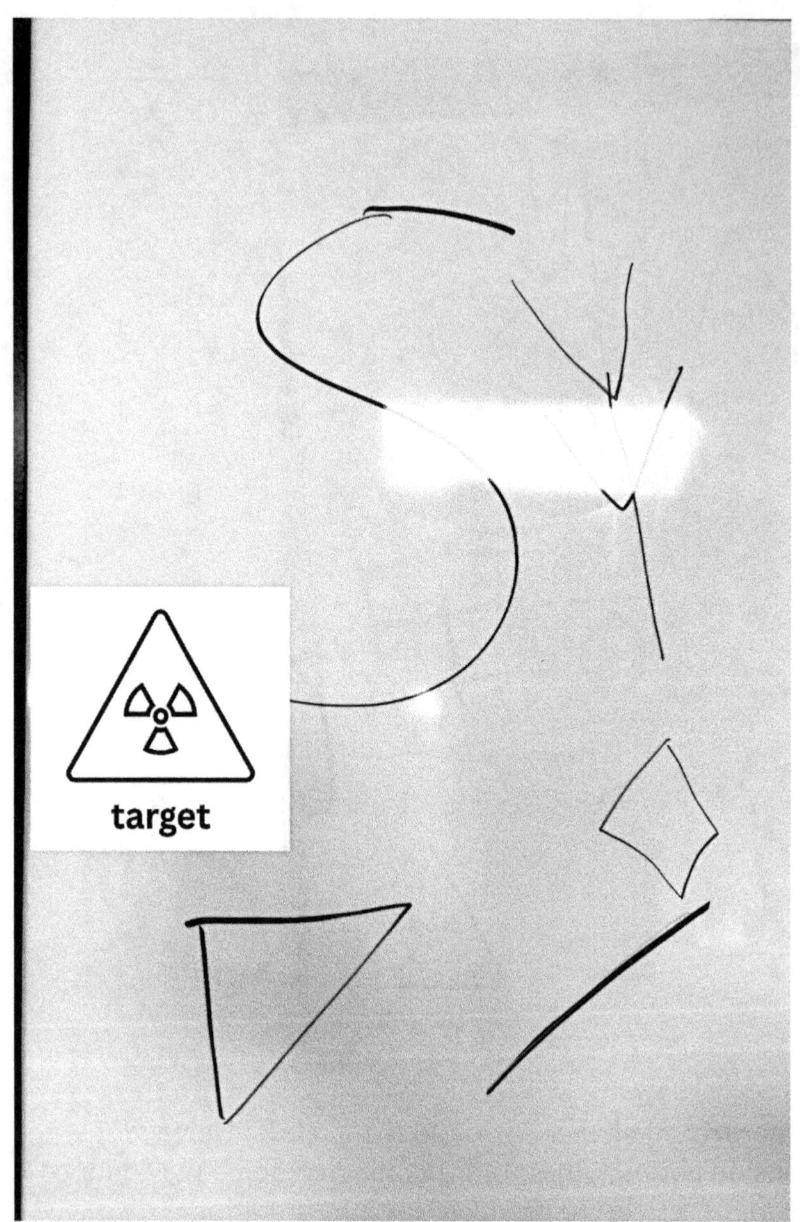

Associative feature: “main shape is triangular” – There is one whole triangle here. How many partial triangles do you see in addition?

Target: Rainbow and two clouds

Associative Features:

- the rainbow is composed of 3 lines
- the lines are parallel
- the lines are in the shape of curves
- both ends of the curves move in a downward direction on either side of the central, and highest, point of each line
- the clouds are mostly composed of curves, conveying a feeling of *roundedness*
- there are multiple (2) clouds (the *rounded* shapes)
- the clouds are *beneath* the central shape (the rainbow)

Associative feature: "the lines are parallel"

Associative feature: "both ends of the curves move in a downward direction on either side of the central, and highest, point of each line"

Associative feature: "the clouds are mostly composed of curves, conveying a feeling of *roundedness*"

Associative feature: "the clouds are *beneath* the central shape (the rainbow)"

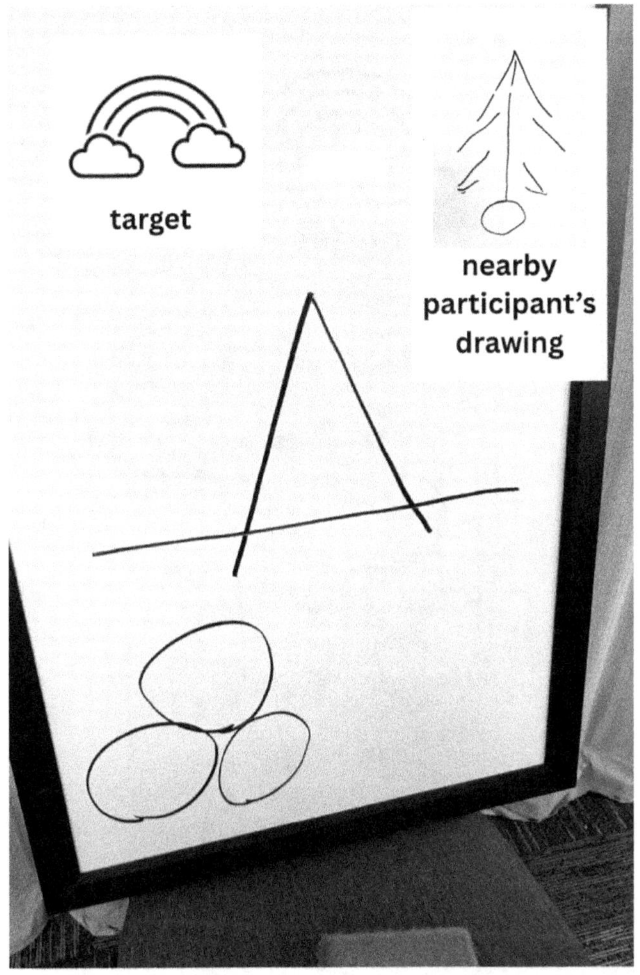

Associative feature: "there are *multiple* (2) clouds (the *rounded* shapes)" – 3 instead of 2 in the transcript.

Associative feature: "both ends of the curves move in a downward direction on either side of the central, and highest, point of each line" – The mind may have translated the curve of the rainbow into the large, central, angular shape in the transcript.

Observed attribute: Psychic soup. Compare the circles with the one on the previous page as well as the one on the next page.

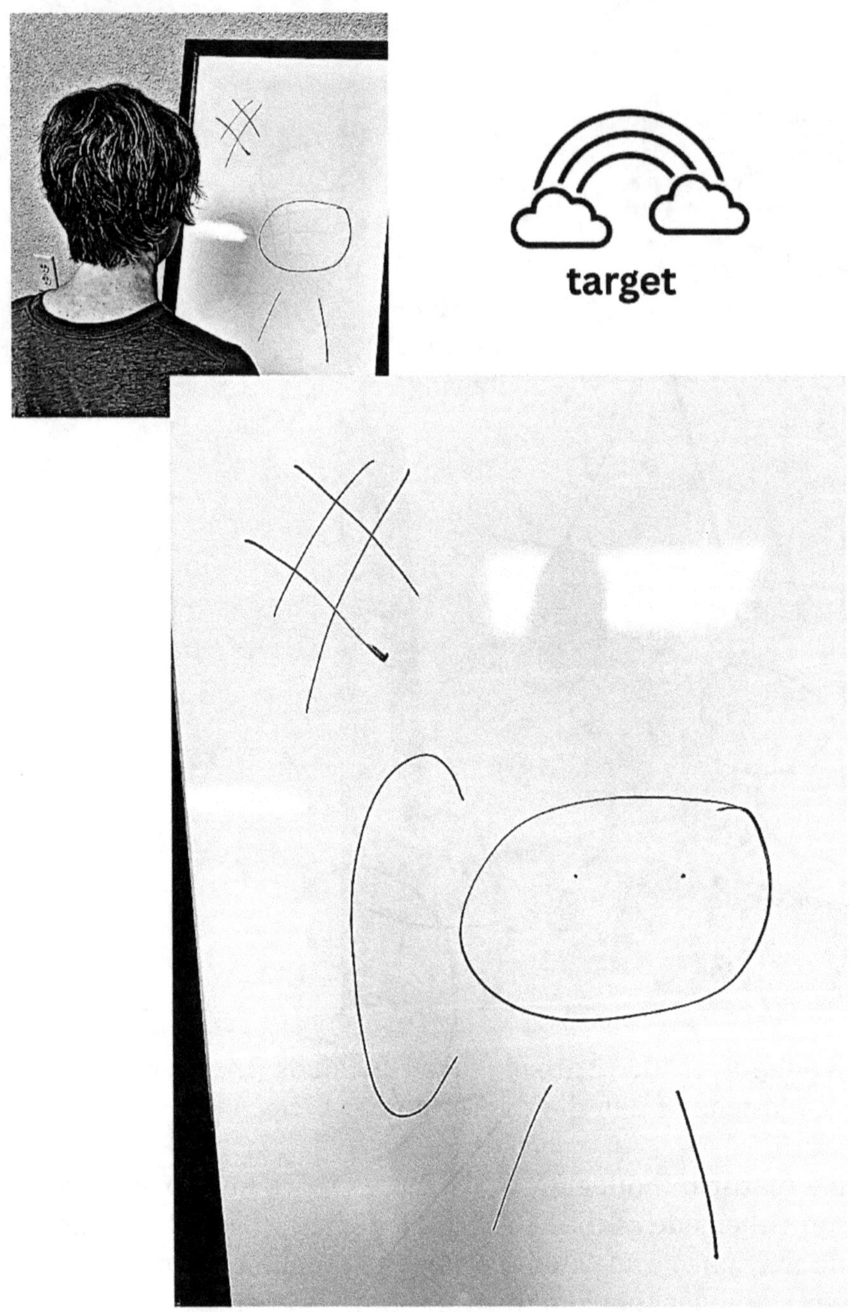

Associative feature: "the lines are parallel" – See the hashmark at the upper left? It's composed of perpendicular pairs of *parallel lines*.

Associative feature: "there are multiple (2) clouds (the *rounded* shapes)" – How many rounded shapes do you see in the transcript?

Associative feature: "the rainbow is composed of 3 lines"

Associative feature: "the lines are parallel"

Associative feature: "the lines are in the shape of curves" – See the curved lines inside the central shape.

Associative feature: "the clouds are mostly composed of curves, conveying a feeling of *roundedness*" – Here, there is a rounded shape in the center.

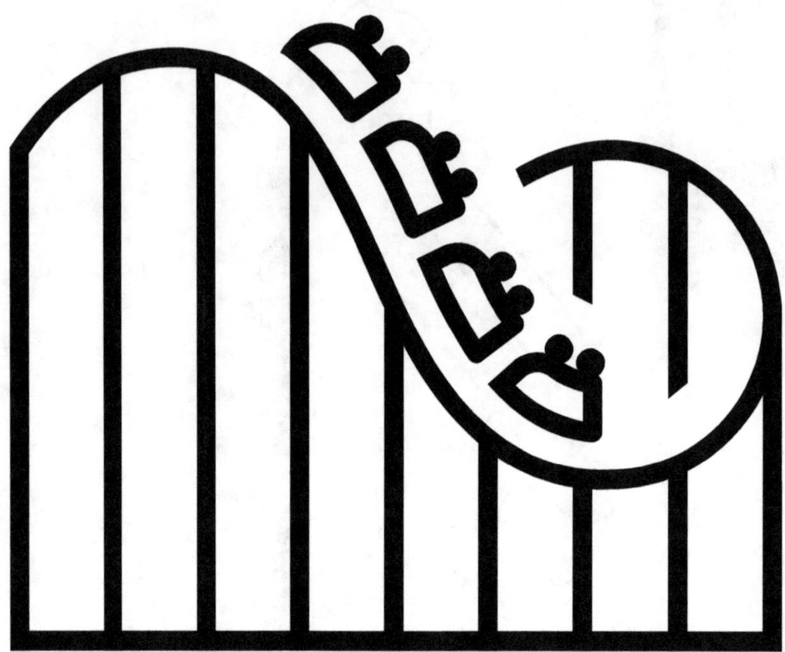

Target: Roller coaster

Associative Features:

- includes a prominent curve along the top
- the right side of the curve resembles an unclosed circle
- the bottom of the drawing is a horizontal line
- multiple lines
- parallel lines
- segmented shapes are aligned with the top of the curve
- each segmented shape is topped with 2 circles

Associative feature: “includes a prominent curve along the top” – Curves present inside the triangle.

Associative feature: “the right side of the curve resembles an unclosed circle” – The transcript features a whole circle.

Associative feature: “the bottom of the drawing is a horizontal line”

Associative feature: “parallel lines” – Except the lines in the transcript are horizontal (bottom of transcript) instead of vertical (target).

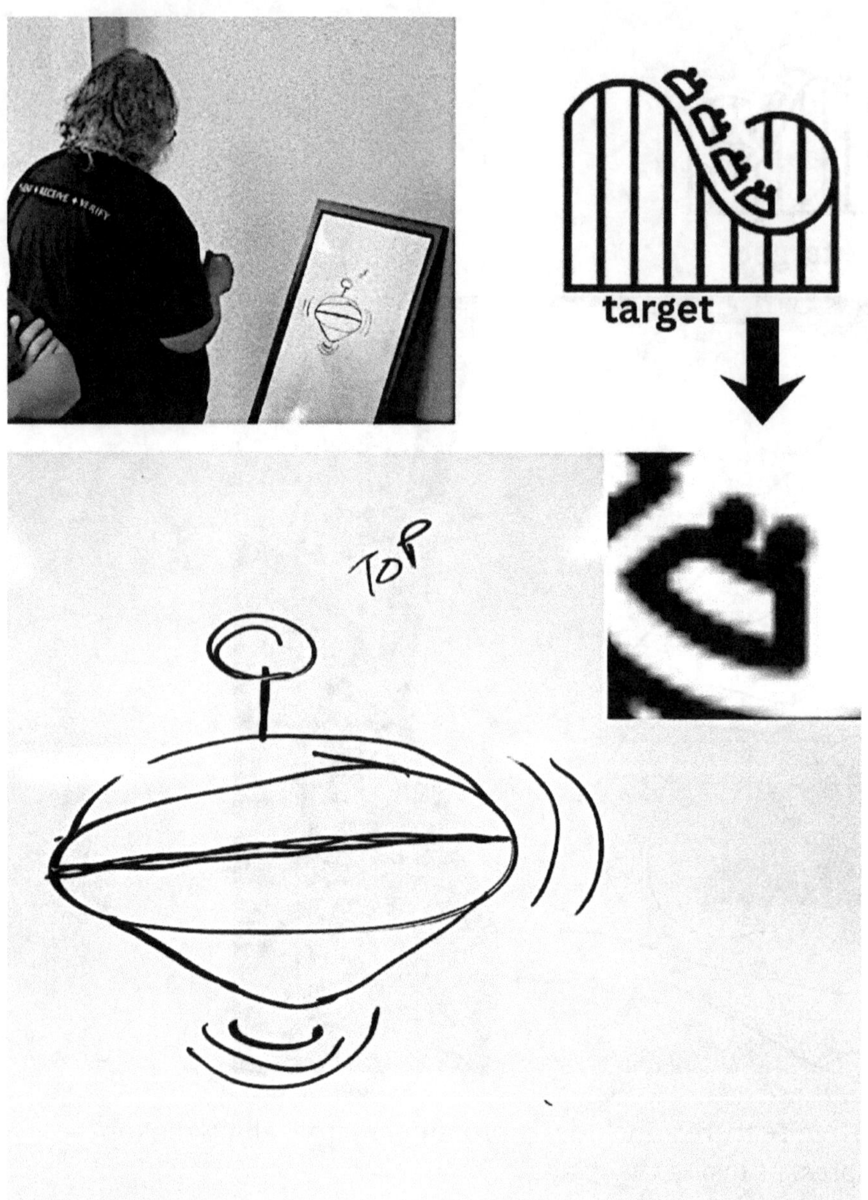

Associative feature: "each segmented shape is topped with 2 circles" – just 1 circle here, though.

Observed attribute: Thematic similarity. The mind appears to have focused on one of the cars atop the roller coaster, featuring a single circle on top, presumably a rider. The curved lines to the right and beneath convey a sense of movement.

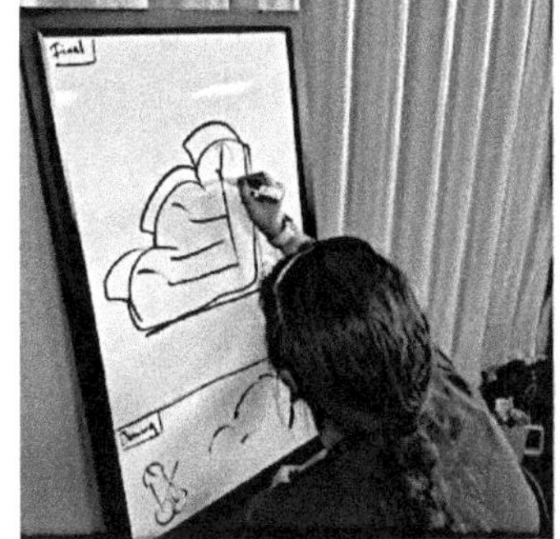

Associative feature: "includes a prominent curve along the top"

Associative feature: "the bottom of the drawing is a horizontal line"

Associative feature: "segmented shapes are aligned with the top of the curve"

Associative feature: "parallel lines"

Target: Rose bud with leaf

Associative Features:

- vertically oriented shape with shapes extended from it
- larger extension on top
- small extension to the side
- rounded top at the center
- multiple (2) shapes with triangular (pointed) ends at their tops enfold the rounded center
- thin line with curved object on one end

target

Associative feature: “vertically oriented shape with shapes extended from it”

The participant decided to erase this image and start over. Her second attempt is on the next page and contains more information.

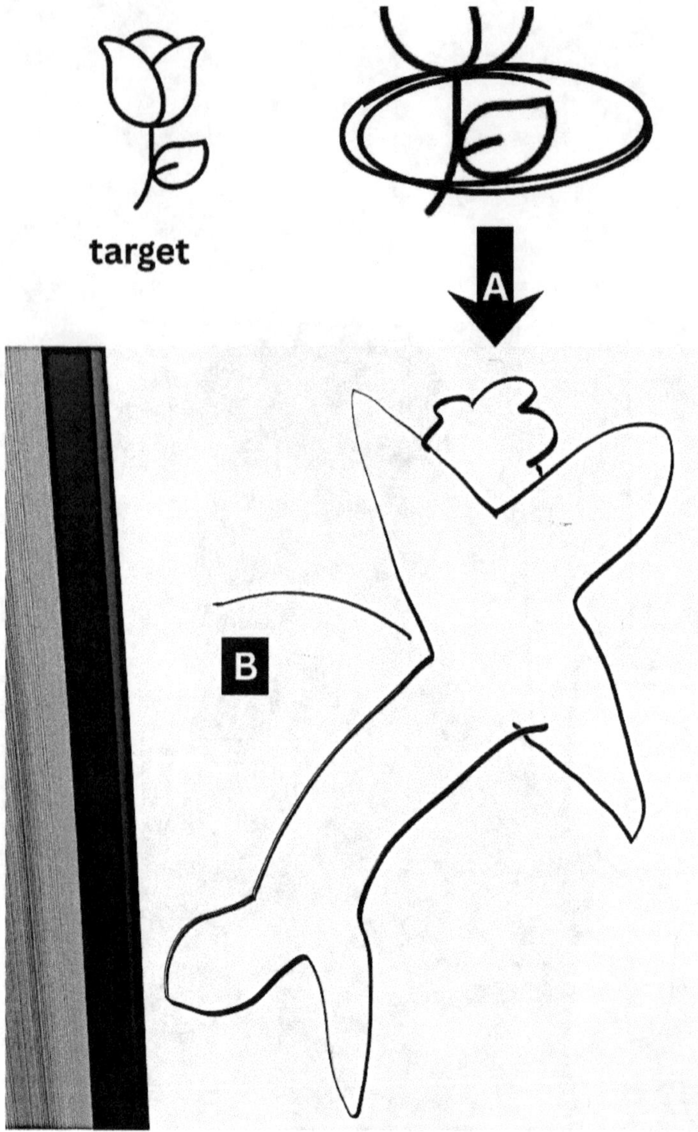

Associative feature: "vertically oriented shape with shapes extended from it"

Associative feature: "small extension to the side" (A)

Associative feature: "rounded top at the center"

Associative feature: "thin line with curved object on one end" – Here, the *thin line* has been separated from its attachment. (B)

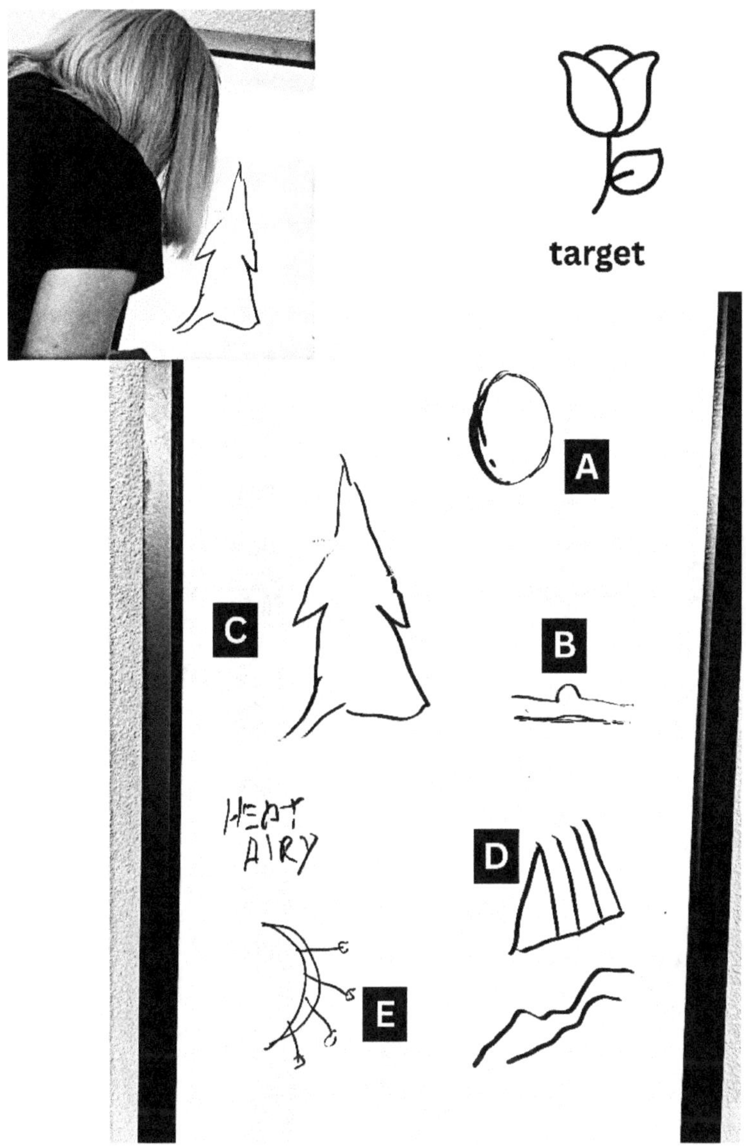

Associative feature: "rounded top at the center" – "Roundedness." (A and B)

Associative feature: "multiple (2) shapes with triangular (pointed) ends at their tops enfold the rounded center" – Here we see triangular shapes, some layered (or *enfolded* perhaps?). (C and D)

Associative feature: "thin line with curved object on one end" – (E) Concept is repeated here.

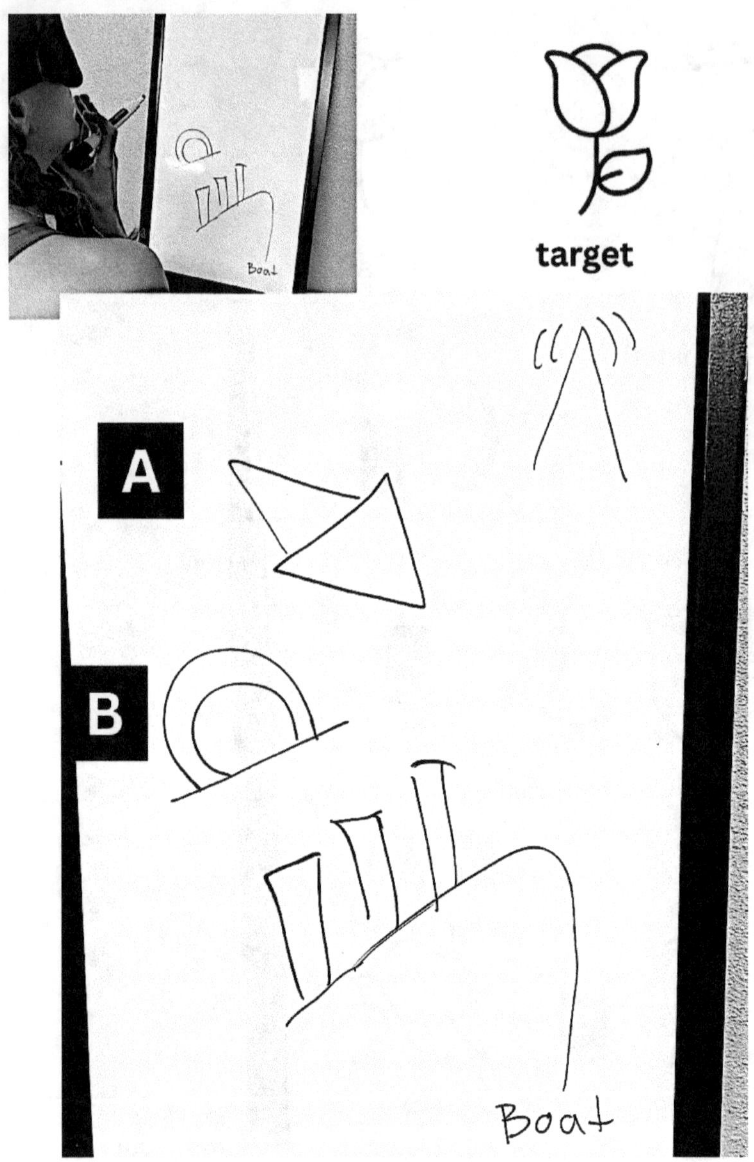

Associative feature: "multiple (2) shapes with triangular (pointed) ends at their tops enfold the rounded center" – Here the two triangular shapes seem to enfold each other. (A)

Associative feature: "rounded top at the center" – (B)

Observed attribute: Analytical overlay (AOL). See how the mind incorrectly labeled the drawing "Boat" at the bottom.

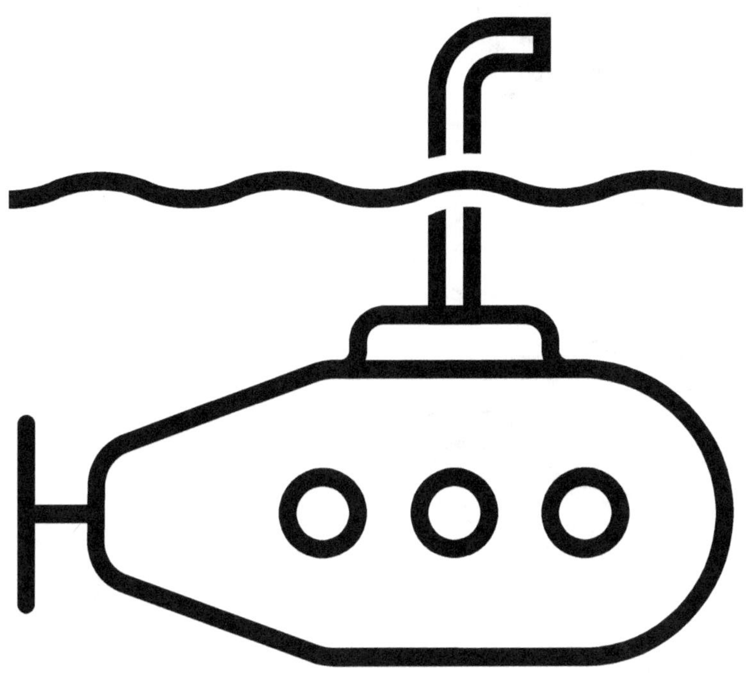

Target: Submarine

Associative Features:

- the extension on the left side is normally associated with a *propeller*
- circles figure prominently
- there are 3 perfect circles inside of the main shape
- circles are aligned
- circles are *horizontally* aligned
- main shape is horizontally oriented
- main shape is oblong
- long, horizontal wavy line across the top of the image
- circles serve as *windows of a structure*

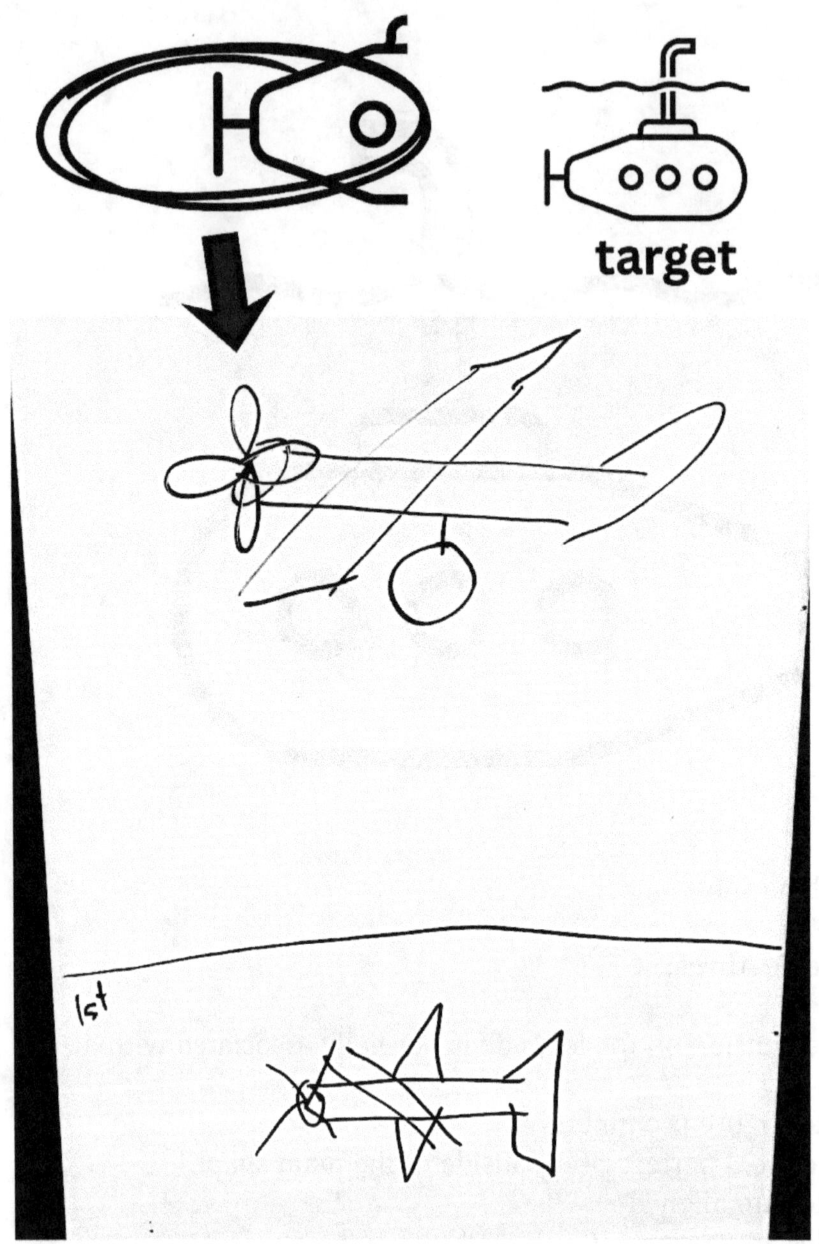

Associative feature: “extension on the left side is normally associated with a *propeller*”

Associative feature: “main shape is horizontally oriented”

What else do you see in common?

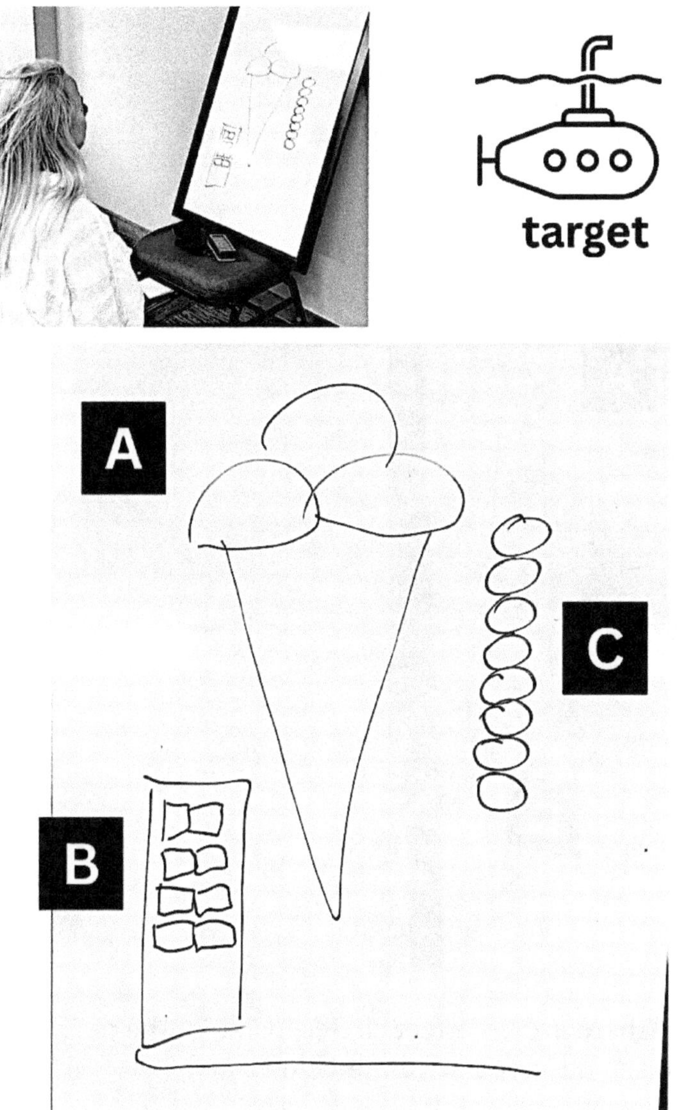

Associative feature: "circles figure prominently" (A & C)

Associative feature: "there are 3 perfect circles inside of the main shape" – (A) Three circles.

Associative feature: "circles are aligned" – But vertically here, not horizontally. (C)

Associative feature: "circles serve as *windows of a structure*" – (B) resembles a building

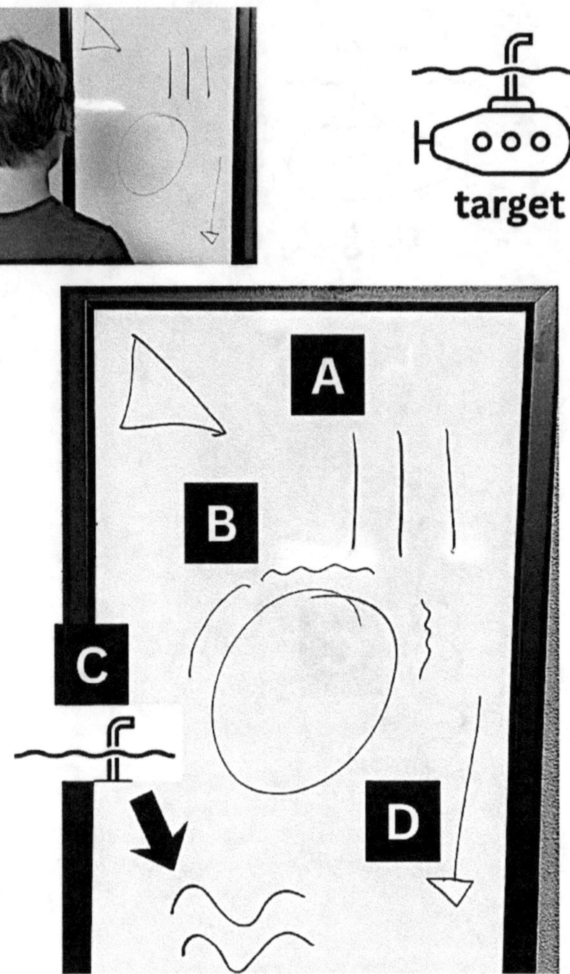

Associative feature: "there are **3** perfect circles inside of the main shape", (A) Relates to the observed attribute below.

Observed attribute: Recognition of multiples (**3**) – symbolic. (A)

Associative feature: "main shape is oblong" – (B)

Associative feature: "long, horizontal wavy line across the top of the image" – Here, the wavy line(s) are at the bottom of the transcript. (C)

Observed attribute: Thematic similarity. The downward arrow (D) is indicative of "down" or "beneath," as a submarine is in water.

Target: Radio

Associative Features:

- prominent shape is a quadrangle (rectangle)
- prominent shape contains another quadrangle (smaller rectangle)
- prominent shape contains a circle
- prominent shape contains 3 horizontal lines
- lines inside prominent shape are parallel
- long diagonal line on top of the quadrangle
- long diagonal line originating from the RIGHT side of the shape and moves UPWARD at a diagonal angle toward the center (to the LEFT)
- diagonal line is long and thin

Associative feature: "prominent shape is a quadrangle (rectangle)" – Square in the transcript.

Associative feature: "prominent shape contains another quadrangle (smaller rectangle) – In this case, multiple quadrangles (the house windows).

Associative feature: "long diagonal line on top of the quadrangle" – Here, 2 diagonal lines form the roof.

Observed attribute: AOL with primary shape recognition. They're both mainly quadrangles, but the mind interpreted it as a house.

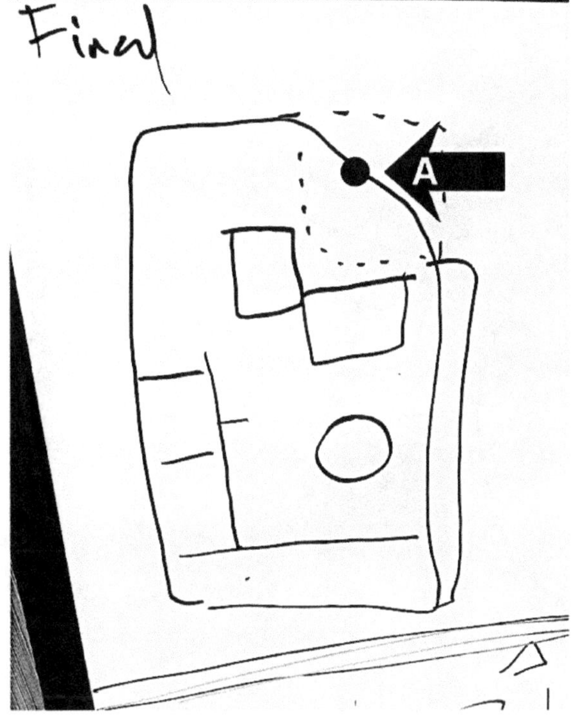

Associative feature: "long diagonal line originating from the RIGHT side of the shape and moves UPWARD at a diagonal angle toward the center (to the LEFT)" – Similarity (A) [The dot was added to the image by the author to help identify the line indicated by the arrow.]

Associative feature: "prominent shape contains a circle"

Associative feature: "prominent shape contains another quadrangle" – Transcript contains multiple.

Associative feature: "lines inside prominent shape are parallel"

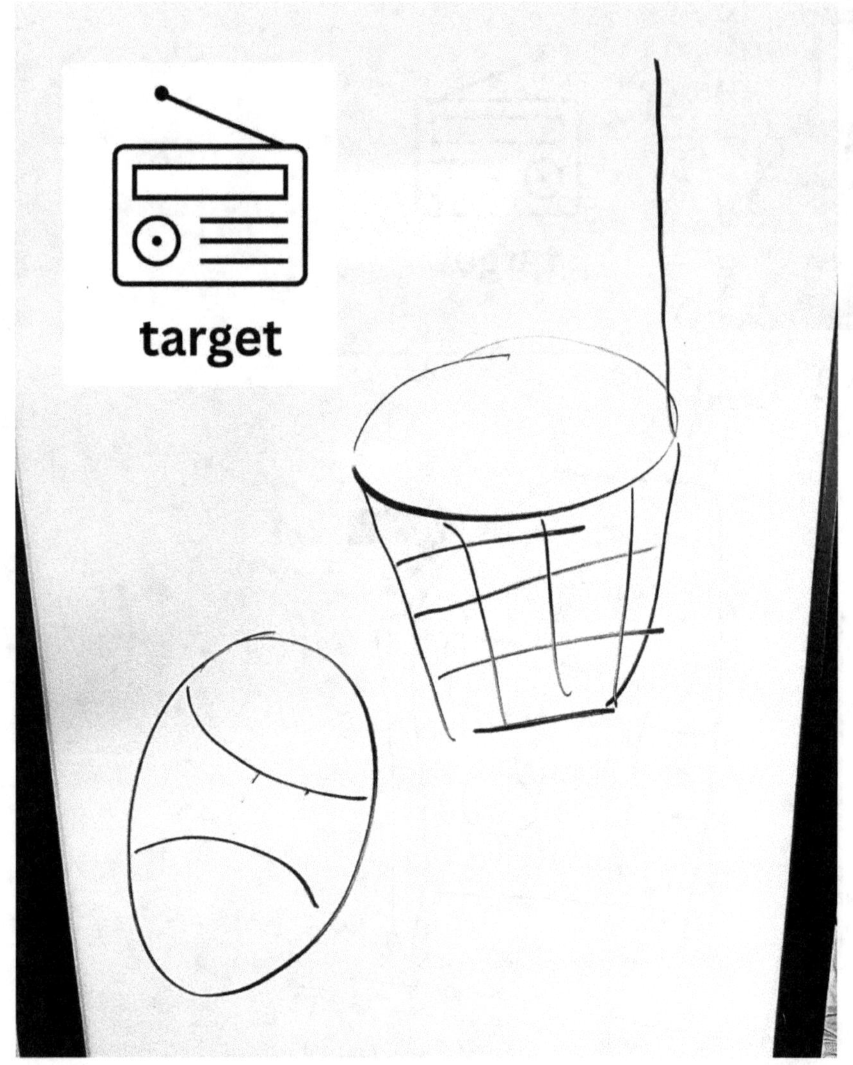

Associative feature: "long diagonal line originating from the RIGHT side of the shape and moves UPWARD at a diagonal angle toward the center (to the LEFT)" - Here, it is not diagonal.

Associative feature: "prominent shape contains a circle" – Here, the circle is outside the prominent shape.

Observed attribute: AOL with Primary shape recognition. The mind interpreted the information as what appears to be a basketball hoop and a baseball.

Target: Award ribbon

Associative Features:

- top shape is composed of 2 spherical shapes (a plain circle within a "ruffled" circle)
- ruffled edge is composed of curves (lines moving up and down in sequence)
- pair of vertically/diagonally oriented shapes extend downward from top shape
- downward shapes are primarily created from long lines
- the bottoms of the downward shapes are composed of 2 outward points (triangles from the inside) and/or 1 inward point (triangle from the outside)

Associative feature: "top shape is composed of 2 spherical shapes (circle within a "ruffled" circle)" – Do you see the 2 circles in the transcript?

Observed attribute: Deconstruction. The "ruffles" have been separated out and placed at the bottom.

What else do you notice?

Observed attribute: Deconstruction.

This is like the transcript on previous page, especially the "ruffle" being placed beneath all the other deconstructed parts. Is this the result of another observed attribute, *contamination by another telepath*?

Associative feature: “top shape is composed of 2 spherical shapes” – Here we see 1 spherical shape at the top, and 2 near the bottom.

Associative feature: “pair of vertically/diagonally oriented shapes extend downward from top shape”

There are still more similarities from the main list of associative features on page 317. What do you find?

Associative feature: "top shape is composed of 2 spherical shapes (circle within a "ruffled" circle)" – Here, the ruffled circle is replaced by three large, curved shapes above.

Associative feature: "pair of vertically/diagonally oriented shapes extend downward from top shape"

To me, this was the most accurate transcript of the round, and perhaps of all the line drawing transcripts in the book. Not just by the look of it, but by its *feel.* For that, I chose to show it last as a celebration of this participant's, and indeed everyone's, hard work throughout the week.

THE CLOSING CIRCLE

On the final night of the intensive, we rearranged the tables and chairs to form one large circle. Not to sing this time, but to see each other… and to be seen *by* each other. I was happy to express my gratitude for everyone's participation, especially to my friends Jill and Cheryl who'd been exploring psychic phenomena with me for several years. And I was grateful to have made new friends.

Spontaneously, everyone decided to take turns telling the group what they were grateful for and what the intensive had done for them. There was laughter, and there were tears. In my heart, I felt that this is what it was all about. The meaning we created together.

Over the week, we formed new connections with each other. Or, using telepathy terms, we'd formed new *associations* with each other. And through those connections and associations, we produced something meaningful. I regard our shared experience as the Great Mystery working through us, continuing its eternal evolution.

Our part in that evolution continues, and it now includes *you* since you're holding this book in your hands. We probably have never and will never meet, but now we share a thread in the cosmic web by our mutual association with this book.

But everything's *already* connected, isn't it? That's the basis for the spiritual trope "We're all one." Yet we're not all one, exactly. You and I have our personal lives, with unique lessons to learn, and experiences only we can have, given the time, location, personality, body capacity, and countless associations particular to us.

We cannot say that we're separate, either. Aside from our interdependence on the physical plane (I am who I am because you are who you are), telepathy reveals that we share a common, non-physical source of information. Perhaps it is that Great Mystery, or some organic, non-physical database, or the Akashic records.

Maybe we're just memories within those cosmic records, replaying ourselves over and over again, a little differently every time. Or maybe we're already in heaven, united, but our temporary physical brains serve as veils to maintain the illusion of separateness for a greater, sacred, purpose.

So, maybe we're *not* two. Maybe, we're not separate. But we're not *one* either because we're not the same. We are like a murmuration of starlings.

Photo credit: Brian Robert Marshall / *Starlings over Rodbourne, Swindon (2) / https://creativecommons.org/licenses/by-sa/2.0/*

Reality, carefully contemplated, doesn't lend itself to tropes. It's ineffable. Sometimes symbols do a better job.

At some point during the intensive, I discussed the idea of "not two, not one" and held my hand up in a *mudra*, a symbolic hand gesture, to make my point. You can see it in the photo in the *About the Author* section at the end of this book.

It resembles the yogic *prana mudra* used to harmonize one's life force. It also resembles the gesture of benediction often portrayed in paintings and statues of Jesus holding up two fingers. It's said that the two fingers represent the duality of being human and divine. I like that. I believe we all possess human and divine natures, as evidenced by our interactions within a non-physical reality that transcends time, and in our ordinary day-to-day contact. Touch is essential to thrive.

The "not two, not one" mudra shows two fingers, but they become one by touching. They are both, and they are neither. But what to do with these thoughts?

Although psychic exploration has been part of my spiritual path, it's important for me to state that psychic abilities are not spiritual in and of themselves and certainly have nothing to do with religious beliefs. To say telepathy is spiritual is like saying gravity, space, or time are spiritual. They are not.

Telepathy may be included in spiritual beliefs and practices, but whatever that *thing* is that makes psychic abilities possible is probably as natural, and as neutral, as the wind, planetary orbits, and subatomic fields.

Yet I can't help but regard our universe, even the dirt beneath our feet, as sacred. Dirt and gold are equal in this view. They're of the same nature, as are we. So, please allow me to offer some advice.

Two months after the intensive, I woke up in the middle of the night feeling short of breath and pressure on my chest. Soon, I was overcome by a sense of impending doom, which I quickly learned is a clinically recognized symptom of a heart attack. I spent the next few hours in the nearest urgent care center waiting for test results to reveal whether I'd had a cardiac event. That gave me time to think. Perhaps I was overdue for a life review.

It wouldn't be the first time a heart condition caused me to re-evaluate my life. Last time, I was half my age and underwent a minor heart procedure. Afterward, I decided to go to Machu Picchu, quit my high-paying career in telecom afterward, and went on to pursue a more meaningful life.

This time, lying in a hospital bed waiting for a prognosis, I realized I needed a slight course correction. The in-my-face reminder that this physical life is temporary and can end at any time made it easy to reset my priorities.

I realized I wanted to slow down and do less. I wanted to reclaim the time I spent focusing on psychic development and devote it to learning to play music and being outside in nature more instead. And I realized I'd let my meditation practice slip.

My purpose for meditating was always to cultivate profound levels of peace by reducing suffering and changing my relationship to that suffering at an existential level. This kind of meditation isn't for stress reduction, productivity, to be more psychic, or other worldly goals. Like psychic development and psychedelics, meditation doesn't help with certain psychological issues. It can even worsen them. Psychotherapy would be better. But certain types of meditation are effective for something much, much deeper. Yet, for the last few years, I'd let my practice lag. There was a reason, of course.

Discovering psychic abilities had been extremely helpful to me at a certain point in my life. I'd been hurt by spiritual teachers who, it turned out, were just as prone to human failings as the rest of us. I walked away from them and pursued psychic development to continue my spiritual development unhindered by dogma and power differentials.

Psychic training became a mode of self-empowerment for me. And as some readers already know, this became my motivation to teach psychic development to others[68], so that they could empower themselves.

But after years of exploring the psychic world, one thing is clear. It does not lead to peace. It may lead to awe, to personal growth, to a sense of adventure, to connection with the divine, and certainly to a more meaningful experience of being alive. And it's a beautiful way to make new friends. These are all important.

---

[68] The details are in my memoir, *Renegade Mystic: The Pursuit of Spiritual Freedom Through Consciousness Exploration.*

Still, psychic development has its limitations. It does not necessarily make one a better person. I've personally seen and met very psychic people (and other types of experiencers) who exhibit psychological conditions causing them to engage in harmful, aggressive, egotistical, and exploitative behaviors.

Especially in the age of social media, I've seen people rushing the digital stage to become instant stars. I've seen unscrupulous profiteers use consciousness events as cash machines. I'll stop my rant here by simply restating that psychic development has its limitations.

I'm not suggesting we should stop investigating our non-physical reality. A lot of good has come and will continue to come from both scientific and amateur exploration, especially in healing applications.

But I don't prioritize becoming more psychic myself anymore. I'll continue teaching those abilities, though, because I love connecting with people and helping them achieve their goals, especially to understand their deeper natures. For those interested in learning meditation, I'll continue teaching that too.

Here's my advice, if I may. Practice moderation and make sure you don't neglect your other interests and responsibilities. Are there other things in your life that could deliver as much or even more meaning and fulfillment than psychic phenomena?

Take those dance lessons. Learn a new language. Go camping. Visit your friends and family more. Look at the stars. Run, climb, and jump. Avoid screens, especially scrolling; they damage our mental health by disconnecting us from the felt experience of being alive. And if you're ready to seek fundamental peace, consider meditation.

This is your life, and only you know its purpose. Only you can choose how you'll contribute meaning to our collective oneness. You are divine, but don't forget you're also a human being. That experience is as precious as it is brief. So, make your own way. It's okay to make mistakes, and it's all right to get lost once in a while.

Thank you for being a part of my life. I wish you the best on your journey.

APPENDIX 1

The next two pages contain scanned copies of the author's handwritten notes from the Zoom call with Dalia and Lidu Burgoin.

Magdalia [illegible] Dalia 4/18/25

Cidoving [illegible] Lidu

Cida

it will be why on the

[illegible] elevated frequency

I told you

Everyone who wants to hear should

ask their angels to help

team of angels always w/ you, will help
but only interfere when asked

catacombs

other religions?

the angels are the same beings across
spiritual categories but with different names
just are used

they want him to know that his view is a healthy one
in his etymology, viewpoint →

but it eventually will evolve to include   1/18/25
a love for expressing the spiritual religious world interpretations as it's showing me that
he will evolve to help the spiritual teachers of all religions e.g. the secret ones and those that help progress emerge their ability creatively (telepathy).

---

with that, not everybody aligned

---

what about private stuff?
I telepathically can see everything that you experience but I easily can turn my attention elsewhere

---

more to Logan's mission?
we are in telepathic teams to bring a paradigm shift to the world

---

how can he help?
he can help by asking non-speakers to telepathically tell their story on his network on TV and have them see them spell
- can I say I am pleased with his desire to help and his channel will grow exponentially with early expressions of telepathy using the letterboard and telling others the teachings

APPENDIX 2

The 2025 Psychic Training Intensive's Complete Schedule

***Not all activities shown in the schedule are discussed in this book** due to space limitations and other reasons. Also, a couple of nights were concluded with sky watching, but the exact dates weren't recorded.

Sunday Sept. 21 – Arrival Day

5 pm - 6 pm	Check-in and playing Blank Slate™ together
6 pm – 7 pm	Dinner
7 pm - 8:30 pm	Orientation and lucid dreaming Instructions

Monday Sept. 22 – Day 1

7 am – 9 am	Breakfast
9 am – 10 am	Spoon Bending Session #1
10am – 12 pm	Telepathy with line drawings
12 pm – 2 pm	Lunch
2 pm – 3:15 pm	Clairvoyance & telepathy with colors
3:30 pm - 5:30 pm	Psychometry session #1
5:30 pm – 7 pm	Dinner
7 pm – 8 pm	Lucid dreaming instructions – dream incubation to meet partner in the dream realm

Tuesday Sept. 23 – Day 2

7 am – 9 am	Breakfast
9 am – 10 am	Blake F.'s presentation about energy clearing
10 am – 11:15 am	Clairvoyance with colors and small objects
11:15 am - 12:15 pm	Telepathy with Complex Images in small groups
12 pm – 2 pm	Lunch
2 pm – 4 pm	Remote viewing
4 pm - 4:30 pm	Spoon Bending #2
4:30 pm - 5:30 pm	Psychokinesis with the Owls (random number generated lights)
5:30 pm – 7 pm	Dinner
7 pm – 8 pm	Remote viewing session for outbounder feedback

Wednesday Sept. 24 – Day 3

7 am – 9 am	Breakfast
9:30 am – 12 pm	Travel to outbounder target location as feedback
12 pm – 2:30 pm	Lunch
2:30 pm – 4 pm	Psychometry Session #2
4:15pm - 5:30 pm	Team-Style telepathy games (using the Horserace for score-keeping)
5:30 pm – 7 pm	Dinner
7 pm – 8 pm	"What's in the Box?" session #1

Thursday Sept. 25 – Day 4

7 am – 9 am	Breakfast
9 am - 10:00 am	Feedback and discussion for What's in the Box? #1
10:15 am – 12 pm	Heart Rate Telepathy #1 (DMILS - Direct Mental Interaction with Living Systems)
12 pm – 2 pm	Lunch
2 pm – 3 pm	Participant leading group in directly seeing Pick 3 lottery
3 pm - 3:45 pm	Rapid telepathy
3:45 pm - 5:00 pm	Associative remote viewing
5 pm – 7 pm	DINNER
7 pm - 8:30 pm	What's in the Box? Session #2

Friday Sept. 26 – Day 5

7 am – 9 am	Breakfast
9 am - 9:30 am	Feedback and discussion for What's in the Box? #2
9:30 am - 10:30 am	ARV groups led by teacher-trainees for mid-day Pick 3 drawing
10:30 am – 12 pm	Heart Rate Telepathy #2 (DMILS - Direct Mental Interaction with Living Systems)
12 pm – 2 pm	Lunch
2 pm – 5:30 pm	Team-style MAT (matching abacus test) with colored shapes Team-style telepathy with line drawings Team-style telepathy with complex images Team-style telepathy with small objects Team-style telepathy with blinking shapes
5:30 pm – 6 pm	ARV feedback for mid-day Pick 3 drawing
5:30 pm – 7 pm	Dinner
7 pm – 8 pm	Closing circle

Saturday Sept. 27 – Departure Day

APPENDIX 3

QR codes to see the remote viewing target images in color.

Sahrawi tribal men performing fantasia at the Tan-Tan (Moussem) Festival in Tan-Tan, Morocco. Photo by Максим Массалитин (Maxim Massalitin).
Source: https://commons.wikimedia.org/wiki/File:Муссем_(фольклорный_фестиваль)_в_Тан-Тане_(Марокко).jpg

View of Blue Mosque in Istanbul, Turkey. Photo by Moonik. Source: https://commons.wikimedia.org/wiki/File:Exterior_of_Sultan_Ahmed_I_Mosque_in_Istanbul,_Turkey_002.jpg

Dragon 2 Hover Test. Photo by Msaynevirta/SpaceX photos. Source: https://commons.wikimedia.org/wiki/File:Dragon_2_hover_test_(24159153709).jpg

360-degree video of the light rail →

APPENDIX 4

Below is the QR code for the video of the author doing **telepathy under the influence of LSD**.

Note: The video will open at the start of the specific telepathy test discussed on page 11.

Below are the QR code and URL for the **Mind Possible YouTube Channel**, which you can subscribe to if you'd like to be notified when new videos are posted.
https://www.youtube.com/@SeanMcNamaraandMindPossible

Below is the QR code and URL for the **360-degree remote viewing practice targets** on the website for Sean's other book *Signal and Noise*. https://www.SignalAndNoiseBook.com/360.html **Have fun!**

APPENDIX 5

QR codes for other recommended websites

Dalia Burgoin
www.DaliaBurgoin.com

Dalia and Lidu Burgoin
www.Extra-Ordinaries.com

Wendy Gallant
www.SeeingBeyondEyes.com

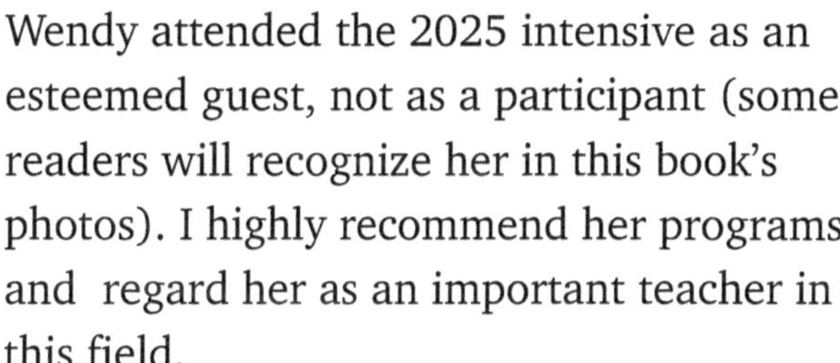

Wendy attended the 2025 intensive as an esteemed guest, not as a participant (some readers will recognize her in this book's photos). I highly recommend her programs and regard her as an important teacher in this field.

Mind Possible Authorized Teachers

www.mindpossible.com/mind_possible_authorized_teachers.html

PLEASE WRITE A BOOK REVIEW

In some ways, society has not changed very much since the medieval witch trials (1400 to 1775)[69]. In fact, it was only in 1944 when the last person, Helen Duncan, was arrested for witchcraft in England under the Witchcraft Act of 1735, which was still on the books at the time.[70]

The attempt to control society by manipulating people's beliefs and preventing independent thought, largely by major religions, biased media, and governments, continues.

These days, a common form of censorship by pseudo-skeptics, religious zealots, and other agents is to write misleading, unfair, or libelous reviews on booksellers' and other websites. Their primary goal, of course, is to dissuade potential readers from being exposed to the book's information. To prevent *learning*.

If you enjoyed this book and support the human right to explore one's own consciousness, the easiest and **most powerful act you can perform** is to write a positive book review where you purchased it. If you're an Amazon customer, please visit your account's Orders page, locate your book order, and click on "Write a product review." It only takes a minute, but it makes a tremendous difference.

Thank you for your support.

---

[69] https://en.wikipedia.org/wiki/Witch_trials_in_the_early_modern_period

[70] https://www.historic-uk.com/HistoryUK/HistoryofScotland/Helen-Duncan-Scotlands-last-witch/

ABOUT THE AUTHOR

Above: Displaying the *Not Two, Not One* mudra discussed in the final chapter.

Sean McNamara is a teacher, researcher, and explorer. The primary aim of his *Mind Possible* platform is to provide others with the tools and knowledge to explore consciousness in a self-empowered way, free of dogma. Sean works as a clinical mental health counselor and hypnotherapist for clients in Centennial, Colorado. He plays various musical instruments for personal enjoyment. He and his wife Cierra enjoy meandering through mountains and deserts, tarrying in cute coffee shops, and watching baking shows at home.

www.MindPossible.com
Psychic exploration and development.

www.WisdomWithin.space – Meditation for mental health, developing wisdom and compassion, understanding the nature of existential suffering, and cultivating the experience of fundamental peace.

www.ingramcontent.com/pod-product-compliance
Lightning Source LLC
LaVergne TN
LVHW081256100826
845148LV00005B/894

* 9 7 9 8 9 8 8 3 1 1 9 6 6 *